Beyond the Workshop

Kingston University Press Ltd.,
Kingston University,
Penrhyn Road,
Kingston-upon-Thames,
Surrey KT1 2EE

British Library Cataloguing in Publications Data available.

ISBN 978-1-899999-52-1

Set in Palatino
Typeset by: PK Editorial, www.pkeditorial.co.uk
Cover design by Gudrun Jobst

Kingston Writing School

Kingston Writing School is home to courses in Creative Writing, English Language and Communication, English Literature, Media, Journalism and Publishing.

Kingston Writing School fuses the talents and experience of professionals from the areas of Creative Writing, Journalism, Publishing and Digital Media. The KWS team includes academics, novelists, journalists, playwrights and poets who develop courses to suit writers of all levels, and who contribute in multifaceted ways to outreach projects in the wider community, including partnerships with Hampton Court, the Bush Theatre, armed services veterans and writers in prison.

Come join us and spread the word.

www.kingstonwritingschool.com

Contents

Acknowledgements

'And Then There Is That Incredible Moment', from *The Laws of Falling Bodies* (Story Line Press, 1997). Copyright Kate Light. Reprinted by permission of the author, from *Filibuster to Delay a Kiss and Other Poems* (Random House © 2007)

The poem 'Instructions for How To Put an Old Horse Down', originally appeared in a chapbook entitled *Instructions for How To Put an Old Horse Down*, published by Longhouse Press, 2009. Reprinted by permission of the author.

'Filibuster for Life,' copyright by Alicia Vallarta. Reprinted by permission of the author.

'The Queerosphere: Musings on Queer Studies and Creative Writing Classrooms' from *Queer Girls in Class* by Lori Horvitz, ed., Peter Lang Publishing, 29 Broadway, 18th Floor, NY, NY 10006, reprinted by permission of Peter Lang Publishing.

Deirdre Fagan's essay *Creative Writing Teaching Theory and Practice* first appeared online, ISSN 2040-335, accessible at http://www.cwteaching.com/#/issue-3/4546769027, reprinted by permission of the author.

The Editor would like to thank Frances White for her diligent preparation of the manuscript.

Foreword

As Paul Perry writes in his Introduction, the workshop has been at the centre of the teaching of creative writing in the academy since the inception of university creative writing programmes more than two generations ago, and the ever-growing attraction of such programmes, in the U.K. as well as the U.S., testifies to its success and value as practice. Yet the increase in creative writing programmes has also been accompanied recently by an understandable and timely reflection on that practice. For today's students of creative writing in the academy are much more diverse than in the past. The majority of them continue to want to become published writers, as they should, and they continue in many respects to judge the success of the teaching they receive on the basis of their publication record and the publication records of the other graduates on their course. Yet more and more teachers of creative writing now appreciate the variety of other benefits that creative writing courses provide their students, whether those students are undergraduates, postgraduates, promising professionals or keen amateurs whose main motives for enrolling on a course relate to personal growth and satisfaction.

It is because of that collective appreciation that committed university writers/teachers have begun to consider alternative, complementary methodologies, methods of teaching 'beyond the workshop'. Their interest should not – does not – imply the end of the workshop. The workshop will no doubt remain vital to the curriculum of creative writing in the future. Their interest does, however, indicate a welcome understanding of the need to examine the conventional practices associated with workshopping – for the sake of the discipline, certainly, but, more importantly, for the sake of the legion of students to whom creative writing means so much, as writers and prospective teachers.

Creative writing programmes dedicated to their students, and attentive to the range of ways in which they may legitimately define success, thus have an obligation to help their students fulfill their potential, in all areas, and from wherever they start. As a sign of our dedication, and the dedication of colleagues and writers in residence associated with the new Kingston Writing School, Kingston University Press is especially pleased to publish this outstanding collection. Both KUP and KWS want to promote continuing discussions of the pedagogy involved with all forms of writing, including creative writing. We are certain that the contributors to *Beyond the Workshop* will not only help with that promotion but also play a leading role in inspiring further critical reflection.

David Rogers

Head, School of Humanities
Kingston University, London

Desire Paths or 'The Workshop is Dead. Long Live the Workshop': An Introduction to *Beyond The Workshop*

Paul Perry

Beyond the Workshop arrives at a crucial time in the creative writing studies debate. More and more writers, students and scholars are asking the questions: What is the role and future of creative writing in the academy? Does the workshop remain central to creative writing studies? What comes 'beyond the workshop'?

Unlike many other studies on the evolution of the creative writing workshop, *Beyond the Workshop* not only provides a compelling suite of essays on the subject, but the collection also contains a range of practical creative writing exercises.

The exercises are original and compelling 'triggers' from the *Beyond the Workshop* contributors, all of whom are writers *and* teachers of creative writing. Their expertise has an international dimension: they write from the United Kingdom, Ireland and the United States of America. They are poets, novelists, short story writers, creative non-fiction writers, and essayists all in their own right. In this sense, *Beyond the Workshop* is a collection of essays and exercises that will be of interest to teachers and students of creative writing in an international context.

One of the most striking elements of the *Beyond the Workshop* is the variety of ways in which the contributors have understood the title itself and the concepts embedded in the phrase 'Beyond the Workshop'. *Beyond* is variously interpreted as what comes 'after' formal creative writing education, what 'reaches out' beyond the academy into the community, and what 'extends' beyond the written text into the realm of the digital and virtual world.

Within the 16 chapters you will find a balance of both theory-driven and practice-driven essays and the journey you take as a reader will lead you from what a workshop is to how it is practised and what it may become.

Nigel McLoughlin's 'Within Limits: Examining the Occupied Space and the Spaces Occupied by the Creative Writing Workshop' opens the book by explaining the practice of a workshop as 'a transformative space'. The 'horizon of expectation' of the student is investigated and the potential for different interpretations to a student's work detailed. McLoughlin makes a strong case for the workshop as 'a microcosm of the critical and selective processes to be found among creative industries', a place where students can 'self-actualise', but warns against knowledge transfer as something which can achieve this directly.

Many of McLoughlin's concerns are echoed and debated in a number of different chapters. Heidi Lynn Staples in 'Metaphors We Teach By' challenges the guiding metaphor of the workshop and demands a revision of the workshop concept so that the writing class is constructed as a 'community of practice'. The learning in a workshop becomes thus collaborative and social, rather than individual and psychological. Writing is learned rather than taught, Staples contests. Students learn *to* rather than *from*. Cultural relativity and a resistance to decontextualising an artwork are paramount to Staple's vision of the writing community.

In contrast to this vision, and to the ethos of many of the 'revisionary' books on creative writing now appearing, is Todd Swift's essay 'The Workshop as Stage', in which he defends passionately the need for the workshop to remain a 'unique space' and contends that the workshop is in danger of being undermined by too much 'tinkering'. He argues for the process of workshopping 'as a good in and of itself' and raises the workshop to a mystical status, invoking ritual and offering a 'quasi-ethical model' of the workshop as 'The Stage', a process that has to be undergone by all writers.

After the opening gambit by three poets, two non-fiction writers carry the concept of the workshop toward a social arena. Ben Ristow, in 'Bridges Between: Articulation in Narrative Form and Public Argument in Creative Non-Fiction', writes about the space between creative writing and rhetoric, and asks his students to interrogate the relationship between their own lives and narrative form. His idea of a 'braided essay' is realised through encouraging students to take risks and combine autobiographical content with atypical narrative forms. The division between the private and public is explored by bringing the workshop out of the classroom and into the public arena with a public reading. By contrast, Joseph Rein in 'What *Really* Happened: Rethinking "Truth" in Creative Non-Fiction' tackles the notion and nature of truth itself. His audience-based approach to creative non-fiction in many ways refutes David Myers's claim that 'students take it as a betrayal to do basic research or to handle abstract ideas'.[1] Rein encourages students to 'research' personal narratives, something he argues helps them step outside 'the confining labyrinths of their memories'.

---

[1] D.G. Myers, *The Elephants Teach* (2006), p. 175.

He writes that the goal in an essay is to discover its own truth. Perhaps the same can be said of the creative writing workshop.

Margaret Lazarus Dean writes, in her essay 'Tough But Fair: Honesty and the Management of Emotion in the Creative Writing Workshop', of the emotional risks in the writing workshop and how a tutor might minimize the damage of 'toughness' on an emerging writer. Lifting the 'gag' rule, outlawing evaluation and global comments, she opens up a discussion on workshop etiquette with her students from day one. In a fascinating experiment, Dean allows her students to make the decision as to whether they are to be workshopped in a 'tough' or 'gentle' manner, and places the onus on the student: with intriguing results.

The workshop becomes then, the site of independence, initiative and self-reliant learning, a sentiment broached by and expanded in Ursula Hurley's 'Standing on Deep Shale: the Problem of Originality'. Hurley not only introduces her students to the concept of 'reading as a writer', but also espouses a holistic pedagogic philosophy that includes a collective agreement written by the class that then is transformed into a 'class constitution'. A tutor's own enthusiasm, a commitment to innovation, and the 'deep shale' of the writing of others become the cornerstones of resisting the traditional workshop.

The importance of creating a community is paramount to Deirdre Fagan's essay 'Creative Writing Creating Community: The Power of the Personal'. Fagan devises an egalitarian workshop where the teacher becomes one of the 'students' and carries out and shares the in-class writing assignments the other students attempt. Michael Theune, in his essay 'Other Arrangements: The Vital Turn in Poetry Writing Pedagogy', invokes Tom Hunley's argument that the workshop 'was designed for gifted, elite writers who needed very little instruction', and proposes studying poetry by looking at rhetoric. Theune's 'filibuster poem' exercise embodies his theory of taking the workshop methods to a more challenging and structural level.

Jenny Dunning, on the other hand, in 'Making the Writing Process Strange: New (and Recycled) Approaches to Teaching Creative Writing', advocates making the act of writing 'strange' for students. Turning to the studio art classroom as a model, she shifts the balance of how class time is spent in order to reflect a more realistic composition process. This rebalancing involves no workshops in introductory classes, as Dunning believes that the workshop acts against creative composing strategies. She therefore emphasizes 'front-loading' classes with 'interventions' in the writing process. Students are encouraged to take 'risks, experiment and play' and to engage in small-group peer review sessions with 'student facilitators' that are distinct from workshops in that the 'centre of gravity' shifts to the student-reader response. 'Radical revisions' and new media in the writing classroom help contribute to a 'draft culture' that Dunning sees as vital in teaching creativity.

Stephanie Vanderslice moves further beyond the traditional workshop model in 'A Whole New Creative Writing Classroom: Daniel Pink, Digital Culture and the Twenty First Century Workshop'. Requiring her students to start a blog, upload audio and video, and create digital literacy narratives, Vanderslice aims to equip her apprentice writers to negotiate digital culture with meta-cognition and cultural awareness. Story, empathy and right brain thinking are all important in the evolution of the workshop, she argues, and how a writer 'stays abreast of trends in these foundational skills'.

Whether future developments of creative writing workshop technique create a 'diffuseness of the literary text' remains to be seen, but it is something addressed in Fiona Sampson's wry and insightful 'Twelve Syllogisms in Search of an Editor'. With the publishing industry undergoing major changes, the literary editor is, Sampson declares, a 'profession under threat'. Her pseudo-Wittgensteinian piece interrogates notions of value, and pertinently questions whether 'excellence has been replaced by success'.

Success of another sort is sought in Adam Baron's essay 'Permission, Potency and Protection in the Creative Writing Workshop'. Baron makes a psychological investigation of the student body. He emphasizes understanding the two-way process of teaching and learning from a Berneian perspective, sketches notions of 'Permission', 'Potency' and 'Protection', and questions how a tutor might persuade a student to 'engage' rather than 'impress'. The 'Transactional Analysis' he describes outlines the psychological role a tutor can play in a student's engagement. Baron's essay recognizes that the workshop is not purely an exercise in teaching the technical aspects of writing or craft; it also suggests that the creative writing workshop is permeable to other disciplines, both as a way for teachers of creative writing to develop their pedagogic practice and to aid a student's own development and identification of themselves as writers.

The student's experience within the workshop is also addressed in Maureen Seaton's essay 'The Queerosphere: Musings on Queer Studies and Creative Writing Classrooms (On Poetry, Creativity, and the Fleetingness of Things)', an essay which 'borders on the prose poem', resists 'a straight predictable line', and embraces the fluidity of the workshop's constant motion. Seaton's collaborative writing exercise emphasizes the collective enterprise within her workshops.

Another way of developing students' writing, and at the same time taking them beyond, or in this instance, 'out' of, the workshop, is demonstrated in Éilís Ní Dhuibhne's compelling case study in 'The Archive of the Imagination: Using Oral Tradition in the Teaching of Creative Writing'. Ní Dhuibhne describes how as a creative writing tutor she escorts her students to the National Folklore Collection in University College Dublin and asks them the compelling question: 'How can oral narratives be useful to writers?' Even if, as she concedes, literature has progressed away from oral narrative, introducing students to a new discipline like folklore can revolutionize the way a young writer works. The cross-fertilisation of archetypal structures with contemporary material can, she argues, work to 'outstanding effect' and the rich imagery of oral narrative provides a counterpoint to the textual economy championed in many writing workshops.

Finally, Siobhan Campbell and Patricia Clark's co-written article 'Writing Without a Safety Net: Guidance for Writing after the Creative Writing Classroom' combines Irish/U.K. and U.S. perspectives in a generous offering of some of their most successful strategies, strategies that students can take from the workshop environment and develop alone after formal creative writing education finishes. These strategies include students devising their own assignments, employing amplified self-reflective practice such as 'auto-critique', creating their own manifestos, and building their own anthologies.

Given the opportunity, the contributors of *Beyond the Workshop* have not suggested the workshop's demise, or argued for its disregard. They could have. Michelle Cross, in her essay 'Writing in Public: Popular Pedagogies of Creative Writing', cites R.V. Cassill, 'founder and first president of the Associated Writing Programs', who is reported by George Garret to have made 'a strong case for the de-institutionalization of creative writing characterising the programs as "a good idea whose time had come and gone" '.[2] Cross suggests that a 'decentring of workshop hegemony would remind the writer that the MFA program is a fundamentally temporary and contingent community'.[3]

Of course, there is nothing wrong with a healthy scepticism of creative writing workshops. The workshop is a more productive space for being a contested space. These essays do not create a

---

[2] Kelly Ritter and Stephanie Vanderslice, eds., *Can It Really Be Taught? Resisting Lore in Creative Writing Pedagogy* (2007), pp. 67-76 (p. 73).
[3] Ibid., p. 74.

consensus culture of what is made and what is valued within the workshop. Rather, engaging with the authors of *Beyond The Workshop*, I feel that the workshop is a place that is enriched by the debate and that many writers, facilitators and student-writers will find their own 'desire paths'. Apprentice writers may be directed a certain way by teachers and workshop leaders and then it is up them to find their own way. It may not be the path laid down by the academy at all; it may be the other less trodden path, not a short-cut, but a deviating, playful, path, a line or trajectory suggested by many other forces, cultural or even environmental.

Either way, it is clear to me as both a writer and a teacher of creative writing that the workshop does require a continuing re-invigoration. The individual passions of writers will help guide their pedagogic focus and of course the changing needs of the student body and the forms our poems, stories and essays take, which are ever-shifting, will also guide us toward the best way to pass on what we have learned and know. The writer has a peculiar duty, writes James Liddy: 'He has to create other writers'.[4] Right now, I believe, the workshop has arrived at a moment of 'criticality', that is a point where systems are poised on the verge of something, a point where a near-instantaneous transformation is possible. While the term has been applied to crystal formation, avalanche-movement, and the murmurations or flock dynamics of starlings, I also see it as an apt metaphor for the crucial evolution of the creative writing workshop.

As I write this I have returned from Robert Coover's demonstration of CAVE (Computer Assisted Virtual Environment) Writing, an example of 'immersive technologies' or 3-D computerized environments, which may, Coover believes, become a dominant art form in our culture. Creative writing students of the future might replace, 'See you at workshop next week', with 'See you in the CAVE.' It's hard not to think of those first markings in the caves of Lascaux. How far we have come; far enough to return to the cave? Is it a case of *plus ça change, plus c'est la même chose*?

Or rather, 'The workshop is dead. Long live the workshop.'

---

[4] Dennis O'Driscoll, ed., *The Bloodaxe Book of Poetry Quotations* (2006), p. 37.

Works Cited

D.G. Myers, *The Elephants Teach* (Chicago, Illinois: Chicago University Press, 2006)

Dennis O'Driscoll, ed., *The Bloodaxe Book of Poetry Quotations* (Northumberland, Bloodaxe Books, 2006)

Kelly Ritter and Stephanie Vanderslice, eds., *Can It Really Be Taught? Resisting Lore in Creative Writing Pedagogy* (Portsmouth New Hampshire: Boyton/Cook, 2007)

Within Limits: Examining the Occupied Space and the Spaces Occupied by the Creative Writing Workshop

Nigel McLoughlin

The title of this book, *Beyond The Workshop*, implies a boundary to be crossed or a limit to be exceeded. The notion is an inherently spatial one, and looking at the workshop as a creative space is helpful in many ways. To call something a workshop implies that something within that space is being worked on; that something is being produced; and that there are artisans at work. In that sense the workshop refers to the physical arena in which production takes place, and also to the imaginative space where the participants engage with the particular artifact under construction. If Lefebvre's ideas hold, the process of constructing those spaces is a signifying process. The way in which space is created, and by whom, and indeed the very fact that it has been created at all, carries information related to the epistemological ideas which underpin the decisions.[1] This raises a number of questions: Who does the encoding? How is that encoding achieved? To what end is the encoding carried out? It also raises issues that tend towards the political, in terms of power relations and who controls the 'means of production' of such spaces. Once such a space has been constructed, it can be decoded or read.

The terms 'workshop method', and sometimes more specifically, 'the Iowa workshop method' are generally applied to the teaching methodology practiced in these arenas. But, as we will see, this is not really one method at all, but a very varied set of methods that may be applied in various mixtures to produce different types of workshop. This chapter seeks to analyse what kind of space the workshop might be, paying regard to the questions above in order to examine the ways in which one might view that space, and what might lie beyond it.

So, what are these different types of workshop? One could make a basic distinction between generative workshops and regenerative workshops. In a generative workshop the main function is to generate new work. This type of workshop may be characterised by writing exercises, the creation of a non-judgemental atmosphere, mutual support, and long periods of silence while the writing is being done. Regenerative workshops on the other hand take work in progress and attempt to improve

[1] Henri Lefebvre, *The Production of Space*, trans. D. Nicholson Smith (1991), pp. 36-138.

it. This type of workshop may be characterised by critical engagement with work in progress; open exchange of views in a space full of conversation, argument and sometimes competition. Most workshops make use of various mixtures of both strategies at different times.

One of the things that characterises both basic forms of workshop is play. Workshops of all kinds are spaces where people play with ideas, structures and rules. Caillois classified play into four types: competitive play (agon), games of chance (alea), mimetic play (mimicry), and vertiginous play (ilinx). All of these can have rule-driven (ludic) or unstructured and spontaneous (paidic) varieties.[2] Workshops can be seen as spaces where all of these varieties of play, play themselves out. The ubiquitous workshop exercise, in all its variety, can be seen as offering ways into a number of these types of play. It would not be difficult to see how asking the workshop participants to write a strict Petrarchan sonnet is, at base, a ludic exercise: there are rules to be followed; there is a structure to be maintained or imitated. However, there are also other, more paidic, elements at play in that exercise. Novel images and combinations of sounds as well as meanings are played with through the novel combination of words. Most exercises contain elements of a number of different kinds of play.

For example, an exercise I have used in the past consists of giving out copies of old newspapers (each student gets a different one) and asking the participants to turn to the page number that corresponds to their day of birth. That is, someone born on the seventh would turn to page seven. Then I'd ask them to pick a story that catches their eye and go to the line in the story that corresponds with the month of their birth. So if they were born in June, they'd go to line six. I then ask them to take that line and use it as the first line of a poem, structured however they please. This exercise contains elements of ludic and paidic play through the initial set of rules that produce the first line, and the removal of rules and structure at the end. The exercise contains a high element of chance in the generation of the first line, and one might be lucky or unlucky with that – one might even cheat! It allows opportunities for mimetic play if one was to imitate the style of a poet one admired, and vertiginous play if one decided to be experimental with image and language and see where it led. It may also be competitive if one is trying to outdo one's neighbour. Students can also use this as a 'take-away' exercise. In that case, I generally ask them to use a newspaper that they would not normally read and to follow the

---

[2] R. Caillois, *Man, Play and Games*, trans. M. Barash (2001, 1961), p. 36.

instructions as above. I find that an unfamiliar newspaper may offer more challenging views and different modes of expression that may be more noticeable than the idiom of a newspaper that they read regularly.

The workshop is not just a space full of creative play, there is critical play too, in the sense that ideas relating to the theme, structure, tropes and language of the piece under consideration are communally played with in order to provide ideas for improvement of the piece and to understand it fully in relation to the wider literature and culture. This too can have a competitive edge; can be mimetic; can contain chance elements; and vertiginous play. This play too can manifest itself in the various guises of rule-driven or spontaneous play, but it tends towards a type of play that Caillois omitted from his classification: and that is collaborative play. Every text that passes through workshop is to some extent collaboratively produced through suggestions for changes that may be adopted, or new ideas offered and/or reacted against.

If we can analyse what takes place in the workshop in terms of play, then we can also design our teaching in order to encourage play. I tend to use exercises much more with beginners' groups and community-based writers' groups when I am invited to run them. At university level, I tend not to favour in-class exercises, because I prefer to use valuable contact time for critical workshop and lectures, rather than watching students write. When I give exercises, I tend to give them at the end of class and students can do them at home. But I have found Caillois' classification useful as a way of thinking about the different types of play that I can encourage in students in order to facilitate the production of creative work. I have found it of help in designing exercises students can do at home through understanding what particular type of play might help them find other ways into their writing. In critical workshops students can be asked to play with ideas they find in the poems and the tropes and structures that they encounter in order to better understand how these work.

One way of looking at what happens in the space of the workshop is that something is introduced to the participants which will require an imaginative response; as Philip Gross put it in a workshop I attended some years ago, a stone is being thrown into someone else's pond. This disrupts the imaginitive space; a set of game rules are given, and the participants are asked to construct a new imaginative space from their imaginitive interaction with the exercise, according to the rules (or by bending or breaking them). This imaginitive space is the space of the poem or story being produced. It must exist in a separate intellectual space from the workshop that produced it, because, using the rules of language, narrative and trope, the writer constructs the 'reality' of the text. If the game is the act of writing, then the workshop is the space within which the game is played. The workshop leader has outlined the rules of the game and thereby facilitates the game initially, but the participants may choose to ignore the rules, or interpret them differently as they play the game. Some may even choose to play an entirely different game. The actual imaginitive space of the writing act then becomes the space of the game itself.

The workshop becomes an inherently transformative space where the participants move between these spaces as they simultaneously engage with the space where the game is played (the exercise set in the workshop) and the space of the game itself (the imaginative space of the language game through which they engage with the making of their own text). The workshop leader provides the framework for the writer to construct their own unique language game through the act of writing which emerges from the general game that all the participants play within the space of the workshop. Each writer controls the space of their own language game and actively encodes that space to create the text through creating its imagined temporal and physical reality, populating it with characters and setting the action in motion across an imagined temporal span.

So, the workshop is a playful space that exercises different ways of playing in order to make or remake text. What else might be at play in this space? The workshop is an artificially constructed space. It normally takes place in a room supplied by, or hired on behalf of, the organisation or individual responsible for the workshop. In most cases, for those of us who work in Higher Education, this means the university supplies a physically appropriate space and furnishes it. The university also supplies the lecturer to run the workshop, an it is he who will set the prevailing rules, at least initially, and he who will dictate the tenor of the workshop, particularly in the early stages.

The workshop exists in an intellectual space which is constructed through the interaction of the participants. Initially each of the participants (including the workshop leader) has an expectation of how the workshop will function and what purpose it will serve. The initial workshop will exist as an aggregate of all of these horizons of expectation. The idea of a horizon of expectation is taken from Gadamer, who asserted that understanding could be viewed as a negotiation between partners in a hermeneutical dialogue.[3] The partners in this scenario are leaders and participants in the workshop. Of course, it is never an entirely equal partnership, there are power relations at play even in the very setting up of the workshop, which as an entity may well pre-exist its participants and will initially be dominated, at least in the early stages, by the perceived authority of the tutor. Participants will bring a variety of levels of experience and confidence to the arena.

The aggregate understandings which are present in the group initially, may provide a common framework or 'horizon' through the fusion of individual horizons, which enables the formation of a new context of meaning integration and the assimilation of what is unfamiliar or strange.[4] There will undoubtedly be tensions in this process because everyone's individual horizon must shift to a degree in order to form a single common horizon which the group can agree on and hold between them.

Where participants have similar expectations and read the prevailing habitus of the workshop in the same way, and tacitly operate a common set of rules or doxa, these horizons reinforce each other, thereby resulting in a workshop which is mutually agreed and strongly delineated in terms of the intellectual space that it occupies. Where such horizons of expectation interfere with each other, participants will have constructed different versions of what they believe the workshop to be, and different versions of the doxa which they believe underlie it. These will not necessarily be shared by other participants, and, as a result, participants may well come into direct conflict with each other regarding their perceptions of the same space.

I take the terms 'habitus' and 'doxa' from Bourdieu (1977) who defined habitus as 'a product of history' which 'produces individual and collective practices' and 'schemes of perspective, thought and action which tend to generate the "correctness" of practices and their constancy over time more reliably than all formal rules and explicit norms'.[5] Doxa is defined as 'the relationship of immediate adherence that is established in practice between the habitus and the field to which it is attuned',[6] and the term relates to the 'commitment to the presuppositions ... of the game'.[7] Given that Creative Writing evolved as a discipline in large part by replicating historical sets of rules learned by generations of teachers through their own participation in similar workshops, particularly in the United

---

[3] Hans-Georg Gadamer, *Truth and Method* (1979), p. 270.
[4] Ibid., p. 273.
[5] Pierre Bourdieu, *Outline of a Theory of Practice* (1977), p. 54.
[6] Ibid., p. 68.
[7] Ibid., p. 66.

States, where the Iowa workshop model was replicated by its graduates at other universities, this mode of thinking about the workshop methodology would seem apt. This process of learning to teach Creative Writing has been described as happening by 'osmosis'.[8]

What Fish refers to as 'interpretive communities' can also be directly related to the operation of the workshop.[9] Fish asserted that interpretive communities which are underpinned by differing epistemologies can be expected to interpret a text differently.[10] If one substitutes habitus and doxa for text, one is left with the notion that there may be interpretive communities operating with regard to the perceived rules of workshop, and this would lead to different expectations with regard to what the workshop is envisaged to achieve and how it might go about achieving the expectations being held among these different communities.

By way of a practical example, consider one possible introductory workshop at undergraduate level: participants who arrive for the first workshop of their undergraduate degree may come from widely dfferent backgrounds. To simplify the example I will focus on three commonly encountered and disparate backgrounds. Some may have no experience of workshop at all, because they have come from a school environment where the teacher imparts information and they take notes. They are used to being told how and what to think but not used to voicing opinions and justifying them in a workshop environment. They may expect the tutor to tell them why a text is working or not working, rather than ask *them* if they think it works or what parts work (or don't), and why. These participants may be very quiet initially and require active strategies from the tutor to draw them out. Several others might be mature students who have been used to attending workshops where the workshop leader gives exercises for free writing and the outcomes are then read out and some positives are pointed up for further work. These participants may be quite confident and have very clear ideas about what good literature is and the type of writing that they want to engage in. They may find it difficult that the other groups have other ideas and if the previous environment has been very supportive, they may have problems in giving and receiving constructive criticism initially.

---

[8] K. Ritter, 'Professional Writers/Writing Professionals: Revamping Teacher Training in Creative Writing PhD Programmes' in *College English*, 64:2 (2001), p. 205.

[9] Stanley Fish, 'Interpreting the Variorum', in *Is There a Text in this Class?* (1980), p. 171.

[10] Ibid., pp. 167-73.

A third set of participants might come from a Further Education course where there has been a critical workshop in which work in any genre may be circulated and in which the workshop leader leads criticism on each piece and the students note what works and what doesn't. These participants may be more familiar with the critical workshop format, but they may also expect it to be run in exactly the same way as the workshop they previously encountered. They may also be much more confident and vocal initially, and if, as a group, these participants are already comfortable giving and receiving constructive criticism, this can make the others initially think they are overly harsh, and some participants may find them intimidating. Clearly these three backgrounds will result in three completely different interpretations of what the workshop will actually be, based on participants' own experiences of education generally and workshops in particular. Three very different horizons of expectation will be in operation within each of these interpretive communities and may well result in conflicts as each set of participants struggles to adapt to a habitus which may be very unlike anything they have previously experienced.

Of course, within Higher Education this is normally ameliorated to an extent by establishing an initial set of 'ground rules' and through the group leader outlining the expectations and requirements of the workshop in the initial meeting. This might serve to make manifest some of the doxa, and clarify the habitus of the workshop in general terms. However, some doxa will remain tacit and are only learned by participants through the act of participation and the modelling function of the workshop leader. It is difficult for instance, to clarify exactly what level of criticism is required in advance, and exactly what the expected tenor of that criticism should be when it is delivered. The advice to be constructively critical and to provide detailed criticism on structure, form, and language use, for example, may itself be interpreted differently by different participants. I have found for instance a misinterpretation of the word 'criticism' in many cases among new undergraduates, whereby the term seems to be interpreted as wholly negative, and there appears to be a belief that positive comments are 'not critical'.

In more mature groups many doxa will already be implicitly present within the workshop. The participants may already have prior experience of how the workshop tends to operate in the institution and the habitus may already be well established. This is common in final year B.A. workshops, but it can also be particularly true of groups operating outside the academy, where workshops may be long established and only occasionally take new members. New participants must be inducted into the prevailing habitus and made familiar with the 'presuppositions of the game'[11] in order to be able to develop a doxa – a feel for the game. This is a very important part of the process and will ensure that all of the partipants have the same information from which to construct their horizons of expectation. This means that it is less likely that they will construct widely divergent expectations and the workshop participants will have a much more coherent idea of the workshop as an entity, because all participants broadly understand, and agree on, the prevailing habitus and doxa within the social space.

Depending on the habitus that has been engendered within the workshop, a variety of theoretical concerns may become manifest. Take for example the common requirement that the writer is silent while the workshop discusses their work. In a very tangible sense the writer enters into, and experiences what Barthes referred to as the 'death of the author'.[12] Without the distraction of replying to criticism, they have the opportunity to observe the birth of their fellow students as 'readers' and the difficulties those readers face when they no longer have recourse to the writer as 'authority'.[13] This dialogic process is also decodable in terms of what Hirsch called the 'babel of interpretations'.[14]

The workshop is filled by a number of these interpretations as each student puts forward the interpretation they have constructed through their reading of the text. The space at this point is a dialogic space, since these interpretations enter into dialogue with each other in order to establish how the 'interpretive community'[15] of the workshop may ultimately view the text. Sometimes, several interpretive communities will arise where the workshop group may disagree as to the interpretation each feels is most appropriate. The workshop leader may add to this babel of interpretations by adding their own view, or they may initiate a synthetic process. Such synthesis may not be entirely possible, but the summary of views provided can prove very useful to the group and to the writer particularly. The process can open up the writer to the realisation that their text contains the potential for different interpretations and indeed that this may well be something that they might wish to use as a deliberate artistic strategy.

Some workshops offer the writer a 'right to reply' when the

---

[11] Bourdieu, p. 66.
[12] Roland Barthes, *Image-Music-Text* (1977), p. 242.
[13] Ibid.
[14] E.D.Hirsch, Jnr., *Validity in Interpretation* (1967), p. 127.
[15] Fish, p. 171.

discussion is over and this may result in the writer defending their work, asking further questions of the group or acknowledging the criticism received. Such defence of the work may sometimes enlighten readers and cause them to change their original interpretation of the text, but the original interpretations still remain valid, since these are the likely interpretations the text as it stands may receive once it has been cut loose of its author through the act of dissemination. In the process the writer has gained a rare chance to observe what readers may struggle with, misunderstand, or impose upon the text through their own reading. Sometimes, especially when dealing with early apprentice writers, the feedback is more mundane, but this too can help the writer in the editing process through pointing out clichés and metaphors that don't quite come off, for instance. Writers may wish to change the text in the light of what they have learned, or they may be comfortable with allowing the intended and unintended meanings that are generated to remain and choose to let the text stand. Either way, they make an informed decision in the light of what other writers have said about the text.

The workshop is undoubtedly a social space, and sometimes a contested social space, but it is also an experimental and intellectual space, where questions are asked and answered, sometimes directly, sometimes tacitly. It may be thought of as a model which conforms to the social aspects of creativity as described by Csikszentmihalyi in his tripartite social model of creative interactions between the artist, the domain and the field.[16] Through examining the processes that occur in workshop we may better understand what we as writers believe is worth adding to the domain; and how we, at various levels, act as gatekeepers to that domain and what processes are used to maintain that system.

Part of that development is the tacit learning that goes on through the workshopping process, whereby the student learns what those who read literature and those who write literature value *as literature* and what is seen as 'good' and 'bad' writing by those who are currently engaged in writing (and in some cases editing and publishing). The workshop leader is invaluable in this regard, since they are more than likely an author who is currently publishing within the genre that the workshop deals with, and aware of the current habitus within the genre. Part of what is transmitted through the workshopping process is the doxa which constitute the current habitus within the genre as a domain and the expectations of the current field (made up of the

---

[16] Mihaly Csikszentmihalyi, *Creativity: Flow and the psychology of discovery and invention* (1996), pp. 36-47.

editors, publishers and reviewers) which acts as gatekeepers to that domain.

By such mechanisms the workshop can act as a reliable test for a piece of writing, in terms of how a piece of writing confirms or challenges the prevailing cultural habitus within the genre, and the mechanisms whereby it goes about doing that. The workshop may be used to address questions about who controls the system and who or what it serves and to examine the power relations at play through that system. In that sense, the workshop is a microcosm of the critical and selective processes that are to be found among the creative industries more broadly, and it can function as a proving ground where apprentice artists attempt to find new modes of expression and attempt to prove them in the wider domain, while also generating an awareness of the processes which may be at play within the domain and between the gatekeepers of that domain and themselves as emerging creative individuals.

The workshop is a space where experimentation is possible and where the 'what if?' questions can be answered: what if I do this? Will I be understood, will it make the text more intertextual/experimental/interesting? There are also the 'why didn't that work?' questions, and these are just as important because the answers that the apprentice writer receives will allow them to make a potentially more successful attempt next time. The workshop provides a space where boundaries can be pushed in relative safety. Adverse comments in workshop are not as public as a bad review notice in the press, but they may well throw up many of the same issues, which the writer can then address, should they wish to. This process may be viewed in terms of what Weisberg has described as a heuristic approach to problem solving through finding strategies to search the problem-space of the writing project in order to generate a creative solution.[17] These strategies can often involve a hill climbing approach which attempts to break the major problem down and solve it in sections, or can involve using strategies that have previously worked and combining them in novel ways to address the new problem. It may involve looking at how others solve similar problems and identifying if there is something in their approach which may be of use in the problem at hand.

It may well be anathema to some to think about the process of writing, or indeed creativity more generally, in terms of algorithms and problem solving strategies. But at base that is as much at the heart of any creative endeavour as it is in other domains where the approach is more usual, in engineering for

---

[17] R.W. Weisberg, *Creativity: Understanding Innovation in Problem Solving, Science, Invention, and the Arts* (2006), pp. 141-52.

example. Recognising and learning to use these strategies can produce new approaches to writing through generating novel combinations of the strategies we see in other writers and those strategies we have used previously. In effect, we learn to connect two previously unconnected matrices of thought, as Koestler put it, and that process is at the heart of all creativity.[18]

The workshop is a place where the student can explore the process of making text; analyse the creative processes which they use to make and remake their text; and a space where they can self-actualise as a creative individual and a writer. These processes take time and they are not something that can be achieved directly through knowledge transfer. Instead, they are organic and developmental self-reflective processes and the workshop provides the dedicated time, space and interaction with other writers in a formalised environment needed to focus on these processes through their manifestation in raw and redrafted text, while encouraging the writer to engage self-reflectively with their art. It provides a framework for the development of the artist, alongside and through the development of the texts.

In these economically difficult times, the workshop has often been the target of those who want to maximise teaching efficiency. One can see why. In order to have an optimally functioning workshop, numbers must be small. A number of industry standards have suggested optimal sizes between 12 and 16 at undergraduate level and smaller still at postgraduate level. Many in Higher Education would prefer the staff–student ratio to be somewhere in the mid–high twenties. Colleagues talk of being asked to run workshops of 40. This has resulted in a number of strategies for separating elements of creative writing courses that may be taught to large classes in order to protect the workshop group size. This has met with varying degrees of success. Now, with the removal of the higher HEFCE Band C funding that Creative Writing previously enjoyed, the pressure will undoubtedly become more intense. However, I for one, would be loath to lose the workshop as a teaching environment. It is difficult to imagine what might economically replace the level of individualised expert feedback that it provides to the student. One might find, of course, that contact time becomes much more important to the student when faced with paying fees of £8,000–£9,000. Workshop is actually quite an economical way of providing dedicated, individualised tuition and feedback to the student, and it may well now come into its own.

In looking beyond the workshop, I think we need to look

---

[18] Arthur Koestler, *The Act of Creation* (1964), p. 35.

beyond the surface of what the workshop teaches, and how it teaches, in order to see the many complex processes at play within it, and to examine their importance for writers. We need to examine not just the hard skills that the workshop teaches, but the soft skills and the more generally transferable skills that students learn through the process and how they might be of more general use to the student. I am thinking particularly of critical, creative, and problem solving skills, and the skills gained in articulation of opinion, the ability to examine the arguments of others, and the ability to work collaboratively towards a common goal. All of these are highly marketable skills, and all are taught and learned through workshop. In workshop, students observe these skills modelled by the tutor and have the opportunity to practice them for themselves.

In order to remain economically viable, it is true that we need to be looking for a much more mixed method approach to our teaching practice. We will also be asked to revisit the structure of our courses in order to refresh them as a result of this new funding landscape. These new course designs will undoubtedly include lectures, seminars, online exercises, directed research projects and employment-focused sessions, as well as creatively and academically challenging aspects. Many courses already include a number of them. We will be asked to examine what each method offers to the student and to the learning process in order to pick the most appropriate methodology suited to our course aims. It may well be that the workshop ceases to be the default mechanism by which creative writing is taught (and it already has in some places). However, this must be for sound pedagogical reasons rather than as a knee-jerk reaction to financial constraint. Not to have workshops at all would short-change the student. It would be a bit like trying to teach fine art without crits, chemistry without lab work, or medicine without dissection.

Writing Exercise

At exactly 10.43 a.m. or p.m., one day next week, go to a window in your house that overlooks a street, a farmyard or another place where things might happen. Open the window. Describe exactly what you see, hear, smell and feel. Be as detailed as possible. Use all the senses and use simile and metaphor to build as exact a picture as you can. Spend ten minutes doing this. Put the piece away. At exactly the opposite time of day one day the following week (so 10.43 p.m. if you did a.m. the first time) go to the same window. Open it again. Again describe exactly what you see, hear, smell and feel. Again use all the senses, use metaphor and simile. Put the piece away. Then in a few days take both pieces out. Try and combine the pieces, either as two views in two separate stanzas or as two voices using interlinked descriptions. Use your imagination to find ways to draw these together to resolve the poem. Don't be afraid to add or cut away.

Works Cited

Association of Writers & Writing Programs (AWP), *Director's Handbook: Guidelines, Policies, and Information for Creative Writing Programs,* (Fairfax VA: Association of Writers & Writing Programs, 2011)

Barthes, Roland, *Image-Music-Text* (Glasgow: Fontana, 1977)

Bourdieu, Pierre, *Outline of a Theory of Practice* (Cambridge: Cambridge University Press, 1977)

Caillois, Roger, *Man, Play and Games*, trans. Meyer Barash (1961); (Chicago: University of Illinois Press, 2001)

Csikszentmihalyi, Mihaly, *Creativity: Flow and the psychology of discovery and invention* (New York: Harper, 1996)

Fish, Stanley, *Is There a Text in This Class?* (Cambridge Mass.: Harvard University Press, 1980)

Gadamer, Hans-Georg., *Truth and Method* (London: Steed and Ward, 1979)

Hirsch, E.D., Jr., *Validity in Interpretation* (New Haven: Yale University Press, 1967)

Holland, Siobhan, *Creative Writing: A Good Practice Guide* (London: English Subject Centre, 2003)

Koestler, Arthur, *The Act of Creation* (London: Pan, 1964)

Lefebvre, H., *The Production of Space*, trans. D. Nicholson Smith (Oxford: Basil Blackwell, 1991)

National Association of Writers in Education (NAWE) *Creative Writing Subject Benchmark Statement and Creative Writing Research Benchmark Statement* (York: NAWE, 2008)

Ritter, K., 'Professional Writers/Writing Professionals: Revamping Teacher Training in Creative Writing PhD Programmes', *College English*, 64.2 (2001), pp. 205-27

Weisberg, R.W., *Creativity: Understanding Innovation in Problem Solving, Science, Invention, and the Arts* (Hoboken, New Jersey: John Wiley & Sons, 2006)

Metaphors We Teach By

Heidi Lynn Staples

> *As civilized human beings, we are the inheritors, neither of an inquiry about ourselves and the world, nor of an accumulating body of information, but of a conversation, begun in the primeval forests and extended and made more articulate in the course of centuries. It is a conversation which goes on both in public and within each of ourselves.*

Michael Oakeshott[1]

A professor of mine once lifted a workshop poem he did not like into the air and lit the piece on fire. I was not there. But I believe the story. I gave him my didactic feminist rant about encountering no women artists on my first visit to the Guggenheim in New York City. 'But there *are* no female geniuses,' he declared. I resisted of course. He swivelled in his chair and conceded, adding maybe Gertrude Stein was the exception. He said more I do not recall, except: 'and after all, men have the *penis*.' I can still see his expectant blue eyes. I did not register the look then, but now I recall hilarity. He was baiting me. At one point, he asked how I got started on a poem and added that to write he often drank. In the middle of our independent study, I arrived to find a note taped to his office door stating he had been removed from his tenured position for a drunken outburst in which he called a literature graduate student a 'Marxist bitch' and threw a drink in her face at an off-campus party. Maybe he will not win any teaching awards. But he remains one of my favourite teachers.

Since that independent study, I have had more than six years of creative writing classroom experience as a student in M.F.A. and Ph.D. programmes and just as many as a teacher myself. I have taught creative writing at the Irish Writers' Centre; the National Forensic Psychiatric Hospital in Dublin, Ireland, Syracuse University, and the University of Georgia. What continues to prove exemplary about that early exchange is the professor's participatory stance. As I recall, he did not much edit my poems. He did not focus on any piece as an individual object, a product, making editorial comments to suggest he might shape

---

[1] Michael Oakeshott, *The Voice of Poetry in the Conversation of Mankind: An essay* (1959), p. 11.

my efforts into a well-polished piece of individual writing for positive reception in the marketplace. The guiding metaphor was not that of a workshop. Instead, he invited – okay, goaded – me into conversation. He emphasised conversation about poetry and the writing process, offering descriptions and asking questions that prompted me to engage in discussion. Despite the disparity in our artistic accomplishments, he somehow made me feel we were, as cognitive anthropologist Etienne Wenger describes it, just two 'people who share[d] a concern or a passion for something they do and learn how to do it better as they interact regularly'.[2] My professor's emphasis on description and insistence on conversation implied my participation in a 'community of practice'.

Wenger and his research partner, Jean Lave, coined the term 'community of practice' after studying apprenticeship as a learning model in the 1990s. They observed Yucatec midwives, native tailors, navy quartermasters, meat cutters and alcoholics in A.A. to discover how learning functions. They have found learning does not usually involve the traditional 'relationship between a student and a master' but a 'more complex set of decentralised social relationships through which learning takes place'.[3] They note 'very little observable teaching; the more basic phenomenon is learning',[4] which takes place as community members move from 'legitimate peripheral participation' to 'full participation',[5] and change their identities in the process. Since Lave and Wenger's findings, many colleges and universities have established campus-based learning communities throughout the U.S. post-secondary system and emphasised what Lave and Wenger call 'situated learning'.[6] The learning communities assume learning is mostly not individual and psychological, but collaborative and social. Rather than one individual student learning *from* an individual teacher, people develop by learning *to* engage with other community members in 'communities of practice'.[7] This reorientation is pretty standard fare in progressive education. Many creative writing workshops, meanwhile, continue to attempt the teaching of writing. As creative writing instructors with our students' best interests in mind, we would do well to stop trying to teach writing. Writing cannot be taught. Writing, however, can be

---

[2] Etienne Wenger, 'Communities of Practice: A Brief Introduction', online
[3] Jean Lave and Etienne Wenger, *Situated Learning: Legitimate Peripheral Participation* (1991), p. 94.
[4] Ibid., p. 92.
[5] Wenger, 'Communities of Practice'.
[6] Lave and Wenger, p. 93.
[7] Ibid., p. 109.

learned. Our job is to find ways to help students learn. The shift from teaching to the facilitation of learning requires we construct the writing class as a community of practice, revising the workshop conception accordingly.

Isn't a 'writing workshop' fundamentally a 'community of practice'?

The writing workshop is a metaphor applied to the writing classroom and points to an understanding of the writer's education as involving a period of apprenticeship. The workshop is cast as promoting active engagement, that students *do* learn *to* rather than *from*, as Louis Menand suggests in his article 'Show or Tell' when he says that 'creative-writing courses follow naturally from the "learning by doing" theories of progressive education: they add practical, hands-on experience to traditional book learning'.[8] The workshop as an experience does imply a community of practice, and many workshops may facilitate participation in the writing community. But as commonly understood, the creative writing workshop as a tradition has several limitations which need review because the guiding metaphor may thwart full participation by students.

We can begin with the word itself. A reductive, mechanistic, industry-oriented word, 'workshop' implies uniformity of intention, of material and of final outcome. The word most directly references a small room into which participants enter, leaving the context of their daily lives in order to create a 'work', a product fit for consumption. The purpose of the workshop in practice is the enhancement of this product, a purpose that emphasises writing as a noun, a thing. The discussion of the writing aims for the writing's beautification in order to receive a positive reception by an imagined discriminating reader like the workshop leader, who has final reading of the work. The leader assigns all readings and writing assignments. With the leader's representative mastery in mind, workshop participants wield pens and preferences. Lines are drawn. A process of informal learning is assumed – that by pursuing editorial rigour, students will gain the ability to write better. Unfortunately, however, an imbalance can develop between generative and critical voices, and with the rigour comes mortis. Not only does the emphasis on the writing as a product too often result in a lively piece becoming a beautiful corpse, the cognitive habit of emphasising

---

[8] Louis Menand, 'Show or Tell', *New Yorker* (8 June 2009), p. 2.

reception and 'high standards' can cut deep. The critical voice can slip lethally into the messy, ungainly, awkward, inelegant wilds within the poetic imagination.

The historical context out of which the creative writing workshop arose helps explain the standardising impulse. The first writing workshops in the U.S. came about in the 1920s, and the workshop's rise coincided with that of New Criticism. Within the context of New Criticism, which aimed for decon-textualisation of the aesthetic object in order to judge its aesthetic value using purportively objective measures, the workshop metaphor for the writing classroom seemed to make sense. Accomplished teachers might rest easy approaching a piece of writing as an object and compare its accomplishment and merit to those of works deemed worthy by canonisation. But after the second half of the twentieth century, specifically given the insights of post-modernism, we can no longer so easily decontextualise an artwork. The workshop metaphor fails to reckon with what we now understand about cultural relativity, and we can no longer assess writing through appeals to the literary canon without performing a potential violence. To approach a writing classroom with the presumption of objectivity and to wield one's own cultural biases as final truths can violate difference in subtle and not-so-subtle acts of cultural imperialism.

By contrast to the workshop's emphasis on the art object, a writing class conceived as a community of practice foregrounds the social interplay between writers and the action of writing. The classroom is not a place to polish an object but a meeting ground where members bring offerings around which 'to interact and learn together'.[9] A holistic, organic, anthropologically oriented term, 'community of practice' implies a multiplicity combined with active co-operation in a 'shared domain of interest'.[10] The word 'community' evokes diversity of point of view. The word most directly references a group of people, a potentially expansive group that participants join, bringing their diverse experiences in order to create a fruitful discussion about writing practice. The word 'practice' most directly refers to the writing process, a richly various activity in which participants engage on personal and highly particular creative journeys. An emphasis on 'practice' allows us to remain alert to the individual needs of each student and to define 'the work' not only as a production for public consumption but as a process for private transformation.

The process-oriented classroom privileges generativity in

---

[9] Wenger, 'Communities of Practice'.
[10] Ibid.

order to support a writer's effort at perception. The instructor facilitates discussion and navigates group dynamics. Observations are made and multiple viewpoints established. The purpose of the community of practice is ongoing cultivation, a purpose that emphasises writing as a verb, an activity. With new ways of being and knowing as aims, we yield to each other. Judgement is suspended while patterns are recognised and described. The entire class contributes in the selection of course texts, while compositional approaches are explored as entry points into the imaginative landscape. Editorial suggestions are expressed as part of articulating a work on its own terms. A process of informal learning is assumed in this approach also – that by opening to possibility, students will gain the ability to write better – and writing better means thinking more flexibly and deeply. Participants will have a sustainable writing practice and an individual inquiry with which they are profoundly, personally and particularly engaged. Foregrounding the writing process helps the creative voices survive the influx of critical insights that can challenge the writer's courage, while the cognitive habit of emphasising perception and relative standards orients the writer toward a dynamic interplay between her conscious mind and her imagination.

The idea of 'situated learning' arose well into post-modernism. Our current writing classes are developing during an era of heightened cultural sensitivity, deconstruction and international globalism. The radical insights of the period are naturally producing attendant shifts within education, as easily observed in the well-established emphasis on multiculturalism, group work and the New Literacy in the U.S. university system's first year writing sequence. The writing classroom articulated as a community of practice has begun to make sense. Accomplished teachers are free to explore writing as a dynamic process of cultural exchange and help students move toward 'full participation' with the intention 'to do justice to the diversity of relations involved in varying forms of community membership'.[11] The writing is repeatedly recontextualised by varying viewpoints, including the author's. The community of practice metaphor allows for 'a reciprocal relation between persons and practice',[12] and the parameters of aesthetic values shift as participants engage. The authority in the classroom remains decentralised and unstable as 'continual interaction of new perspectives is sanctioned, everyone's participation is legitimately peripheral in some respect. In other words, everyone can to some degree be considered a "newcomer" to the future of

[11] Lave and Wenger, pp. 36-7.
[12] Ibid., p. 117.

a changing community'.[13] To approach a writing classroom with this emphasis on listening, and to remain open toward encounters with difference, facilitates collaboration within a multicultural community.

The seven habits of highly community-oriented creative writing classrooms

In a course organised as a community of practice, students learn to behave like writers – that is, they read, write, support and discuss writing rigorously and on a regular basis. The following seven practices can help facilitate full engagement.

1. *Assume a learner's stance*
    Rather than a set of behaviours, a learner's stance is a mindset. Do not expect yourself, or allow students to expect you, to have all the answers or all the questions. Instead, anticipate that your thinking will be altered during every class, and by students. When you model comfort with this position, you help students accept the uncertainty learning involves and informally teach that full participation in the writing community includes perpetual learning. For this stance to be more than theatre, however, include practices that give students access to expertise beyond your own.

2. *Foster co-participation*
    Co-participation is more than leaving silence for students to fill during the discussion of student writing, although a learner-centred teacher certainly does that. Students also need to speak from a position of some expertise. Presentations can help provide students with positions from which to speak and points of entry into lines of inquiry particular to their own predilections. During a semester of student-led presentations that involve not only biographical data about authors, but also the creation and fulfillment of an exercise generated in response to the creative works, students begin to gain frames of reference and vocabularies with which to talk *to* each other about their projects. A great multiplicity develops in the course, and a sense of possibility emerges. As students are exposed to a variety of writers and encouraged to make choices of their own, a sense of adventure arises.

---

[13] Ibid., p. 117.

3. *Give choice whenever possible*
   Choice in the classroom means that each individual student plays a significant role in plotting her experience of the course and actively engages her unique creative journey. The decision making also orients students and gives them a position from which to speak so they can genuinely participate.

4. *Design major process-based assignments*
   Process-based assignments are those that do not involve the critique of a final product but rather the management of an ongoing rigorous engagement with writing. The inclusion of a major process-based assignment contributes perhaps the most to redefining the creative writing class from a workshop to a community of practice.
   An example of a major process-based writing assignment is the writer's notebook assignment described at the end of this essay. The writer's notebooks function throughout the course as a decentralised text from which we all learn. The collection of notebooks evolves into 'a field of learning resources in everyday practice viewed from the perspective of learners', rather than 'a teaching curriculum ... constructed for the instruction of newcomers'.[14]

5. *Cultivate interdependence*
   Students feel a sense of interdependence when their success depends in some part on that of their classmates. A buddy system can facilitate this experience. As part of the writing notebook assignment, a student's buddy will read and respond to her notebook several times during the semester. Consider having students take responsibility for leading the discussion of each other's writing during the workshops. Student-led workshops profoundly decentre the authority and help generate a connective rather than competitive community.

6. *Emphasise descriptive feedback*
   Descriptive feedback focuses on suspending judgement and delaying advice in order to note carefully and articulate fully as many patterns in a writer's work as possible. Readers also speculate on the philosophical implications and aesthetic alignments presented by the writer's choices. This type of rhetorical analysis can create for writers the self-consciousness necessary for effective writing without

---

[14] Ibid., p. 97.

presuming a shared worldview or aesthetic. A student writer is not forced to learn *from* the group's discussion as members recreate the student's work into a form more suitable to their tastes. Rather, descriptive feedback gives students vocabulary through which *to* talk with themselves and others about writing. When discussion of a student's best effort begins and sustains itself with a description of that effort, the class becomes less pressurised and more driven by a pleasurable curiosity.

7. *Be festive*
    A writing class that values festivity pursues a pleasurable, even joyous engagement with writing. We might even say that the creative life is one that values and so seeks the festive experience. Collaborative writings, public readings and chapbook and broadside creation are all ways to generate particular festive moments within a course. But if you are happy enough to participate in a creative writing community of practice as a teacher, then wherever your students go for the rest of their lives, it will stay with them, for the writing community is a moveable feast.

Writing Exercise

The Writer's Notebook

The writer's notebook is a large ring-binder with loose leaf paper, divided into four sections. **Please bring your notebook to class every week.** At the beginning of each class, you will have the opportunity to share and listen to notebook entries.

- **Section one:** *Personal observation* – Several times a week, record anything you find interesting – a drawn sketch, found words, dictated conversations, freewrites, diary, etc.

- **Section two:** *Exercises* – Each week, please choose and perform an exercise from the book on craft you are reading, from the Bernadette Mayer compilation, or one of your own devising.

- **Section three:** *Imitations* – Each week, please perform what Charles Bernstein has described as 'wreading' – that is reading by writing a close imitation of a work by any published author you like.

- **Section four:** *Writers' Events* – Please attend at least two writers' events this semester. In this part of your notebook, please describe and respond to these experiences.

Works Cited

Lave, Jean, and Etienne Wenger, *Situated Learning: Legitimate Peripheral Participation* (New York: Cambridge University Press, 1991)

Menand, Louis, 'Show or Tell', *New Yorker* (8 June 2009)

Oakeshott, Michael, *The Voice of Poetry in the Conversation of Mankind: An essay* (London: Bowes & Bowes, 1959)

Wenger, Etienne, 'Communities of Practice: A Brief Introduction', available at: http://www.ewenger.com/theory/ [accessed 31-10-2011]

The Workshop as Stage

Todd Swift

My question in this chapter is easily summarised: is Creative Writing at university level (and its attendant pedagogy) meaningful without The Workshop? The very ethos of this book seems to suggest it is possible for there to be 'life beyond' workshopping; I am not so sure such a thing, even if possible, would be advisable, and will discuss why below.

Evidently, not everyone thinks The Workshop (TW) is essential to Creative Writing (CW), at least in the British context. Matt Morrison's *Key Concepts in Creative Writing* has more than 100 entries, from Absurd Literature to Writer's Guild of Britain, but seems to have a curious, and telling, blind spot – there is no entry for workshopping.[1] This is surely surprising, since, from its inception, CW in the university has been connected to TW. In fact, there is a pleasing doubleness to that 'W' – and is not the most famous (and original) M.F.A.[2] in Iowa also called the Writer's Workshop – doubling that W?

Morrison's exclusion of TW from his list of 'key concepts' may indicate two intriguing options – either it is such a given of CW that it requires no further comment or consideration (it has been naturalised, and is no longer problematic) – or that he genuinely felt that TW is an entirely separate concern – more or less just a room in a building where students meet; in this sense, one would not expect a list of key concepts in philosophy or geography to contain an entry on the classroom.

Surely, though, TW is not merely, or only, a room; it is a space – one that has practical, theoretical, and symbolic implications. Michelle Wandor's recent study (also from Palgrave), *The Author Is Not Dead, Merely Somewhere Else* (2008) is an impressive survey of the many issues that arise when 'reconsidering' CW. Her first chapter notes that The University of East Anglia (U.E.A.) began the CW M.A. more than 40 years ago (1970) when Malcolm Bradbury and Angus Wilson set it up, inspired by the Iowa Writer's Workshop, officially established in 1939.[3]

Wandor makes a distinction between two meanings of TW – in one case it is the process of 'workshopping' and in the other, it is the very 'academic distinctiveness of CW as an academic

---

[1] Matt Morrison, *Key Concepts in Creative Writing* (2010).
[2] Master of Fine Arts.
[3] Michelle Wandor, *The Author Is Not Dead, Merely Somewhere Else* (2008), pp. 8 and 131.

discipline'.[4] This rather elides the question. TW is neither merely an umbrella term for all CW on campus, nor can it be simply be a verb, like 'reading' or 'writing'. Indeed, its ambiguous status, and potential, is partly connected to its complex significance; it is a term that everyone assumes the meaning of, but no one has quite nailed down. TW is a slippery term, then – like language itself.

TW is not the sum of all the parts of CW, because experience shows that much has to happen beyond the TW space – such as the CW Student (CWS) writing and reading. Indeed, part of the anxiety about whether CW has any value (can be 'taught') is based on the fact, obviously recognised, that much of what CWSs do – reading and writing – is done 'in their own time', outside the academic space, and presumably only becomes 'academic' and appropriately institutionalised when it is returned to the university, to be discussed, analysed, and, finally, graded. After all, such an argument goes, anyone can 'read and write' anywhere anyway.

In this reading of CW at university, and especially graduate level, TW becomes the central academic location where CW can be policed – or less dramatically – validated; it is something the university requires, more than the CWSs themselves. TW has three key actors associated with it – the university; the students; and the 'leader'. The Workshop Leader (TWL) is almost always a member of the faculty, or a visiting lecturer, and is usually a published and successful writer (though not always). University, CWS and TWL each meet, with their intersecting needs, expectations, desires, and abilities, in The Workshop. By definition, this is the only 'place' or space where all three actors do so.

Wandor has done a good job of exploring concerns regarding CW protocol, and the several usual models on which TW is based. These can be boiled down to:

- Anarchy – no one has any authority, and all are equal – though in practice it is hard to imagine the university and TWL relinquishing all control (who would grade the work?) – this perhaps happens most often when students, teacher and institution are all equally lost, weak, or clueless.

- Democracy – TWL is nominally in charge, but respectfully defers to the CWSs, who lead TW.

- Dictatorship – TWL holds the students more than a little

---

[4] Ibid., p. 120.

in contempt, and governs TW by a mixture of fear and awe.

- Theocracy – TWL is treated as an admired 'guru' figure and is worshipped willingly by the CWSs.
- Meritocracy - the favoured or notably best students in TW become *de facto* leaders, working or colluding with TWL.

Despite the cynicism of some of this anatomy (and there may be other permutations) what emerges is a recognisable picture of social interaction – The Workshop as Polis. But so is every classroom, and such an analysis hardly gets to the heart of what makes TW – as opposed to mere workshopping – unique and even invaluable.

Going deeper, we come to the protocol of TW. There are variations, but what seems usually to occur in such spaces is that creative writing by the students is discussed. In fact, to most people, without this, there is no workshop. However, at British universities, especially, this is not an accepted aspect of TW; I have heard of (and witnessed) situations where TWL would silently hand out (return) corrected writing samples; or use TW as a simple classroom hour or hours, to lecture, teach, or provide lists (good books, words to use), or recommend exercises – and this may be the default option at undergraduate level. However, whatever the variations discussed above, I hold to the position that an authentic Creative Writing Workshop must, at the very least, offer the following, every week: *creative writing by the students being discussed*.

My position is this. Mass is a ritual where Holy Communion is offered; no communion, no Mass. Psycho-analysis requires that 'the analysed' lies down and talks for 50 minutes; no talking, no cure. Sure, there are other rituals and other therapies, but at the end of the day, there is also the classical basis in some form of pure (and traditional) ritual. I would hold that Drama is a third such space; no acting, no play. Here is a fourth: Writing itself is a space that requires a basic action – inscription onto a neutral space, the blank page; no words, no writing. I am going to establish a complex trope from the above – TW is a bit of all of these other ritualistic spaces: communion; therapy; play; creation; but it is not simply a trope. It has its own peculiar power, and its own special values, as it is its own kind of unique space.

The Creative Writing Workshop is not merely, as we have seen, an assigned time and place, a room. It is a space where three actors (university, student, teacher) come together, and where writing by students is discussed. This is then a good preliminary definition. But as we know, there are protocols.

These are often simply administrative and revolve around the economics of TW – who gets to present and speak, and how often. The first issue to be resolved is how and when is work submitted for review? Normally, it is either circulated in advance (via some form of media) or at the previous session; or provided sight unseen on the day, and read aloud in TW itself. The key thing here is that TWL and CWSs have access to the text to be discussed. Discussion ensues. Then, depending on how much time there is, this process will be repeated.

I have intentionally been using the word 'discussed' as a temporary marker for now. As Wandor observes,[5] this can also be called evaluation, or criticism, among other things, and is the crux of the entire enterprise. Indeed, the issue of value (for money, as pedagogy, as advice) is almost entirely located around the function of TW as a space where something happens between the creative writing texts (CWTs), TWL and CWSs. Perhaps, there is a text in this room, and it is the fourth actor in the workshopping process.

What this something is, is what is up for grabs, and is likely always going to be somewhat heterodox, ineffable, and unique to every Workshop; indeed, I have heard creative writing teachers proudly claim that what they do cannot be described or prescribed (as in a module guide) since it defies categorisation; and there tends to be a rather exaggerated claim of originality here, as if each creative writer is expected, or able, to create their very own system. Far from that being the case, as we have seen, the clarity and beauty of TW is mainly based on its simple repeatability across countries and cultures. Religions, political systems and therapies do not spread if they are complex and unrepeatable phenomena.

The tendency among some British creative writing teachers to undermine or doubt TW is in fact more often than not a symptom of one of two things – an inherent suspicion of workshopping as a process, a disbelief in creative writing as a pedagogy; or a discomfort with American educational models (predicated on the American ideologies of independence, originality and democracy) that sit uncomfortably with some British writers more used to a hierarchical critical-publishing reception model. As one creative writing teacher said to me once, 'we can teach them, but they won't be published' – a sentiment more likely to occur in London, with its establishment consensus of how good writing finds its way to an agent, than in Iowa, where no such literary establishment impinges.

Let us return to the special moment when The Workshop

---

[5] Ibid., p. 143.

actually does what it does. As I have suggested above, this must not be something so idiosyncratic, eccentric, difficult as to be unrepeatable – a one-off trick to which only one workshop leader has access. I offer a controversial trope here: it must be like lovemaking itself, always different, never original, sometimes procreative. The critical impulses at work at what I would like to call The Stage – where discussion, analysis, debate, advice, insults, defensiveness, anxiety, interpretation, encouragement, mentoring, proofing and rewriting intermingle in a Workshop Discourse – will never be precisely the same. Try recreating any dinner party word for word a year later, let alone The Last Supper or The Symposium. The Stage will always be different precisely because it is not original – further, cannot, expressly, be a search for origins of its own basis.

To sum up – The Creative Writing Workshop must not be in constant search of itself, its meaning, or any number of writers or characters; it must not succumb to becoming an endless meta-workshop, wondering about its necessity or value. To work it must – like Tinkerbell – be believed in.

I believe that Creative Writing Workshops in the U.K. are in danger of being fatally undermined for the very reason that too much tinkering with this meta-critical level will only result in TW being abandoned as a working model – and not because it doesn't work, but because it works too well – as a standard basic model. The very British desire to improve upon the original American model (however justified) also leads to a fixing of the ain't-broke.

What does happen at The Stage? I would like to claim that the power of The Stage is enigmatic, and even quasi-mystical. It is a process, like catharsis, in ancient drama, or Freudian analysis, that cannot, and should not, be entirely understood or reduced to prescriptive elements. What can be done, however is to 'set The Stage' as best as possible, to let this creative mystery of peer-fellowship occur. In my experience, the following rules best set the stage:

- Singularity: Only one text (story, poem, play) is under discussion at any one time;
- Silence: The author of the text cannot speak, but must maintain total silence; listening, in abeyance;
- Solidarity: Each other member must make their comment or comments, in one to three minutes, in a set order;
- Summary: After all students in the group have spoken on the work – in whatever way they choose – the leader briefly summarises these comments; perhaps offering her own further guidance;

- Satisfaction: the author now breaks their silence, satisfying all questions and concerns the other writers and students might have had.

This simple five-part structure forms The Stage.

It should be noted that two important formal elements have not been identified here: one, the length of time, and two, the precise nature of the 'feedback' given. It would be impossible to delimit how people will talk about writing, as each text will initiate its own response-needs. Crucially, the level of creative indeterminacy (that spark of freedom) is therefore transferred to the most important part of the process – the feedback itself. By removing – as much as possible – deviations and difference at the structural level, that creative tension between form and free play that writers discover in the act of writing itself is reproduced, indeed, enacted.

Debate will continue to focus, though, on the value of what happens during The Stage. What is the 'value added' to the text in question? Is it improved? Is it more publishable? Again, I do not think this is a meaningful concern, but a red herring. The Workshop is not – or should not – be about perfecting or improving any one text submitted. Instead, it is about experiencing, going through, The Stage itself. The process of workshopping, in my mind, is a good in and of itself – just as a kiss, or a vote, is an inherent good. One can use a kiss to betray, or vote for a despot – but that is not to besmirch the act itself.

The Workshop Stage aims to produce better writers and readers, not better stories, poems, or plays. This is the fundamental misreading that leads to claims that the work created in workshops becomes 'the same'. Maybe. I have never seen that happen. What is incontestable, in my experience, is that any person who goes through The Stage becomes a better-equipped reader of their own and others' writing.

I am sure it will be argued that this is also a quasi-ethical model I propose. I hope it is. Responsibility is grounded in repetition of tasks in a reliable order. Writers are free (one hopes) to write what they want, at university, before, and after. How they are guided through the act of turning this writing into a serious, repeatable, and profound activity that can be shared with others, bringing to bear criticism, compassion, and thought, is up to the university, in tandem with its teachers. The Creative Writing Workshop exists as an ideal space in which to do this. Like every other blank space, it invites you to do your best, or worst.

Writing Exercise

Each student is asked to compose a 300-word critical statement of how they intend to respond to writing in the workshop. This can be wildly comical, a manifesto, list poem, or in dramatic monologue, for instance. It should then be submitted anonymously. The class should be given copies of each one, and they should all then be workshopped (briefly), discussing both the style, but also the ideas that come up, regarding ideas of evaluation, critical reception, and review styles. This should break the ice, raise valuable insights, introduce theories and ideas relating to workshopping, and actually be an ideal first or second week exercise.

Works Cited

Morrison, Matt, *Key Concepts In Creative Writing* (London: Palgrave Macmillan, 2010)

Wandor, Michelene, *The Author Is Not Dead, Merely Somewhere Else: Creative Writing Reconceived* (London: Palgrave Macmillan, 2008)

Bridges Between: Articulations in Narrative Form and Public Argument in Creative Non-Fiction

Ben Ristow

In my advanced composition course, we concentrate on creative non-fiction writing in a manner that connects with my background and training as a fiction writer and rhetorician. The course is often taught by a diverse group of graduate students and faculty in the English department, especially those associated with the rhetoric and composition studies programme. Within the same course taught by my colleagues, an emphasis is placed on argumentation and analysis and the course description provided by the Writing Program may be interpreted to focus primarily on rhetoric or composition; it reads:

> This course introduces students to the theory and practice of writing within multiple genres of expository prose. Students will engage in projects that require them to analyze and respond to a variety of rhetorical situations and to write for an identified audience.[1]

The challenge in planning the course was trying to imagine how a creative writer's skill in the 'practice of writing in multiple genres' might connect with a rhetorician's commitment 'to analyze and respond to a variety of rhetorical situations and to write for an identified audience'. In order to achieve the objectives of the course, I needed to secure a clear union between what might seem the disparate space between creative writing and rhetoric.

Advanced composition courses within the United States have historically included creative writing components.[2] As an upper-

---

[1] 'English 306: Course Description', *Writing Program*, University of Arizona English Department. Online.
[2] Both D.G. Myers' *Elephants Teach: Creative Writing Since 1880* (1995) and Mark McGurl's *The Program Era: Postwar Fiction and the Rise of Creative Writing* (2009) identify advanced composition courses at Harvard University as among the first places for creative writing instruction in American universities. Myers (p. 49) and McCurl (p. 94) point to Barrett Wendell's 'verse-making' course as the first creative writing course to give credit for imaginative writing, and it is important to recognise advanced composition courses as sites where creative writing may continue to expand in the future.

division writing requirement, the students in my class included majors in English (literature and creative writing), journalism, education, business, pre-med, pre-law, psychology, sociology, computer science, and the visual and performing arts. By drawing from such a diverse group of students, the course was made more dynamic by the fact that many students were upper-classmen and already trained to write within their major. In such a classroom context, students were not able to rely on insider knowledge or specialised language to navigate the course or speak to their peers. As a result, my instruction could not be directed to an audience of English or creative writing majors and the classroom took on the qualities of a collective who had to negotiate their beliefs about reading and writing. What was common among the students was that they valued writing and that it would continue to be part of their personal and professional lives.

I also focused the course on creative non-fiction because it appeared that even English majors were not familiar with the content and form of the genre. Sharing an uncommon language proved beneficial to students and I began the semester by offering a definition of creative non-fiction that characterised it as 'a hybrid of literary elements, employing the techniques of fiction in dialogue, characterization, and detail while also including the intimate "true" content of nonfiction'.[3] The definition was presented as flexible and alongside those offered by Lee Gutkind, Robert Root, Wendy Bishop and other writers discussing the genre, though the creation and expansion of the definition really began when students started to speculate: 'So creative non-fiction *can...*' or 'So creative non-fiction *could...*'. When students pushed back against mine and others' definitions of the genre, they began to understand (or were reminded) that definitions are flexible and an important stage in forming an argument.

I contextualised the first writing assignment of the course, an autobiographical essay, by asking students to interrogate the relationship between their own lives and narrative form. Writing students conceived of narrative in terms of written genres despite the fact that they encountered different forms of narrative throughout their day and in other visual or sensory mediums. Through class discussion, students generated a personal inventory of narrative forms that intersected their lives. From forms in poetry, fiction, and playwriting, students were able to move toward non-traditional or atypical forms of narrative in family heirlooms, recipes, internet pages, T.V.

---

[3] Ben Ristow, 'English 306 Course Syllabus' (Fall 2009/Spring 2010), p.1.

commercials, etc. By imagining a range of narratives, students began to establish connections with those forms that parallel the content of their lives or their academic studies. Through taking calculated risks in writing about themselves, students were better able to challenge their previous conceptions of autobiography.

By challenging students to explore unique narrative forms that intersect their lives or their academic majors, I found that students were more willing to take the chances associated with improving as writers. I believe *experimentation* is paramount to developing writers. As a writing student myself, my professor, Darrell Spencer at Ohio University, asked me pointedly, and in front of the whole class, 'Did I plan to write about the same thing in the same way for the rest of my life?' I was puzzled at first, but from that question I began to write in forms about subjects that were new, and felt new. I feel the writing teacher serves their students poorly when they ask students to produce versions of what they know and have written before. After my students surveyed definitions of creative non-fiction and listed various kinds of narratives in their lives, students read autobiographical essays that experiment with literary convention. We read from John D'Agata's edited collection *Next American Essay*, Judith Kitchen's collection *Short Takes: Brief Encounters with Contemporary Nonfiction*, and Lee Gutkind's series *The Best of Creative Nonfiction* (Vols. 1-3).[4] From these three collections, we also read Joan Didion's 'White Album' and Dinty W. Moore's 'Son of Mr. Green Jeans' along with more recent experimental work such as Jenny Boully's essay 'The Body' (using footnotes) and 'Life Story' by David Shields (using bumper stickers).[5]

The published essays set a tone for further inquiry into the parallel between the form and content of autobiographical writing, and I posed questions to the students: what forms have portions of your life taken? How might the parts of your life render or conjure a form? How does your life present challenges to formulaic methods of essay writing? In discussing the course readings, we analysed Ander Monson's essay 'Outline Toward a Theory of the Mine Versus the Mind and the Harvard Outline' within his collection *Neck Deep and Other Predicaments*.[6] The form

[4] John D'Agata, ed., *The Next American Essay* (2003); Judith Kitchen, ed., *Short Takes: Brief Encounters with Contemporary Nonfiction* (2005); Lee Gutkind, ed., *The Best of Creative Nonfiction*, Vols. 1-3 (2004).

[5] Joan Didion, 'The White Album' in *The Next American Essay*, pp. 339-41; Dinty W. Moore, 'Son of Mr. Greenjeans' in *Short Takes: Brief Encounters with Contemporary Nonfiction*, pp. 283-91; Jennifer Boully, 'The Body', in *The Next American Essay*, pp. 435-66; David Shields, 'Life Story' in *The Next American Essay*, pp. 339-41.

[6] Ander Monson, 'Outline toward a Theory of the Mine Versus the Mind and

is the Harvard outline and the essay acts as a meditation (or excavation) of the essayist's relationship to the mines, bodies, family, knowledge, and writing he has experienced. Monson writes:

> II. My family has a background in the Michigan mining
> industry
>> a. a history in copper, iron, the cast-off leftover materials
>>   necessary
>> b. though less my recent family
>>
>>> i.   i.e. not my father who is a professor – whose job,
>>>   like mine, is (reductively) the mining and refining,
>>>   then the distribution of information for (small sums
>>>   of) money
>>>
>>>> 1. though perhaps this is a cynical view of the
>>>>   profession
>>>>   a) and light-as-knowledge metaphor is
>>>>   hardly breaking new ground
>>>> 2. still I like the imagine of the light-helmeted
>>>>   professor plowing through the darkness
>>>> 3. "like mine" (from above) – mining is a story of
>>>>   possession
>>>>   a) of legal ownership of land and rights, the
>>>>   permission to go below the crust.[7]

Monson performs the act of self-inclusion through the sterile narrative form of the outline, and the tension created in his exploration of metaphor literally 'mines' the raw material of the essay. In the passage above, Monson connects the metaphor of mining with his family's history, the search for knowledge in writing, and later on, the problems of environmental damage. The metaphors continue as veins of digression, a labyrinth tunnelling through the earth, and within Monson's essay students found inspiration and exemplars for their own essays.

Among the first drafts I received there was considerable variety, especially as students began to see methods for remixing and splicing narratives. A student produced an essay using an epistolary correspondence between herself, her mother, and Martha Stewart, another student utilised the parameters of a Monopoly game to reflect on a meeting with her estranged

---

the Harvard Outline', in *Neck Deep and Other Predicaments* (2007), pp. 3-12.

[7] Ander Monson, 'Outline toward a Theory of the Mine', (2007), p. 5.

father, another female student parodied the Communist Manifesto and wrote her own version called 'The Crazy Bitch Manifesto,' in which she confronts and defines the label 'crazy bitch'. For this writer, Cathy, the harassment she may have experienced through being labelled is transformed through an act of self-empowerment. She explores the label in the following passage, and writes:[8]

> Frequently, a crazy bitch will find herself in situations in which, through the repeated lack of acknowledgment of those skills possessed by crazy bitches by the world at large, she begins to question her own reactions and impressions. Leading to circumstances under which a crazy bitch can find herself operating alone for long stretches of time as she attempts to come to terms with the chasm between what she feels and sees and what the rest of the world does.[9]

Within the passage and the essay as a whole, the writer concludes that being a crazy bitch – far from being a signifier of instability or shame – must be recognised as a hyper-sensory perception and resolute knowledge. The 'chasm between what she feels and sees and what the rest of the world does' is taken to be a gift or power that allows the writer to navigate the world. Between a sensory awareness akin to a superhero and a knowledge more pronounced than others, the crazy bitch is in many ways an intellectual and political radical. 'The Crazy Bitch Manifesto' surprised and enlivened the students of the class into the possibilities of the assignment.

The challenges of self-definition were prevalent throughout many of the essays for this assignment, and another student, Sergio, wrote an essay titled 'Human Java' using his background as a computer programmer to create a Java script that examines humanness and the deterioration of life. He writes:

```
/**
* Shuts down the human by ending all biological
functions and beginning
* decay process. Also ends lifetime timer.
*/
public static void death() {
```

---

[8] Permission has been granted the writer for the inclusion and use of student sample essays. The names of all student writers and their subjects have been changed to preserve anonymity.
[9] Cathy Kartchner, 'Crazy Bitch Manifesto', Student Essay, p. 2.

```
try {
this.death();
} catch (IOException e) {
/ / Prints out reasons for death failure.
e.printStackTrace();
}
/ / Finishes the timer counting total milliseconds
/ / lived by Human object.
lifetime.cancel();

System.out.println("Human is disconnecting
biological processes");
shutdown();
System.out.println("Human is attempting to save");
saveHumanData();
System.out.println("Human is beginning decay
processes");
decay();
System.out.println("Human is shutdown");
System.out.println("Have a great day =)");
System.exit(0);[10]
```

The script represents a playful investigation, and much like Monson's essay, it examines the tension between form and content. Sergio was somewhat disconcerted that the program would not run properly and that the freedoms he was taking as programmer came into conflict with the parameters of technology. I encouraged him to imagine ways to disrupt the restrictions of the form through the personal content of his writing. In the final version, the programmer duels with an 'Editor' in a dialogue that draws the programmer into a defence of his liberties. Both 'Crazy Bitch Manifesto' and 'Human Java' were provocative experiments and another student writer, Susan, wrote an essay 'Regulation of the spiritual cancer pride in *Callahan susan*' as a biological lab report. The essay presents an abstract, background, methodology, and a conclusion that is consistent with the lab study of a disease. In creating a patchwork of 'the truth of pride's identity (C.S. Lewis, 1952), the warnings of family history (S. Roger Callahan, 1953), an undeserved love (Joseph G.P. Stevens, 1989), and the fibreglass trail I left behind at the intersection of St Cyril's and the I-5 (Agnes P. Rogers, 1926, may God bless her soul)', the essay examines the life of the writer through the spirituality and pride she identifies with.[11] Pride is examined in the sense of spirituality

[10] Sergio Jacobson, 'Human Java', Student Essay, pp. 2-3.
[11] Susan Callahan, 'Regulation of the spiritual cancer pride in *Callahan susan*',

and the perfectionism that plagues the writer, and she analyses C.S. Lewis's definition of pride as 'spiritual cancer: it eats up the very possibility of love, or contentment, or even common sense'.[12] The scientific abstract later states that 'the goal of this experiment is to identify its [pride's] effect and potential cures in the species *Callahan susan*'.[13] By utilising the lab report as a formal investigation of pride and its pitfalls, the essayist demonstrates honesty toward her attitude as one who seeks perfection in all things. This drive toward perfection is disruptive in that it makes the writer an outcast and spiritually and emotionally unavailable. This 'cage', as described by the writer, imprisons her in a competition with others and most of all – herself. As examined within the report's conclusion, the species '*Callahan susan*' has the potential to be forgiven her pride and the secrets that conspire to keep her from the love and deeper knowledge of others.

Through all the student essays written during the unit, I found that students took more risks with the autobiographical content of their essays when they sampled from atypical narrative forms. Two other short essays were assigned during the class, one of which focused on the subject of *memory* while the other concentrated on the *lyric*. After students generated three short essays over the course of the semester, they were asked to write a braided essay for their final.[14] For the braided essay, the class read Ben Quick's essay 'The Boneyard' originally published in *Orion Magazine* and republished in the *Pushcart Prize XXXIV* anthology. The essay uses three narrative modes: 1) A scene in an airplane graveyard (a.k.a. 'The Boneyard') in Southern Arizona; 2) An exposition on the historical-political-scientific evolution of the herbicide Agent Orange; 3) A narrative about the essayist's hand deformity – a result of his father's exposure to Agent Orange during the Vietnam War.

Using Quick's 'The Boneyard' as their exemplar, students attempted to transform their personal narrative essay (or another short essay) into a longer essay that focused on a larger context in public argument. The shift here from the more personal to a more public discourse allowed students to see the social and

---

Student Essay, p. 1.

[12] C.S. Lewis, 'The Great Sin', in *Mere Christianity* (1952), pp. 121-28.

[13] Susan Callahan.

[14] A braided essay is a multi-modal non-fiction piece that often relies on the juxtaposition and interweaving of different narrative modes and forms to create a central theme(s). The rhetorical effect of a braided essay is often different from a more traditional essay in that the former treats seemingly disparate narrative modes as an advantage rather than a disadvantage. By weaving an essay in this manner, as seen in the essays of Monson, Quick, and Moore, the essayist becomes decentralised and the scope is widened to capture cultural subjects.

political dimensions of their writing, what Paul Dawson would call the 'sociological poetics' of their work.[15] At this point in the course, I began to push their short personal essays and ask questions: what is beyond your narrative and in the reader's world? How might this essay be transformed to perform as a more public *argument*? In prompting my students with these questions, I tried to act as a gentle and antagonistic force pushing their work beyond the 'navel gaze' and into the context of a more public expression. I was not interested in turning their creative work into academic scholarship, or some hybridity, but I was interested in making them aware of the function of art in the world and having them trace the diaphanous line between the poetic and rhetorical. To affect such an outcome, I drew from the work of Jeffrey Walker's *Rhetoric and Poetics in Antiquity* and Doug Hesse's essay 'Aristotle's *Poetics* and *Rhetoric*: Narrative as Rhetoric's Fourth Mode' in order to argue that narrative, like the lyric poem or enthymeme, functions as a form of argumentation within our work as creative writers.[16]

By navigating the line between private and public, poetic and rhetorical, students answered the question Hesse examines in another of his essays, 'The Place of Creative Nonfiction'. Hesse analyses claims made against creative non-fiction about its inability to engage with the public and civic discourses of the humanities; he writes:

> As scholars explored the local nature of academic genres and workplace discursive conventions, they questioned the assumption that writing abilities could generally be transferred from belletristic genres to local rhetorical situations. Further, and most important, their arguments about the nature of civil discourse not only questioned the political work that creative nonfiction could do but also critiqued the authorial subjectivity constructed through those genres.[17]

Hesse and Walker are unified in their claims that the poetic functions as rhetorical argument and affects the world through a different mode of expression than formal scholarship. Our role as

---

[15] Paul Dawson, *Creative Writing and the New Humanities* (2005), p. 208.

[16] Jeffrey Walker, *Rhetoric and Poetics in Antiquity* (2000); Douglas Hesse, 'Aristotle's *Poetics* and *Rhetoric*: Narrative as Rhetoric's Fourth Mode' in *Rebirth of Rhetoric*, ed. Richard Andrews (1992), pp. 19-38.

[17] Douglas Hesse, 'The Place of Creative Nonfiction', *College English* 65:3 (2003), pp. 237-41 (p. 239).

artists in a postmodern (or post-postmodern) era depends upon the recognition that creative writing has a political and social function within the world and that creative writers can articulate this functionality to those inside and outside the university.

Within Quick's essay 'The Boneyard', students saw how the personal narrative traverses the immediate world of the writer and expands into the world beyond them. The first section (what we call 'braid') begins with the essayist searching for the retired C-123 planes that dropped Agent Orange on the jungles of Vietnam. The scene and dialogue between Quick and a government official named Terry is brief and provides the rationale for the writer's journey to see the planes 'that devastated a vast and peopled landscape, the ones that maimed me before I was born'.[18] The second braid encompasses a broader context and portrays the Kennedy inauguration, the escalation of the conflict in Vietnam, and the initial research, development, and distribution of the chemical Agent Orange. The final braid is personal narrative that begins at Quick's birth and follows the reaction of his family to his hand deformity. This braid identifies themes that are personal to the writer and follow the slow recognition of his difference (and non-difference) from other children. The sequencing, braiding, and repetition of the scene from the Boneyard trip, the historical-political exposition from the cultural past, and the childhood narrative within 'The Boneyard' overwhelmed the students initially and it was important to remind them that the essay may have begun as personal narrative much like their own autobiographical essays.

Whether students chose their autobiographical essay or one of their other short essays, the braided essay served to fuse the skills learned in experimenting with narrative form to those skills required to articulate a public argument. In the case of 'The Boneyard' the essayist uses his personal narrative and extensive research as a foundation to advocate recognition of the continuing effect of Agent Orange on American and Vietnamese citizens. Students identified the structural landmarks of 'The Boneyard' and imagined ways to braid different narrative modes. There were many exemplary braided essays produced by students in the class, and Susan's final essay 'Guilty' presented an interesting marriage between private guilt and public forgiveness.[19] The essayist, a devout Catholic, analyses the public condemnation of priests involved in the sexual abuse scandals while connecting the debate with her own personal guilt over a car accident in which the other driver was killed and she was found to be at fault. The writer combines Bible passages,

---

[18] Ben Quick, 'The Boneyard', *Orion Magazine* (March/April 2008), p. 21.
[19] Susan Callahan, 'Guilty', Student Essay (Spring 2010).

Catholic faith blogs, news reports, statements from lawyers, a priest's homily, and a personal narrative tracing her guilt and reconciliation after the car crash.

The line between guilt and innocence is complicated through the discussion of the writer's devotion to her faith and how the accident destabilised her attitude toward guilt and set her on a path toward forgiveness. Through her own narrative, the writer argues for a reassessment of the notion of guilt as it applies to Catholic priests involved in abuse, and though she imagines the severe punishments for them, she attempts to recast the discussion about ways to affix guilt to fellow humans. She argues that guilty priests should be punished, but the narrative sets the reader on an alternative path – not toward an absolute judgement – but on a journey toward personal forgiveness and the secession of emotional pain. There is a sleight of hand used by the writer that conflates her car accident with the sexual abuse scandals of Catholic priests, and though we might argue with this comparison, the result is a compelling argument for rethinking the possibility of reconciliation.

The braided essay assignment allowed students to explore the division between private and public, and I tried to keep this division in mind when assigning their writing workshop groups. Students began with small group workshops (three or four students) for their short essays and conducted whole-class workshops for their final. Through small group workshopping, students were able to take chances in their choice of personal subjects without exposing the subject of their work to the critique of the entire class. The class itself culminated with a public reading of student-chosen work at the University of Arizona Poetry Center.[20] The evening was facilitated through a faculty-interaction grant and we invited department, family, and community members to attend. The readings at the U.A. Poetry Center allowed students to present their work to a public audience, and this activity enacted the final step for the course: a direct engagement between artistic expression and public argument.

The students read from essays that testified to who they are and what they have witnessed. There was the spouse of a troubled ex-soldier demanding emotional support, an artist depicting scenes of her childhood home in Pittsburgh, and the son of a Mexican undertaker arguing how humour must play a role in death. The list could roll on and on, and for me as a writer-teacher, this advanced composition course served to bridge the rhetorical and poetic. Through the course I came to

---

[20] University of Arizona Poetry Center. Online.

understand how creative writing might challenge students' conception of narrative form while empowering them to use narrative as an argument reaching beyond themselves. The course helped me to conceptualise how creative writers might use their unique tools as artists to function within the academy and the public beyond; in this effort, I can now imagine coalitions with rhetoric that will serve to expand our creative writing pedagogy and further illuminate our work as artist-teachers.

Writing Exercise – Form Experiments in Autobiography

> *It isn't that you subordinate your ideas to the force of the facts in autobiography but that you construct a sequence of stories to bind up the facts with a persuasive hypothesis that unravels your history's meaning.*

Philip Roth

What if you were able to bend autobiographical form to parallel the themes and events in your own life? The autobiographical essay that plods forward from your birth into the scenes of your life often relies on a linear and chronological narrative that is rather stale. Reading an essay such as this may feel like being forced to sit and listen to a monotone tour guide lead you on a tired procession through a city that is too familiar to be interesting.

For this writing exercise, you will begin by brainstorming definitions of autobiographical essay that should recognise that no short essay will capture a comprehensive account of your life. After reviewing the potential limits of the essay's content, the teacher should gather students in groups and have them list as many types of narrative forms as they can. The teacher may also ask students to bring examples of written, visual, or other narrative forms from outside of class. In either case, the lists produced by students and the teacher should demonstrate a range of traditional forms in writing (poem, food recipe, brochure) as well as non-traditional forms in visuals (photos, websites, film) and sensory narrative (smell, taste, touch). The lists may be compiled and later dispersed to students or the instructor may have students compile and write in the same class period.

After students have gathered and/or received the list of narrative forms, they should use class time to compose a short scene or exposition from their life. Students may choose the form at random or be assigned one, but in either case, the writing produced by students should be shared aloud and serve as a primer for their short autobiographical essay.

Works Cited

Bishop, Wendy, 'Suddenly Sexy: Creative Nonfiction Rear-Ends', *College English*, 65:3 (2003), pp. 257–75

Boully, Jennifer, 'The Body', in *The Next American Essay*, ed. John D'Agata (St Paul, Minneapolis: Graywolf Press, 2003), pp. 435-66

Callahan, Susan, 'Guilty', Student Essay, Spring 2010

Callahan, Susan, 'Regulation of the spiritual cancer pride in *Callahan susan*', Student Essay, Spring 2010

D'Agata, John, ed., *The Next American Essay* (St. Paul, Minneapolis: Graywolf Press, 2003)

Dawson, Paul, *Creative Writing and the New Humanities* (New York: Routledge, 2005)

Didion, Joan, 'The White Album' in *The Next American Essay*, ed. John D'Agata (St. Paul, Minneapolis: Graywolf Press, 2003), pp. 339-41

'English 306: Course Description', *Writing Program*, University of Arizona English Department [accessed 2 May 2011]

Gutkind, Lee, ed., *The Best of Creative Nonfiction*, Vols. 1-3 (New York: Norton, 2004)

Hesse, Douglas, 'Aristotle's Poetics and Rhetoric: Narrative as Rhetoric's Fourth Mode' in *Rebirth of Rhetoric*, ed. Richard Andrews (London: Routledge, 1992), pp. 19-38

Hesse, Douglas, 'The Place of Creative Nonfiction', *College English: Special Issue Creative Nonfiction* 65:3 (January, 2003), pp. 237-41

Jacobson, Sergio, 'Human Java', Student Essay, Fall 2009

Kartchner, Cathy, 'The Crazy Bitch Manifesto', Student Essay, Spring 2010

Kitchen, Judith, *Short Takes: Brief Encounters with Contemporary Nonfiction* (New York: Norton, 2005)

Lewis, C.S., 'The Great Sin', *Mere Christianity* (London: Macmillan, 1952)

McGurl, Mark, *The Program Era: Postwar Fiction and the Rise of Creative Writing* (Cambridge, Massachusetts: Harvard University Press, 2009)

Monson, Ander, 'Outline toward a Theory of the Mine Versus the Mind and the Harvard Outline' in *Neck Deep and Other Predicaments* (St Paul, Minneapolis: Graywolf Press, 2007), pp. 3-12

Moore, Dinty W., 'Son of Mr Greenjeans' in *Short Takes: Brief Encounters with Contemporary Nonfiction*, ed. Judith Kitchen (New York: Norton, 2005)

Myers, D.G., *Elephants Teach: Creative Writing Since 1880* (Chicago, Illinois: University of Chicago Press, 1995)

Quick, Ben, 'The Boneyard' in *Pushcart Prize XXXIV: Best of Small Presses*, ed. Bill Henderson (Wainscott, New York: Pushcart Press, 2010)

Quick, Ben, 'The Boneyard' *Orion Magazine* (March/April 2008), pp. 16-23

Roth, Philip, *The Facts: A Novelist's Autobiography* (1998), (London: Vintage, 2007)

Shields, David, 'Life Story' in *The Next American Essay*. ed. John D'Agata (St. Paul, Minneapolis: Graywolf Press, 2003), pp. 339-41

University of Arizona Poetry Center, http://poetry.arizona.edu [accessed 2 May 2011]

Walker, Jeffery, *Rhetoric and Poetics in Antiquity* (New York: Oxford University Press, 2000)

What *Really* Happened? Rethinking 'Truth' in Creative Non-Fiction

Joseph Rein

When I first incorporated creative non-fiction in one of my introductory creative writing courses, I understood that the first challenge would be to define what exactly the genre *is*. I decided to start at, seemingly, the easiest entry point – personal narratives, or memoir – because not only would this be the genre with which my students were most familiar, but also because it seemed the most logical segue from fiction writing. Both are narratives, I told my students. Both need to tell an intriguing story with complex characters and tense situations. The difference, simple enough as it seemed, was right there in the definition, almost equation-like: non-fiction=true, fiction=untrue.

After assigning a few published personal narratives, I set my students to the task of writing one with few stipulations. The next class period, when I inquired as to how the writing was going, more than half of them looked up with disgruntled eyes. 'This is so much harder than making things up,' one said. 'I don't even remember last night,' another said with that undergraduate flair of pride. 'How am I supposed to remember something my mom said to me ten years ago?'

We took another look at the published essays I'd assigned as I scrambled to remind them that what we'd learned about narrative still applied. But no matter how many times I told my students to consider the aspects of good storytelling – tension, plot, scene, dialogue, characterisation – their preoccupation inevitably landed on the 'truth' of their narratives. And why wouldn't it have? My earlier equation set them up for such preoccupation. In class they barraged me with truth-based questions: how true does my writing have to be in order to qualify? What if I don't remember what day of the week it was? How can I write dialogue when I don't remember exactly what was said? As for the texts I offered as examples, the focus did not change; instead of engaging the work as a whole, students responded to the writer's ability to capture truth with either applause ('She has a way better memory than me') or scepticism ('He must have made some of this up'). I realised that, though, as Carol Bly states, 'anyone's mind has the potential to focus on larger issues than his or her own',[1] my approach had caused my

---

[1] Carol Bly, *Beyond the Writers' Workshop: New Ways to Write Creative Nonfiction* (2001), p. 89.

students to fall directly into the 'truth' trap of their own memories.

I needed to change my approach. I could have opened a discussion on the complexities of memory and truth, but ultimately, that still would have missed the point. I needed instead to shift the focus of the word 'truth' itself. I needed to broaden my students' definition of the term, in order to bring back that oft-forgotten truth in creative non-fiction: facts and details about the world not *within* us but the world *around* us. My students' personal essays needed to, as Phillip Lopate states, 'go beyond the self's quandaries, through research and contextualization, to bring back news of the larger world'.[2] I knew the best way to accomplish this was by engaging my new concept of truth rhetorically – by examining their essays with an audience-based approach.

Redefining truth: An audience perspective

Ultimately, my early definition of creative non-fiction was too simplistic. Equating creative non-fiction to truth can lead students to believe truth means only accuracy, only *getting it right*. Students then look mostly inward; the goal of their works, and subsequently their own gauge of success, becomes a question of whether or not they can accurately recall details of their own lives. But if this is a goal of creative non-fiction, it is only one of many; and most would agree that it is not the foremost. Like with fiction and poetry, our students must strive to connect not only with themselves but also with a reader.

In my next creative writing course, I began a discussion of creative non-fiction with this audience-based approach. I asked, 'Why do people read non-fiction?' My students immediately provided rich and insightful answers. One said: 'My father reads only World War Two narratives. He's obsessed with military strategy.' Another said: 'My grandma will read any autobiography by southern writers. Doesn't matter who.' Already, these answers zeroed in on a better, broader definition of personal narrative than my earlier truth-based discussion provided.

Through this discussion my students and I came to the realisation that though creative non-fiction is difficult to define, the term itself just might include a hint at audience expectations. Through our discussion we realised that the 'creative' and the

---

[2] Phillip Lopate, 'Writing Personal Essays: On the Necessity of Turning Oneself Into a Character', in *Writing Creative Nonfiction*, eds. Carolyn Forché and Philip Gerard (2001), p. 44.

'non-fiction' parts merged two (somewhat dissimilar) readerships.[3] Like journalism enthusiasts, creative non-fiction readers often read for factual information, but like fiction or poetry readers, they also read 'for the quality of the reading experience itself'.[4] They read – and my students' responses seemed to confirm this – for both. They want to *enjoy* literary reading, but they also want to *learn* something.[5]

Taking this audience-based approach can lead to a broader definition of what is 'true' in our creative non-fiction. It asks students to understand that – aside from our family members and close friends, of course – readers are not only engaged by our personal experiences but instead by the *ways in which she can relate those experiences, and thus her own, to the larger world.* Many readers will agree with Ander Monson when he says: 'I still don't want to read what most people have to say about themselves if it's just to tell their story. I want it to be art, meaning that I want it to be transformed, juxtaposed, collaged'.[6] Readers like Monson focus less on the accuracy of an author's memory than the author's inquisitive nature and unique understanding of the world.

Now, when I teach creative non-fiction, instead of allowing students' preoccupation with examining the accuracy of their memory, I ask about another truth: an audience-based truth, a communal truth. I ask students to examine the outer truths – social, historical, cultural – that can be applied to their inner truth to create a meaningful reading experience. Their first impulse is to ask: what is true about my life? Instead, I ask them: what truth will readers learn from your retelling of it?

Shifting the focus: A practical approach

Helping students understand the need for a truth outside themselves – particularly when discussed in terms of audience

---

[3] I am indebted to one student in particular, who suggested that, when thinking of audience, I write the term 'creative non-fiction' on the board and divide it in half – 'creative/non-fiction' – to help visualise how the genre's audience lies directly between the two.

[4] Becky Bradway and Doug Hesse, *Creating Nonfiction: A Guide and Anthology* (2009), p. 6.

[5] I don't mean to suggest that fiction or poetry readers seek only the pleasure of the experience, or that newsreaders demand facts stripped of eloquent diction. Naturally, in all cases, these two impulses will interact on a sliding scale, dependent on reader and text. I simply hope to show that creative non-fiction creates a unique blend of the two, in which the scales are often more evenly distributed.

[6] Ander Monson, *Vanishing Point: Not a Memoir* (2010), p. 13.

expectations – came relatively easily. Putting that understanding into practice in writing, however, proved a challenge. Perhaps this is because as writers, in any genre, we often mine our personal experiences for subject matter. Thus, when presented with the genre that calls explicitly for recreation of those experiences, students often dig not carefully, as with a shovel, but instead widely and indiscriminate, as with an industrial excavator.[7]

I begin this exercise with a brainstorm. On a sheet of paper, I have students list significant events in their lives. I ask them to think outside the typical significant events – graduation, first sexual encounter, a grandparent's death – unless that moment was exceptionally unique.[8] Alongside these events, I ask them simply to write whatever words enter their minds, focusing on particular details that allow their writing to take associative, rather than chronological (or plot progression-type), leaps. This method – which I often teach in poetry courses – asks them to focus on the concrete, the tactile, not the thing itself but the things with which this memory is surrounded: a snow-lined beach, rainbow toe-socks, a windowless factory building. After five to ten minutes, I allow them to share lists with each other, in groups or as a class. Not only do students enjoy hearing the odd things that appear on each other's lists, but often such listening will conjure more associations for their own memories.

For the next class period, I assign two personal essays that highlight my new audience-based approach. I like to use Frank Conroy's 'A Yo-Yo Going Down, a Mad Squirrel Coming Up' and Chris Drew's 'Bringing Up the Markers', though any number of recognisable and canonical personal narratives (by George Orwell or E.B. White, for example) are similarly applicable.[9] To begin discussion, I ask the simple, general, but ever-important question: what are these essays about? In the case of 'Yo-Yo', like most coming-of-age narratives, Conroy's overall message about life seems simple: I grew up.[10] The question I ask, then, is why does Conroy's essay persist? Why return to something that can be so easily summated? The overall message of 'Markers' invites a lengthier discussion. Drew's essay is part coming-of-age, but

---

[7] In class I often compare this process of mining our personal experience with digging for dinosaur bones. Archaeologists often find incomplete skeletons, and are left to assemble the rest – the 'whole story' as it were – on their own. The inefficient archaeologist would continue digging and digging in the same spot, finding nothing, creating nothing, and lost in the search.

[8] A first sexual encounter at graduation, for example.

[9] Frank Conroy, 'A Yo-Yo Going Down, a Mad Squirrel Coming Up', in *Creating Nonfiction*, eds. Bradway and Hesse (2009), pp. 241-56; Chris Drew, 'Bringing Up the Markers', *Concho River Review* 22:1 (2008), pp. 62-6.

[10] Or, as my students like to say: 'I replaced childish games with girls.'

also part intergenerational family connection and part nostalgia for outdated technologies.

This discussion often leads to the use of 'outside information' – most notably in these essays, yo-yos and trains respectively – within the essays themselves.[11] Some students might argue against these inclusions, but I've found that most students are eager to defend the text, stating that, without the outside information, the essays would be boring and unoriginal. At this point I direct students to each essay opening, where the necessity of the outside information becomes apparent. Conroy begins, 'The common yo-yo is crudely made, with a thick slank between two widely spaced wooden disks. The string is knotted or stapled to the shank'.[12] Before even a sentence about our narrator, we encounter (likely) unfamiliar terms like 'slank' and 'shank.' Conroy goes on to catalogue and describe his array of tricks, the 'Loop-the-Loop' and 'Eating Spaghetti' and 'Cannonball' and 'Turkish Army' which immerse readers further into the childish yet intricate world of yo-yo-ing.

'Markers' is even more drastic; the 'I' doesn't appear until page three. By dividing 'Markers' into sections, Drew allows himself space simply to discuss trains, in particular the function of the caboose:

> As part of a full train, the caboose was a base of operations for monitoring important readings, such as brake pressure or slack in the couplings....Most cabooses were wired with bright lights aimed down the tracks behind the train, called markers.[13]

This information, placed before we even have a sense of Drew as narrator – or even details of his life, of him as a *character* – boldly emphasises the objects and their history.

In both essays, the openings focus not on the 'I' but on things outside of the authors, on objects important not only to their lives but to the essay as a whole. The history, information and terminology exist right alongside the authors' lives. Therefore, these two parts, paradoxically, become both intertwined but also retain their own importance. Conroy uses the yo-yo as a symbol for childhood, yes, but he explicates its intricacies so minutely that we can't but see it as its own entity. Similarly, for Drew the caboose may represent a simpler age before technological

---

[11] If the conversation doesn't lead there, you can always steer it in that direction by asking, 'Why all the yo-yo stuff?' or 'Why all the information about trains?'

[12] Conroy, p. 241.

[13] Drew, p. 63.

advance, or an emotional connection to his grandfather, or innocence lost. In any case, the caboose functions as more than symbol; in fact, we learn more about it than Drew himself.

Ultimately, these details juxtaposed together create a reading experience during which we both *enjoy* and *learn*. As readers we leave with not only an understanding of the author's life – the narrow focus that stifles early non-fiction writers – but something larger. We understand a little more about how the small things in our lives that make us individuals, things like mastery of yo-yos and working on trains, also make us human.

The power of juxtaposition

To put my students to practice, I return to one of Monson's concepts: juxtaposition. I ask them to return to their brainstormed lists from the previous class period and highlight one object that seems interesting or important. This object then, whatever it may be – the beach, the toe-socks, the factory – and *not* the memory that spurred it, becomes the focus. Another brainstorm asks them to jot down everything they know about this object: terminology, sensory information, history (that steers clear of personal accounts). I encourage them to draw a picture if it helps. I ask them to report the details without the impulse to narrate. The choice of object from their list is theirs; I only ask that it be something that they can feasibly see themselves writing about for more than, say, a page (for which nearly everything qualifies).

Over the next week, students must research their object.[14] Whether it be on the internet, in museums, through library or 'field' research, I ask them to uncover historical facts, pricing, culture, jargon, or anything else that interests them, even if at the time it seems irrelevant to the idea of their essay. If they know a great deal about their object – which many of them will – their first instinct may be to 'uncover' inside their memory. Instead, I ask them to supplement memory with objects from their (often literal) basements – pamphlets, rusty weight bars, old children's books.[15] Go to that beach, I tell them. Find out when rainbow toe-socks became popular (unsurprisingly, the 1970s) and why (though unclear – as one would expect – it may have had

---

[14] I have adapted this research-based approach from one of my fiction exercises. For more, see my article 'Write What You *Don't* Know: Teaching Creative Research', *New Writing: The International Journal for the Practice and Theory of Creative Writing* 8:2 (2011), pp. 96-102.

[15] I ask my students to turn in printouts or copies of any source material they may use to enforce academic honesty.

something to do with athlete's foot). Interview one of the factory's former workers. Surround yourself with as much outside information as possible.

From there, they must write a four to five page personal narrative that juxtaposes these unearthed details of their object with a personal narrative. If the connections between the story and the research are not immediately apparent, I reassure them that this is okay, that it might even be preferred, that as Bly reminds us, as 'essayists [we] are best when we combine unlike issues. We place a reference to one kind of memory next to some mention of another kind of memory'.[16] In this case, the act of writing itself can often inspire discovery for its writer; or, in other words, students can uncover *what* they want to say while *attempting* to say it. The goal is an essay combining both personal truth and investigation, or an essay that discovers its own truth.

Before sending them to write, I offer advice that might help avoid pitfalls I've seen in previous classes. One of the biggest risks in this exercise – as with any that uses models – is that students will replicate Conroy or Drew with their own essay. I do not discourage them from using sections like Drew, say, or choosing a childhood obsession like Conroy. I do ask them, however, to allow their personal experiences and their researched objects to feed off one another in an organic fashion. Start with whichever portion seems natural, I say. Include researched details where they seem relevant. If something doesn't seem to fit, write it anyway and worry about its place later. This advice often helps with another major concern I encountered, that of my students worrying at too early a stage in their writing, 'What is my essay about?' or 'What does it all mean?' This preoccupation is almost as stifling as the concern with accuracy; I remind them that the very point of juxtaposing their lives and their objects is to *create* the larger meaning, and therefore may not be apparent from the start. For students this requires a leap of faith, a belief that the whole will eventually lead to something greater than its two parts. Admittedly, this doesn't always happen. Students may struggle while trying to bring disparate parts together, relying too heavily on one or focusing on balance to the detriment of the overall narrative. Of course, the two parts may never coalesce in the neat fashion of Conroy or Drew. On the whole, however, I have found that this approach most often produces interesting writing and, perhaps more importantly, growth for my students as writers.

I have admired many of the essays my students have produced from this exercise. One student, a gymnast, wrote an

---

[16] Bly, p. 111.

account of his grandmother's death in the form of a three-hour daily practice. Another juxtaposed her sixteenth birthday party with a how-to-style discussion on building a backyard fence. One combined her personal account of the events of 9/11 – like all, a poignant story in itself – with the life cycle of cicadas. In these cases and many more, my students expressed a truth far greater than the accuracy of their own memory. And even though some students may have missed the mark, on the whole their conception of creative non-fiction seemed much improved. When responding to each other's work, fewer students asked, 'Did this *really* happen?' More focused on how the pieces came together, what they as readers learned from the essay, and how each piece might more strongly resonate.

Conclusion: Toward a new understanding of truth

As an avid creative researcher, this approach obviously plays into my sensibilities. At first glance, encouraging research in personal narratives may seem to undermine the very thing that makes personal narratives great: the power of an individual's true story. But even writers who favour personal experience, particularly our beginner creative writing students, can benefit from stepping outside the confining labyrinths of their own memories in order to see their experiences in a broader context, in order to move from the *accurate* into the *connective*. That our *memories* are fragmented, fallible, and often distorted is inevitable. That our *writing be memorable*, however, may simply be a matter of finding the larger truth of creative non-fiction.

Writing Exercise

Exercising Truth

1. In the spaces below, write five places or things in which you have interest (e.g. Caribbean Islands, roller derby, gardening).

2. Now, write five life experiences that stick out to you for whatever reason (e.g. hitting your first hole-in-one, a beloved pet's death, moving into your college dorm).

3. Cut out the ten squares above, making sure to keep the two categories separate. Shuffle the slips of paper, and choose one slip from each category.

4. On a separate sheet of paper, begin brainstorming the connections between the place/thing and the life experience you have chosen. Write any similarities, differences, and note places these things have overlapped in your life, etc.

5. Choose two more slips, one from each category. (You may also keep one slip from your previous brainstorm if you find it useful.) Write another brainstorm of the connections between these two new items.

6. Repeat this process as many times as it takes until you begin to make some meaningful connections. (If you have to shuffle through the slips to find two that work well, no one will fault you!)

7. Finally, write an essay that combines one place/thing with one personal experience. Don't worry if the connections don't appear right away; as you write, the two may begin melding in interesting ways. Get as detailed as possible. Research if necessary. Try not to let one thing or the other dominate the essay; pay adequate attention to both.

Works Cited

Bly, Carol, *Beyond the Writers' Workshop: New Ways to Write Creative Nonfiction* (New York: Anchor Books, 2001)

Bradway, Becky, and Doug Hesse, *Creating Nonfiction: A Guide and Anthology* (Boston: Bedford/St. Martin's, 2009)

Conroy, Frank, 'A Yo-Yo Going Down, a Mad Squirrel Coming Up', in *Creating Nonfiction*, eds. Becky Bradway and Doug Hesse, (Boston: Bedford/St. Martin's Press, 2009), pp. 241-56

Drew, Chris, 'Bringing Up the Markers', *Concho River Review* 22:1 (2008), pp. 62-6

Lopate, Phillip, 'Writing Personal Essays: On the Necessity of Turning Oneself Into a Character', in *Writing Creative Nonfiction*, eds. Carolyn Forché and Philip Gerard (Cincinnati: Story Press, 2001), pp. 38-44.

Monson, Ander, *Vanishing Point: Not a Memoir* (St. Paul, Minneapolis: Graywolf Press, 2010)

Rein, Joseph, 'Write What You *Don't* Know: Teaching Creative Research', *New Writing: The International Journal for the Practice and Theory of Creative Writing* 8:2 (2011), pp. 96-102

'Tough but Fair': Honesty and the Management of Emotion in the Creative Writing Workshop

Margaret Lazarus Dean

Shark attack

I would like to begin with an ugly story.

As a graduate student, I once took part in a workshop session that could only be described as a shark attack. Seated around a large round table in a cosy, book-filled room, my classmates and I took turns savaging a draft of a story by a classmate of ours (let's call him 'Bob') who was, according to tradition, not allowed to speak up to defend himself. I still remember glancing periodically at that classmate's face (or, more accurately, the top of his head, as he was staring down at his manuscript for most of the hour) as we levelled our criticisms: that his characters were one-dimensional, the emotions clichéd, the climactic moment stilted. I remember another classmate reading a couple of sentences out loud in a sarcastic voice and then trailing off in exasperation. Bob's story was not terrible, as I recall – certainly not the worst thing we had seen all semester – but it was not that good either, and its identifiable weaknesses gave the rest of us plenty of material for our onslaught.

As soon as the workshop was over and people started to disperse, another classmate pulled me aside and asked, 'What was that?'

'What was what?' I asked, already knowing by her expression what she meant.

'Why was everyone so *mean* to Bob?'

I hastened to explain to her that we were not being mean, that this had been a 'tough but fair' workshop. The story had not been very good, and we had responded accordingly. If Bob wanted a nicer workshop, he should have worked harder on his story. This explanation was not entirely true, but in my righteousness I felt it to be true. I would have sworn in a court of law I was offering 'tough but fair' criticism. I was, after all, being fair in the sense that every weakness I seized on I could support and explain clearly in a reasonable tone of voice.

What I was not being honest with myself about was the fact that I, along with most of my classmates, came into this workshop with the intention of punishing Bob for certain perceived wrongs, most of which had nothing to do with the work on the page. These were: a failure to deliver written comments to the rest of us all semester; a tendency to sit through workshops looking bored without contributing anything; a harsh and condescending tone when he did rouse himself to comment on our stories; and, probably worst of all, a braggadocio about the fact that he was hard at work on his 'real' project, fiction too precious to be shared with the rest of us, and that the stories he put up for workshop were ringers, drafts cranked out in an evening or two in order to meet the minimum requirements of the course.

We all found these behaviours offensive. (For the record, I still do.) To take it a step further, we found these behaviours emotionally hurtful. Our hurt feelings seemed to justify, in our minds, using the one tool at our disposal to punish him: his workshop. Punish him we did, and the professor did nothing to intervene or to redirect the discussion. If he was surprised that our tone for this one workshop was so different from the other eleven, he did not show it.

At the end of that semester, Bob decided to leave graduate school, only halfway through the programme. I have never heard of any of his fiction being published. I have lost touch with him, and so have no way of knowing what effect that workshop might have had on his decision to stop writing.

Not long after, I came across a description by Carol Bly of the emotional risks of the writing workshop that reminded me of my experience in Bob's workshop:

> I remember very clearly the first time I saw a student undergoing a 'workshopping' of his manuscript. I had heard of 'workshopping manuscripts' all my adult life, but I hadn't actually seen it done....I then noticed two points: first, the room was filled with the smell of fear, and second, I didn't care for the expressions on the other students' faces. They had the look of cats near a mouse hole. I couldn't quite identify it at the time, but in retrospect and with much experience since, I know that at least one dynamic in that room, whether conscious or unconscious, was low-level, mild, politically sanctioned sadism.[1]

Had I not participated in a workshop that sounded very much like this one myself, I might have been inclined to assume that the students Bly describes were either simply mean human

---

[1] Carol Bly, *Beyond the Writers' Workshop* (2001), pp. 15-16.

beings, or normal people made mean by the workshop process, in much the same way that Stanley Milgram's psychology experiments drew cruel behaviour out of his subjects.[2] But there is often much more to meanness than meets the eye. We tend to talk about emotional situations like Bob's workshop in terms of how they distract from the effectiveness of the workshop, as if the intellectual work of the workshop and our hurt feelings take place on separate planes. But intellectual responses are very much informed by underlying emotions. When deviations from the ideal workshop are caused by emotional rather than intellectual distortions, they are more difficult to talk about in intellectual terms but are no less crucial to solve.

Tim Mayers offers a larger perspective of my specific experience:

> Anyone who has ever taught workshop-based creative writing courses can probably recall at least a few horror stories in which something goes seriously awry: the majority of students are effusive with praise about a piece of work the instructor believes is seriously flawed or even patently offensive; students hurl harsh, unwarranted criticism at a piece of work the instructor believes is quite good or demonstrates a great deal of potential; students divide into warring aesthetic camps that operate much like high school cliques; student writers get defensive about their writing, lashing out at other students, or even the instructor, for not being smart enough to understand their brilliant work. When the workshop does not go well, there is little poetry but much friction and much drama (in the most negative sense of that word).[3]

I tell this story about the ugly workshop in order to bring to the surface some troubling aspects of what we mean by 'tough' in the workshop, or 'tough but honest', or 'tough but fair'. When we talk about emotion in the creative writing workshop, we tend to assume we are talking about the emotions of the student-writer being workshopped. But of course there are many emotions in that room, and in the case I describe here the emotions of the other eleven of us were just as central to the outcome as Bob's.

Workshop emotions can masquerade or morph into legitimate

---

[2] Stanley Milgram, *Obedience to Authority; An Experimental View* (1974).
[3] Tim Mayers, 'Poetry, F(r)iction, Drama: The Complex Dynamics of Audience in the Writing Workshop' in Dianne Donnelly, ed., *Does the Writing Workshop Still Work?* (2010), pp. 94-104 (p. 95).

craft concerns, they can be all but invisible to the instructor, and they can have very real consequences for young writers, and as a result on literature. This may sound like an overstatement, but Bob is not the only young writer I have seen give up the craft permanently after a single disastrous workshop session. It's traditional to assume those writers wouldn't have made it anyway; for instance, Dan Barden writes, referring to rejection and criticism: 'If these are things that stop you from writing…well, I'm sure that other things would have stopped you eventually'.[4] But I don't think Barden's dismissal of the impact of emotion is entirely adequate. If even one important new voice has been lost due to irresponsible applications of 'toughness' in the workshop, then we must address how to minimise this damage.

Many years on from that ugly workshop, and armed with the awareness that came out of it, I am now an instructor of fiction workshops myself, both undergraduate and graduate. I still find myself struggling, from the other side of the table, with the same emotional issues I encountered in that disastrous workshop – specifically the way 'honesty' can so easily become a cover for less pleasant and more amorphous motivations. Over the years, my teaching practice has evolved through two sets of tactics I describe here: one a correction (or preventative) for the conditions that led to Bob's workshop, the other a correction to that correction implemented at the suggestion of my students.

The Scylla of Honesty and Charybdis of Truth

I like to start the semester by discussing with my students the content of a laminated card I once received with a free sample of a fiction writing textbook. The card is entitled 'A Workshop Guide for Creative Writing' and is unattributed. A sub-section entitled 'Workshop Etiquette: Receiving Criticism' counsels students to 'prepare emotionally' for their workshops:

> This rare opportunity for concentrated critical attention will be both helpful and stressful. It may help to remind yourself that you joined the class in order to improve your writing, and that is what the workshop will help you to do.[5]

It may not be entirely clear to the novice workshopper why she

---

[4] Dan Barden, 'Workshop: a Rant Against Creative Writing Classes', *Poets and Writers* (March/April 2008), pp. 83-88 (p. 86).
[5] *A Workshop Guide for Creative Writing* (uncredited), (2010).

needs such assurances, and the overall effect may be less than comforting. The other side of the laminated card, entitled 'Workshop Etiquette: Giving Criticism' addresses itself toward those discussing a classmate's work. A section entitled 'Keep your tone appropriate' advises students to: 'Pitch your voice down; speak calmly and slowly. Avoid sarcasm and jokes, which can misfire when you're talking about someone else's work. Never use a workshop to vent your impatience with imperfection.'[6]

Leaving aside that fascinating last sentence, this passage contains a clear implication that, left unchecked, a workshop will turn angry, sarcastic, and impatient. If the fledgling workshopper were not already nervous about the prospect of sharing her drafts with a group, this passage will certainly alarm her. Shrillness is not only a vocal tone, it is a mindset, and these instructions try to correct for one without addressing the other, leaving the implied hostility of the workshop intact.

Another paragraph in the same section advises workshoppers, after the workshop is over, to 'Speak to the author; re-establish equal status.'[7] (I imagine it may be troubling to the writer to learn that her status had been less than equal.) 'Most people feel pretty awkward and vulnerable right after their workshops,' the passage continues. 'Help break the ice by making conversation. Remember that the writer is probably still feeling a little self-conscious and may be wondering what you thought of his or her work'.[8]

My students are especially alarmed by this passage in its implication that the workshop process, which goes on in a classroom under the supervision of a teacher, would be so degrading that classmates would have to make a point of speaking to the author afterward in order to 're-establish equal status'. The idea seems to be that the usual equality between students is somehow altered by the workshop process, and that the author inevitably winds up feeling subjugated to the judgement of her classmates. Again, we see the language of emotion, and, notably, the emotions are never positive ones ('awkward', 'vulnerable', 'self-conscious').[9] The card addresses itself almost exclusively to patching up the bad feelings that apparently always result from workshopping; the only *positive* exhortations directed toward workshoppers are to 'Be honest *and* sensitive. Honesty does not mean a free-for-all, and sensitivity

---

[6] Ibid.
[7] Ibid.
[8] Ibid.
[9] Ibid.

doesn't mean sugar-coating the truth.'[10] The huge and complex difficulty of workshopping is here summed up and dismissed in a single imperative sentence; the card may as well tell us to 'workshop well'. How to navigate between the Scylla of honesty and Charybdis of truth is left to the neophyte workshopper to figure out on her own. The more closely we look at this laminated card, the less clear it is why anyone would want their work to be the subject of a workshop at all.

I lead my students in a close reading of this card precisely because I wish to unpack these negative emotions that students may have come to associate with the creative writing workshop, even if (especially if) they have never participated in a workshop before. I assure them that in my classroom, they will not have to work to 're-establish equal status' and that they will not be made to feel 'vulnerable' or 'awkward' as a matter of course. These feelings are a sign that something is not going right, I explain, and if something is not going right, we will step back and address it together. Vague exhortations to 'be considerate' etc. don't adequately reflect, to me, the range of things that can go wrong in the writing workshop and what is at stake when they do. I believe workshop instructors must go beyond these simple warnings and instructions in order to address the root causes of the problems that can emerge in the creative writing workshop and actively to create the conditions that allow a healthy workshop to flourish.

For years, I have tried to accomplish these goals using three rules:

1. I outlawed evaluation. Workshoppers could say anything they wanted about the work at hand except to label it good or bad, better or worse.

2. I discouraged global comments, sentences that attempted to say something about the *entire* story or novel chapter. I told students I didn't want to hear 'This story was sad' but rather, 'One particular part of this story that created a feeling of sadness for me was on page nine.'

3. Lastly, I lifted the gag rule that is traditional in writing workshops, based on the idea that, as Carol Bly observed, the writer's forced silence can invite meanness in some groups.

Students' first reactions to my rules usually range between bemusement and irritation. My no-evaluation rule can be especially bewildering; many students had understood

---

[10] Ibid.

evaluation to be the entire point of workshopping, and they have trouble, at first, imagining what else one might say when faced with a peer's draft. So we work through some examples, 'practice-workshopping' stories that were not written by any of them in order to discuss different ways of responding. Once they get used to the range of options for responding to each other's work, our workshops are generally ones that make me proud: lively, on-topic, constructive, specific, and rigorous without being discouraging.

Fair enough and tough enough

Implementing these rules does not constitute a perfect solution, however, as a recent semester has demonstrated. I was teaching a capstone course for senior-level creative writing majors, and the group had been responding well (I thought) to my three rules. They had produced impressive stories all semester, pushing themselves and providing insightful, generous comments to each other. A few weeks before the end of the course, I set aside some time to talk about how the course had gone, and to ask for their thoughts about how I might improve the class in the future. After some hemming and hawing, a brave student raised his hand and told me there was one thing he hadn't liked about our class. 'I didn't like that we always had to say nice things about each other's work,' he said. 'I felt the same way,' another student said. 'It was really hard for me to come up with nice things to say about a story when it just wasn't very good, and I didn't like being forced to lie.'

To say the least, I was disappointed to hear this characterisation of my rules. The no-evaluation rule forbids 'niceness' as clearly as it does 'meanness', but apparently students hadn't been interpreting it that way. I was discouraged by the seeming persistence of the notion that a workshop must be a proving ground, that work must be evaluated (and, presumably, mostly found wanting) rather than constructing the workshop as an aid to process, the model advocated by Wendy Bishop that I had found so inspiring as a new teacher.[11]

When I pointed out, trying not to sound defensive, that I had never told them to lie to each other, had never told them to 'be nice', they allowed that this was true – I had never actually *told* them to 'be nice', but as I had in essence prevented them from *being mean* (or 'tough'), I had left them no other choice than to make up nice lies. My students nearly unanimously expressed a

---

[11] Wendy Bishop, *Released into Language: Options for Teaching Creative Writing* (1990).

desire for their own workshops to be 'tough and honest' –
simply put, they said they *did* want their own work to be
evaluated.

One student articulated it this way: 'I'm a fan of calling people
out. When bad is bad, I like to hear about it.' I suspected that this
student would enjoy hearing the details of another student's
'badness' much more than he would enjoy hearing about his
own, but I had to admit that my students had a point: the no-
evaluation rule resulted in workshops that sounded oddly
similar in tone whether the story was a true achievement or
slapped together. And the fact that weak stories were never quite
called out as such removed the self-preservation motivation that
I know sometimes pushed me, when I was a student, to do my
best work.

I told my students I would consider this carefully, and having
done so I will tell you the conclusion I reached: I believe my
students wanted to have their own work evaluated in large part
because only when their work is evaluated can they be told that
it is wonderful. And that having their work praised is one of the
benefits (though certainly not the only one) they seek in a
workshop. This is not the same thing as expecting to be
congratulated for every single thing they produce, a trait for
which the current generation of college students is sometimes
maligned. My students didn't just want to be praised; they were
willing to risk being told their work was bad in exchange for the
possibility of being told it was good – and only in a 'tough,
honest' atmosphere could they safely believe that possible praise.

My students' desire to hear bad work called out as such might
stem partly from a sense of competition; it also might come from
the same type of dark motivations that drove my graduate-
school shark attack. Students resent classmates who don't take
the work of the class seriously, and calling a thin or unfinished
story what it is allows those students who have poured hours of
sincere work into their own stories to feel that there is some
justice in the world. The fact that these motivations are outside
the supposed goals of the writing workshop does not make them
any less compelling to students.

When I asked my class what we should do to address their
preferences without letting the workshop turn into a bloodbath,
they proposed a simple solution: writers should introduce their
own workshops by announcing what type of criticism they
would like to hear. 'People who want a tough, honest workshop
can ask for it,' they explained, 'and people who want a gentler
workshop can ask for that.' I was very suspicious of this plan. I
thought there was a good chance that each of them in turn
would announce that they wanted a 'hard, honest' workshop

while secretly hoping to hear nothing but praise; when they didn't get it, emotions would run high, resentments would ensue, and I would be powerless to keep the class on track. But I didn't have any better ideas, so we tried it.

What I found was fascinating: some students did express a desire for a 'tough, honest' workshop (and, for the record, no one ever asked for an easy one) – but more often, students refrained from using adjectives like 'tough' or 'gentle' and instead offered a brief history of their work on the story. They wanted to tell each other where their original ideas had come from, how long they had been working on the drafts, where they still felt uncertain, and what they found the story's weak points to be. Students were surprisingly forthcoming and self-aware in these introductions, and these narratives contained quite a bit of metadata about both the state of the draft and the student's emotional state. A wavering, apologetic creation story filled with false starts communicates clearly: *please don't tell me this is a mess, I know it is. Instead please offer help with these specific problems.* A short, confident-sounding 'have at it' communicates: *I feel good about this, please hold it to a high standard.* The group was generally adept at absorbing these meta-messages and giving each writer the workshop that would be most helpful to them.

Donald Hall observed, famously, that workshops 'reduce poetry to a parlor game', that 'they trivialize and make safe-seeming the real terrors of real art'.[12] I have always found his dismissal of the workshop overly simplistic, but I also take his point about terror. When a workshop becomes too warm a bath of mutual support, writing can start to seem easy, and it's not. Writers often fail, and if we are told we are succeeding when we have actually failed, the workshop is doing us no service. Gaylene Perry calls for something similar in her discussion of vulnerability in the writing workshop, that 'what is perhaps needed is *less* safety, in a sense. I am not advocating a lack of care. However...institutional *over*-protection can too easily become the greatest endangerment to learning and quality experience'.[13]

I've gone on to use this approach since in many writing workshops at the undergraduate and graduate levels, and for both fiction and creative non-fiction. After a few 'practice' workshops, most groups become very good at hearing workshoppers' requests clearly and offering rigorous but supportive discussions.

---

[12] Donald Hall, 'Poetry and ambition', Online.
[13] Gaylene Perry, 'Potentially Dangerous: Vulnerabilities and Risks in the Writing Workshop' in *Does the Writing Workshop Still Work?* (2010), pp.117-129, (p. 128).

This isn't a perfect solution, of course. Not everyone is equally skilled at sending meta-messages, as doing so requires a bit of performance, and it's a significant problem that shy students, who may be the most vulnerable to harshness, are also least able to communicate their needs. An equally significant problem is the mismatched two-workshop day: when one story is much stronger than the other, there is a tendency for the governing spirit of the stronger story's workshop to continue. It's hard to shift gears, and even harder for the second writer to ask for a different sort of workshop than the one we just finished. These are serious issues, and my approach to the writing workshop must continue to seek to address them.

Looking back at my experience with the shark attack workshop, I'm struck by my memory of our collective sense of righteousness, our assumption that the instructor was doing nothing to address Bob's shortcomings and that it was therefore our right to punish him ourselves. Only in the writing workshop does one student's failure so directly affect every other student in the class, and only in the writing workshop is it possible for students to punish and reward each other in such a public way. In any other type of class, Bob's poor performance would not have had an impact on the rest of us, might not even have been visible to us. Only in a writing workshop is student emotion – both Bob's emotion and ours – such a salient aspect of the day-to-day workings of the class.

My thinking about 'toughness' and the effects of evaluation continues to evolve. My youthful experience playing a part in an attack on a classmate illustrates how easily the workshop format can be turned into a weapon, how easily students can turn mean in the guise of 'toughness'. My more recent experience as an instructor has taught me just the opposite, that evaluation can play a role in authentic, useful responses, that in fact, student writers crave 'toughness', even if that concept is to some degree a cipher for other desires: the desire for approval for their efforts, the desire for acceptance into a community of writers, the desire for affirmation that they might have what it takes. Meeting these emotional needs may not normally be the burden of an academic course, but as these desires are ones that all writers share, the writing workshop must be prepared to address them.

Writing Exercise (any level)

Pass out a copy of a short story from a previous class or found online, with the name removed and replaced with the name 'Bob'. (Of course, obtain permission to use the work in this way beforehand.) The story should be relatively short (under 15 pages or so) and should have both noticeable strengths and noticeable weaknesses – an 'average' story for the level of the workshop. Ask students to prepare for Bob's workshop as they would any of their classmates. They should read the story carefully at least twice, make line notes, and write up a one or two page note to Bob at the end.

In the next class period, workshop Bob's story. Remind students to speak as if Bob were in the room. Keep the workshop a bit shorter than you generally would allow (e.g. 15 minutes if you would generally allow 20).

After declaring the workshop over (and 'Bob' out of the room), have a meta-discussion of the workshop. Discuss any comments that might have made Bob uncomfortable. (You might appoint one or more students to speak for Bob here). As you discuss, notice that the comments most likely to offend or discourage Bob are often also the ones least likely to lead to a useful craft discussion. ('This dialogue seems really cheesy' is less useful than a general consideration of how emotion is earned in fiction; 'I really just hate this kind of story' is less useful than a broader discussion of genre or tradition.)

Discuss how many ideas about the craft of fiction came out of the workshop. Notice that these ideas were useful in some way to every writer present, even though Bob was not. Agree to remember that the goal for every workshop will be to make it relevant to everyone, not just the writer at hand.

Works Cited

Barden, Dan 'Workshop: a Rant Against Creative Writing Classes', *Poets and Writers* (March/April 2008) pp. 23-7

Bishop, Wendy *Released into Language: Options for Teaching Creative Writing* (Urbana: NCTE, 1990)

Bly, Carol, *Beyond the Writers' Workshop* (New York: Anchor Books, 2001)

Donnelly, Dianne, ed., *Does the Writing Workshop Still Work?* (Bristol: Multilingual Matters, 2010)

Hall, Donald, 'Poetry and ambition', originally published in *Kenyon Review*, new series 5:4 (1983), available at: http://www.poets.org/viewmedia.php/prmMID/16915 [accessed May 2, 2011]

Mayers, Tim, 'Poetry, F(r)iction, Drama: The Complex Dynamics of Audience in the Writing Workshop', in Dianne Donnelly, ed., *Does the Writing Workshop Still Work?* (Bristol: Multilingual Matters, 2010) pp. 94-104

Milgram, Stanley, *Obedience to Authority; An Experimental View* (New York: Harper Collins, 1974)

Perry, Gaylene, 'Potentially Dangerous: Vulnerabilities and Risks in the Writing Workshop', in Dianne Donnelly, ed., *Does the Writing Workshop Still Work?* (Bristol: Multilingual Matters, 2010) pp. 117-29

A Workshop Guide for Creative Writing (uncredited), (Boston: Pearson Longman, 2010)

Standing on Deep Shale: the Problem of Originality

Ursula Hurley

While the argument over whether creative writing can and should be taught in a formal academic setting rumbles on, many people vote with their feet by continuing to swell the ranks of undergraduate and postgraduate writing programmes. For those of us privileged with the responsibility of delivering these programmes, the question is not *whether* we should teach, but what, and how? In the increasingly consumer-orientated context of higher education in the twenty-first century, the expectations of learners need to be carefully managed. Writing students often believe (and who wouldn't hope for this?) that in exchange for their tuition fees they will receive the blueprint for commercial success, the formula for a prize-winning story, or, to put it metaphorically, the 'secret recipe' for turning hopes and dreams into reality.

If we endeavour to give learners what they think they want, we are in danger of doing them a grave disservice. In the 2004 report, *The Short Story in the UK,* one anonymous editor says: 'There is a slight cottage industry feel to this – young writers have been taught how to craft short stories by the creative writing courses.'[1] This observation chimes with Doris Betts's caution about the 'cookie-cutter mould'.[2] Teachers of writing therefore need to be wary of contributing to a perceived 'recipe' tendency: if we produce ever-increasing numbers of well-groomed but homogeneous writing graduates we will choke the well-spring of fresh voices on which our discipline and our industry depend.

The issue boils down to originality. Writers are often plagued by the apparent impossibility of saying something new, finding a unique voice; how to add something worthwhile to the almost infinite body of pre-existing literature? We stand at the edge of a vast uncharted sea – the unformed poems, stories or scripts that we may one day write. And what are we standing on, as we look out into this misty expanse? A vast beach of other people's words, those who have gone before. We walk on the deep shale of other people's work, stretching back into prehistory.

---

[1] J. Brown, M. Forsyth and P. Johnston, 'The Short Story in the UK: an overview of the current state and exploration of opportunities for new initiatives' (2004), Online.

[2] Doris Betts, 'Undergraduate Creative Writing Courses', in *Association of Departments of English Bulletin,* 79 (Winter 1984), Online.

The weight of this pre-existing work, especially to the student just beginning their writer's journey, can be crushing. Harold Bloom calls this troubled relationship with our forbears the 'anxiety of influence'. 'Influence,' according to Bloom, 'is *Influenza* – an astral disease'.[3] He describes a macho, blood-soaked process, whereby 'a writer can devour his father, and…we can watch this cannibalism take place on the page'.[4] Bloom restricts his observations to poetry, and to male authors. However, beneath the dramatic imagery, the process Bloom describes is circular, one of recycling and recirculating the act of authorship – perhaps, rather than the psychic violence of Greek Tragedy, it is possible to interact productively with one's literary ancestors, and to find a way to live peacefully together; to explore the possibility of synthesis.

This is what Marina Warner argues when she observes 'a fundamental misunderstanding of originality', and calls instead for creative writing to be taught as an act of retelling: 'Repetition always entails with it a change of meaning because the circumstances change from the original utterance. By echoing history you change the meanings.' This idea of an 'echo chamber' may prove helpful to new writers trying to find a voice: it allows them to play at ventriloquism, to 'try out' different identities, and even 'to accept the instability of voice as a possible way of speaking'.[5] The knowing irony that such informed repetition provides can offer some protection against the possibility of producing derivative work, and can result in startlingly original reworkings such as Angela Carter's well-known fairy tales.[6]

This paradigm of creative retelling is articulated in a different way by Robin Nelson, who envisions authors writing over each other, in continuous iterations:

> Palimpsest: 'a parchment or the like from which writing has been partially erased to make room for another text'. Or with the contemporary inflection, drawing on an archaeological metaphor, a palimpsest is a multi-layered text, the traces of previous inscriptions remaining visible in the new text.[7]

[3] Harold Bloom, *The Anxiety of Influence: A Theory of Poetry* (1973), p. 95.
[4] Michael Wood, 'The Anxiety of Influence: A Theory of Poetry', *New York Review of Books* (17 April 1975), Online.
[5] Marina Warner, Plenary Speech, Cross-Gendered Voices Conference, University of Warwick, U.K., 31 May 2008.
[6] Angela Carter, *The Bloody Chamber* (2006).
[7] Robin Nelson, 'Set Map Slip = Palimpsest (working title) – "working" because it is provisional and "working" because it is on the move', *Performance Research*, 6:2 (2001), pp. 100-108 (p. 101).

The idea comes from that most fertile of metaphors: archaeology. So powerful is this metaphor for writers in the postmodern age, where originality is a contested, perhaps impossible concept, that Penelope Lively devotes a whole section to it in her experimental anti-memoir *Making It Up*: 'This is August 1973, but it is also the first century AD, and very many other points in time as well.'[8] What the archaeologist (and the writer) can do is to short circuit the linear construction of history by digging through layers that have taken aeons to accrue, reaching in a matter of hours an artefact whose story is actually very distant from us in linear time. Through the use of appropriate tools, linear time can be made to bend, so that someone in the twenty-first century can touch a Roman object. 'Fiction,' argues Marina Warner, 'gives you the possibility of empathising with characters from the past. Fiction writers do not record but plant.'[9]

The concept of creative repetition is described yet again in Christopher Booker's monumental *The Seven Basic Plots*, in which he argues that all narratives, from Genesis to Batman and all points inbetween, consist of a combination of one or more of these archetypal story structures. It is not the stories themselves that have the potential for originality, but their recombinations and recastings in specific cultural milieus.[10]

Such conceptualisations offer alternatives to the suffocating idea of having to fight one's way through an overwhelming weight of pre-existing material in order to reach the oxygen of originality. Possibilities for negotiating the concept of originality inform all of my teaching. Sticking with the 'deep shale' metaphor, I introduce to my first year undergraduates the concept of 'reading as a writer'. When you read as a writer, you walk along the 'deep shale' of other people's words, perhaps in quiet contemplation, feverish excitement or total despair. You look down at what's under your feet: other people's books. They're like the pebbles on a real beach; infinitely varied, numberless, mainly undistinguished, occasionally fascinating. As you walk along this beach, you pick up some of these literary 'pebbles'. Some you will look at and discard. Some you may fling furiously into the distance – and interrogating such a violent reaction can tell us a lot about what we think writing is for and what it should do. But some will attract you, and these you will put in your pocket. Their texture, colour, shape or form may inspire you. You will take them home and make a little pile on your desk, next to your computer screen or your notebook. And these you will turn to as you struggle with your own

---

[8] Penelope Lively, *Making It Up* (2005), pp. 74-5.
[9] Warner, Plenary Speech.
[10] Christopher Booker, *The Seven Basic Plots: Why We Tell Stories* (2004).

writing, holding them up to the light, scrutinising them for the things they can teach you.

This approach, I believe, gives us more choices as writers. We can access techniques, content and styles that we may never otherwise have encountered. We can also disabuse ourselves of the false triumph we feel when what we have actually done is re-invent the wheel. We become informed practitioners who understand our field, we know what's going on out there, who the key players are, and how we can use the work of others as maps that may provide clues as to how we can get where we want to go.

This philosophy is holistic, it underpins my pedagogy, but it's about framing a life-long approach to reflective practice. That's of limited use to an undergraduate who doesn't have a lifetime of reading behind her and just needs to get her 3,000 words submitted by a week next Tuesday. Something more explicit is required, and nowhere more so than in the fiction module that I teach to our final year undergraduates. This is the last thing I can give them before they leave the structured support of their course and have to negotiate the complex terrain of the writing life without anyone to hold their hand.

Betts states that beyond an affirmation of the rudiments (mastery of mechanics and spelling), there are only two approaches to writing pedagogy: wholes-to-parts or parts-to-wholes.[11] The 'wholes-to-parts' method relies upon a process of osmosis, whereby students are fed a constant diet of 'good' writing in the hope that they will internalise its characteristics and reproduce it in their own work. This is where my 'reading as a writer' paradigm fits. It's a valuable habit to acquire, but it's a long-term investment that may not show immediate profit. In the limited time that I have with my students, I need to give them more than a misty beach full of literary pebbles.

In contrast, the 'parts-to-wholes' method picks out and practises one technique at a time. It believes implicitly in the writer's toolbox (advocated so eloquently in Stephen King's *On Writing*): each tool is examined, its use explained, skills to wield it effectively are practised.[12] It returns to the toolbox sharpened and ready for action. At more basic levels of tuition, when students are learning the elements of narrative, this 'parts-to-wholes' approach makes for effective teaching and learning. For example, you don't have to wait until work is submitted for assessment to see that someone needs to strengthen their use of dialogue – you look over their shoulder during the class on

---

[11] Betts, http://www.ade.org/bulletin/frames_browse.htm.

[12] Stephen King, *On Writing: A Memoir of the Craft* (London: New English Library, 2001).

dialogue and you help them sharpen it up. The chances are that they will do better in their assessed piece, gaining confidence and motivation.

However, the problem with the 'parts-to-wholes' approach can be that students have a selection of disparate techniques that they don't know how to combine into an effective, aesthetically cogent whole. It may also be guilty of furthering the 'writing by numbers' paradigm of which we are rightly wary. Final year students should be nearing professional standards. They need a more sophisticated approach, one that facilitates the continued development of skills such as dialogue to very high levels of competence, while also fostering a critical consciousness, a willingness to play and experiment, to take informed risks, to question rules and to break the accepted norms of genre. This is the best hope they have of finding their own voice, and of doing so in the shelter of the academy, before they have to earn a living from the fruits of their writing. We must nurture such an approach if we are to do right by our students, and avoid the 'prescriptive' tendency for which writing programmes are often criticised.

And so I designed my final year fiction module in such a way that the problem of originality is announced from the outset and grappled with explicitly throughout the course. I called the module 'Writing Fiction: Innovation and Experiment', its purpose being to welcome the elephant that has been in the room in every writing workshop I have ever given, and to say: 'Here you are, the question of originality; how can we work with you?' I designed the module to draw on elements of both the 'wholes-to-parts' and 'parts-to-wholes' approaches outlined above, to synthesise the most effective elements of each, and in so doing to create an approach to reading, writing and assessment that allows students to negotiate their own understanding of originality in a supportive academic environment.

My point of departure was a comment by Betts, which I came across early in my career and have tried to live by ever since: 'What works in all writing classes is what the teacher knows best and can transmit passionately – without being doctrinaire.'[13] Being enthusiastic about your material certainly makes you a more engaging teacher. But framing the module around my own practice as an experimental novelist gave me more credibility as an instructor. Students don't always realise that their tutors lead double lives as professional writers. They sometimes assume that if you were any good, you'd be dictating your next bestseller on

---

[13] Betts, Online.

a Caribbean beach, chilled champagne in hand. And because you clearly don't have the 'magic recipe' for commercial success, your teaching can be safely ignored, especially if you're challenging them to do difficult or demanding work.

Setting out the module in the context of my own practice allowed me to share a number of valuable insights with the students: firstly, it is only a tiny minority of writers who make a comfortable living just from writing; secondly, teaching is a rewarding activity that makes both me and them better writers; and thirdly, demonstrates that what I am sharing with them comes from hard-won praxical knowledge – I learned this by doing it, and now I can offer you this guidance.[14] Sharing excerpts of my own work (talking them through the moment when I threw the whole thing in the bin, how I rescued it from the shredder and finally saw it in print) actually provides lessons in editing and drafting (do we ever teach this enough?) and shows students that if I can do it, so can they.

Within this framework, a module reader acts as a 'safari' through a number of key moments of 'originality' in the history of the novel. Students are provided with excerpts from these texts, followed up by guided discussion in class, and also a wider reading list, but the emphasis is on class members discovering their own material. Indeed, each class includes a 'show and tell' where several group members on a rolling, pre-allocated basis bring examples of texts that they feel tell us something about originality. Such texts may be commercial fiction, for example *Holly's Inbox*, which can be seen to build on the tradition of the epistolary novel by presenting the narrative as a series of emails, or much-loved graphic novels, such as Craig Thompson's *Blankets*, that until now had been undeclared obsessions, thought unsuitable for the literary, 'academic' nature of a writing degree programme.[15] Many students respond to the notion that any text, from populist genre fiction to obscure specialist interest, is equally valid as a point of discussion. In a sense, I am asking them to tell me what is interesting and worthy of note. This makes a refreshing change from the 'top down' imposition of a reading list of worthy literary fiction (although I make sure they get their fair share of that, too).

In addition to this guided reading and discussion, each class begins with a writing exercise, designed to introduce and interrogate a concept that pertains in some way to the contested nature of originality, the weirder and wackier the better – one of these is included at the end of this chapter. Students are so

---

[14] For a discussion of praxis, see Robin Nelson's presentation, 'Practice as Research'. Online.

[15] Holly Denham, *Holly's Inbox* (2007); Craig Thompson, *Blankets* (2003).

intrigued by the 'boxes of tricks' and bizarre activities introduced during class that attendance is more regular and there is a lightness and humour to proceedings that allows me to slip in some challenging ideas and techniques. For example, in order to teach meta-fiction, I begin the class by asking students to write a list of things that annoy them. 'Go on, rant!' is the instruction. They have no idea where I'm going with this, but they're intrigued, and it's fun, so they humour me. I then ask them to swap lists. Selected lists are read out to the class anonymously and we have to guess the author. This allows an aside about listing as a literary technique, particularly for efficient characterisation. Then we pick an issue that several people have listed and talk about why it annoys them – issues to do with fairness, transparency, the environment, or human rights are particularly fruitful.

At this point I ask the class to imagine that they live in a regime where freedom of speech does not exist, where state censorship is rife, and where the penalties for speaking or writing out of turn are harsh. It could be a country in the world today, or it could be our own country at a certain point in its history. In Renaissance England, for example, you could have your ears cut off for what the censor decided to be a treasonous comment.[16] No wonder Shakespeare set his political plays in historic Denmark and ancient Rome. Now, how could we get around such constraints? How could you invite your reader to 'read between the lines' and to understand your real message?

Engrossed in the issue at hand, lively and impassioned debate usually follows. With guidance, we get to a rich collection of potential solutions, and exemplar texts. Typical responses include the following:

- Consider how the act of writing can become a metaphor for all sorts of human struggles, particularly to do with power and free will. See, for example, *If On a Winter's Night a Traveller* by Italo Calvino, or *Sophie's World* by Jostein Gaarder.[17]
- Think of a well-known story, legend or fairytale. Rewrite it, allowing the characters in it to comment upon the conventions of the genre. Children's films are good at this. Think of *Shrek*, for example.[18]

---

[16] Julia Briggs, *This Stage-Play World: Texts and Contexts, 1580-1625* (1997), pp. 11-12.

[17] Italo Calvino, *If On a Winter's Night a Traveller* (2007); Jostein Gaarder, *Sophie's World* (2006) .

[18] *Shrek*, dir. Andrew Adamson (2001).

- Find a 'true story' (from a newspaper, or an event that is in the popular consciousness) and fill in the gaps with fictional elements that question the 'official' version of events. This can be done to humorous effect, but it can also offer a profound interrogation of the most traumatic histories. See, for example, the use of Freud and the Holocaust in *The White Hotel* by D.M. Thomas.[19]

By the time I explain to the students that they have been engaged in writing meta-fiction, they are so fired up by the demonstration of how it can generate compelling material that they are quite open to taking the concept on board. This model of praxical pedagogy, where students enact a concept, grasp its practicalities and then discover the theory behind it, seems to be far more effective than the conventional model of introducing a theory by explaining it first. This way around – write first, ask questions later – demonstrates a concept's usefulness to a writer as a way of generating material, rather than as an abstract theory that 'we' have decided they need to know in order to pass the module.

Which is not to say that issues to do with assessment do not arise. The activity and lightness of the classes is often overshadowed by concerns about academic achievement. By this stage in their careers, students on a modular degree programme such as the one I deliver have a pretty good awareness of which degree classification is realistic for them, and what they need to score on each remaining module of the programme in order to reach that goal. The constant question, therefore, is 'how does this wacky exercise translate into marks?' Is this 'innovative' enough, or will I lose marks for being unoriginal? I am sympathetic to these concerns, and have tried to design the assessments for this module in order to address them.

The first assessed element is a 1,500-word 'Writer's Reflection', worth 30% of the final mark. It is a piece of formative assessment, in that it is due towards the end of the taught classes, about a month before the creative piece is due. This unsettles some students. 'How can I reflect on a piece that isn't finished?' they ask. Actually, by forcing them to sit down and reflect, the hope is that such formative thinking will feed into their creative piece, and the clarity that being asked to produce such a 'manifesto' brings will benefit their final submission. In addition to being provided with a model answer, which I wrote about my own practice, students are encouraged to consider the following questions:

---

[19] D.M. Thomas, *The White Hotel* (1999).

- *What does innovation mean to me?*
- *How does this work reflect my engagement with innovation?*
- *Is my work innovative? In what ways?*
- *How might I continue to innovate in future projects?*

Within the framework of innovation, students are also invited to respond to some or all of the following questions:

- *What skills and techniques have I acquired? What are they? How did I acquire and develop them?*
- *What influence has the work I have read or studied on the module had on my writing?*
- *How far has my journal fed into my work?*
- *How has participation in the workshop helped?*
- *Do I wish to continue working in this specific genre?*
- *What kind of writer am I? What kind of writer would I like to be?*
- *What have I learnt about writing in general?*
- *What will I write next?*[20]

In addition to the 1,500-word reflection, the main assessed work on this module is a piece of fiction, word count negotiable (3,000–5,000 words or equivalent), reflecting an engagement with the module syllabus. The word count is negotiable because some students choose to work on visual innovation, and may submit work that contains graphic elements or is not paper based. The office staff know when my module has work due because of the queue of students holding furniture, boxes, CD-ROMs, scrolls and antique-looking books. However, as I emphasise to the students, it is equally possible to do exceptionally well with a piece of work that looks 'normal' but that does interesting things with 'point of view', for example.

Students worry that I 'won't get' their piece, or won't understand that it is innovative *for them*. An oft-repeated worry is, 'What if I submit something that I think is original, but you've read something like it elsewhere?' As a way of addressing such concerns, the piece of fiction must be accompanied by three pieces of evidence documenting a student's engagement with innovation. This material may include excerpts from drafts illustrating a key challenge or decision facing them; extracts from

---

[20] 'Writing Fiction: Innovation and Experiment, Module Handbook', University of Salford, 2010.

their journal; reviews of readings or performances; accounts of visits to galleries, museums, libraries and so on. This material forms a large component of the 'safety net' in this module: it gives me an insight into the context of the creative work, and allows me to reward ambition and intention, even if the execution is not as strong as it could be.

I also advise students that the exact nature of the creative submission needs to be negotiated with me and, to facilitate this, a series of one-to-one appointments is offered in the final stages of the module. This allows anxieties about fulfilling the assessment criteria to be addressed individually. Most of these anxieties congregate around the open-ended nature of the assessment, and students having to negotiate their own understanding of what innovative or experimental practice means for their own development as writers. In many cases, students are concerned that they have not been 'innovative' enough to get the mark they need. In short, the invitation to the student to set their own agenda is not always welcome. It introduces an element of uncertainty that more prescriptive modes of assessment largely avoid.

Dismayed that the explicit reference to innovation was becoming a distraction from productive approaches to originality, I considered strategies for addressing concerns that were being raised with increasing stridency by students. Desperate to resist the traditional workshop model of me as tutor having all the power and all the answers, I used the next class as a forum in which to air these concerns and to forge a collective response. We agreed that we would attempt to grapple with these conceptual difficulties by drawing up a collective agreement on what it is that we think the module is about. In Appendix I at the end of this section, I offer an example 'class constitution' from my recent teaching practice. I have acted as scribe, but this document is generated and owned by all participants, in which we set out expectations, anxieties, collective understandings of key terms, potential problems and their potential solutions. This intervention has been praised by our external examiner, who suggested it be adopted for all the writing modules at Salford. While this document varies from year to year, its underlying principles remain reassuringly constant.

The discussion usually begins with the negatives. The students echo Raymond Federman's cautions about 'the middle-men of literature' who '[give]...the label EXPERIMENTAL to what is difficult, strange, provocative, and even original.'[21] And

---

[21] Raymond Federman, 'Four Propositions in Form of an Introduction', in *Surfiction: Fiction Now and Tomorrow*, ed. Raymond Federman (1975), pp. 5-18 (p.

they are sharply aware of the career implications of such a label: 'Everything that does not fall into the category of *successful fiction* (commercially that is)...is immediately relegated to the domain of experimentation – a safe and useless place.'[22] Even if, as it ought to be, our work is the result of a genuine engagement with issues of concern to us as writers, others will categorise us. The direction of one's own practice and the reception of one's work are both profoundly affected by this act of categorisation. Trying to make it as a writer is a risky enough business. Trying to make it as a writer who will be categorised as 'experimental', riskier still.

A telling example of the heavy price even the best and most respected writers can pay when the 'middle-men of literature' categorise your work as 'experimental' is that of Christine Brooke-Rose with her 1975 work *Thru*.[23] As Brooke-Rose acknowledged, this was too much for the middle-men. In an interview, she said:

> Yes, that really is a very difficult novel...I never thought it would be accepted. It was something I had to do. My publisher loved it; at least my editor loved it, the publisher was perhaps not quite so pleased, and of course, it didn't sell. And after that I did realise that I had probably, career-wise as they say, done myself a lot of harm because I was really dismissed as completely potty...[24]

The students throw this back at me because I include it in their module reader. However, I point out, Brooke-Rose forged a trail for other writers to follow. She produced a 'limit text', showing us what happens when genre is pushed to breaking point. Mark Z. Danielewski's *House of Leaves*, published in 2000, was an international best seller.[25] And yet, as a cursory flick through the text illustrates, it clearly draws on the kinds of things that Brooke-Rose made possible by pushing her practice to the limit.

While Brooke-Rose may have done us all a service in delineating the limits of the novel with *Thru*, her 'very special sort of unreadable book', most of us wish to produce some form of readable text. We don't want to sacrifice our own careers for

---

7).
[22] Ibid., p.7.
[23] Christine Brooke-Rose, *Thru*, first published 1975, this edition in *Four Novels: Out, Such, Between, Thru, The Christine Brooke-Rose Omnibus* (2006).
[24] Ellen G. Friedman and Miriam Fuchs, 'An Interview with Christine Brooke-Rose', *Review of Contemporary Fiction*, 9:3 (Fall 1989). Online.
[25] Mark Z. Danielewski, *House of Leaves* (2000).

the sake of those who may come after. We seek to publish, and possibly to scrape a living from doing so. Thus my students (and I) are sensitive to commercial factors. Can we make a living at this, they asked me. If not, why should we bother? As I trod water, flailing for an answer, one of the students silenced me with his brilliance: experiment, he said, was simply 'a personal challenge to evaluate what you write'. Thus, even a writer engaged in the most conventional of tasks – say, writing a certain kind of genre fiction for a certain kind of reader – needs to innovate in order to stay in the game. As Alain Robbe-Grillet writes, 'Each novelist, each novel must invent its own form. No recipe can replace this continual reflection.'[26] Even the most conventional of novelists has to produce a text which is similar to previous works without being derivative; recognisable without being a clone; and ultimately predictable while disguising this predictability throughout. Expressed like this, the challenge posed to any writer looks almost Oulipian.[27] Originality is not a desirable extra, but rather a prerequisite of the writing process.

What my students and I have begun to understand is that any act of writing is an experiment: it is unique, and, until it is finished, no-one can be sure how it is going to turn out. From this perspective, the concept of 'originality' as something shiny and new, never seen before, is a red herring. If you consciously strive to be original then you will tie yourself in derivative knots, dismissing every idea as hackneyed before it has chance to flourish. Rather, if we revise our understanding of originality in the light of Warner's thinking on creative retelling, on Nelson's paradigm of palimpsest texts, and Booker's thesis that there are only seven plots with which to work, then we begin to see that our anxieties about avoiding repetition at all costs are misplaced. Creative engagement which embraces retellings, recombinations and recastings as part of an ongoing dialogue with our literary forbears can result in the most original work of all. As Gilles Deleuze puts it, 'not the same but the different, not the similar but the dissimilar, not the one but the many'.[28] Thus the 'deep shale' of others' work is not a cause for anxiety but rather a rich seam of creative ore which we may, if our writers' tools are fit for purpose, smelt into treasure of our own. If we keep our minds

---

[26] Alain Robbe-Grillet, *For a New Novel*, trans. Richard Howard (1989), p. 12.

[27] *Oulipo: A Primer of Potential Literature*, ed. and trans. Warren F. Motte Jnr. (1986).

[28] Gilles Deleuze, *Difference and Repetition*, trans. Paul Patton (1968); (1994), p. 126. For further discussion of Deleuze's reworking of Nietzsche's concept of the 'eternal return', the repetition of that which differs from itself, see Jon Roffe, 'Gilles Deleuze', (2002) *Internet Encyclopedia of Philosophy*. Online.

open, and use our creative antennae like divining rods, then under that deep shale, we may find our own wellspring of originality.

Writing Exercise – Textual fossils

This writing exercise sets up a 'narrative generator', whereby students undertake a lottery-style selection of different narrative elements, randomly combined to produce some very challenging situations. For example, a typical result would be: *Charles Darwin meets Genghis Khan at the Super Bowl in the year 3000AD. Genghis Khan is holding a letter from Elvis.* As well as providing resistance-breaking amusement, this exercise demonstrates how recombinations of existing material can produce startlingly original results and invites imaginative resourcefulness while testing students' grasp of narrative craft. Likely strategies include time machines, dream sequences, hallucinations, fantasies, parallel universes, science fiction technologies, films, computer games, reality T.V. shows and found texts.

Preparation

You will need lots of small pieces of paper – 'post-it' notes could work well, particularly if you ask students to use the 'sticky' strip to hold their paper closed once they have written on it and folded it in half to conceal the contents.

Props

You will need two receptacles to contain the pieces of paper, to act as a 'lucky dip' from which the students select their narrative elements. Hats work well (a theatrical 'top hat' would be great), but bags and boxes will also do the job.

Instructions for Students

1. Take a piece of paper. Write on it a date, era or historical period (e.g. midnight on 12 March 1852, the Dark Ages, Jacobean, Neolithic etc.). Fold your paper over and put it in the first hat.

2. Take another piece of paper. Write on it a geographical location, the more precise the better (e.g. 3rd floor, Crescent House; a vineyard in the Champagne region of France; the hold of a North Sea fishing vessel). Fold over your paper and put it in the second hat.

3. Pick a piece of paper at random from each hat. You should now have two pieces of paper that name a date or era and

a geographical place. (Instructor note: it's fun at this point to ask each student what combination of circumstances they have. This also allows you and other class members to offer suggestions as to how the elements could be formed into a narrative.)

4. Begin to write a story set in this time and place. If you don't want to tear a page from your notebook, do this on a separate piece of paper because you are now going to...

5. Swap stories with someone else. It doesn't matter if the stories aren't finished. In fact finishing mid-sentence or even mid-word could be interesting. Everyone should now have a text that they didn't write themselves. Put that to one side.

6. Repeat steps 1 to 3. Try to make your places and dates as different as possible from what you wrote the first time. You should now have a second time and place. The text you have just acquired in step 5 has been found (as an artefact, manuscript, book, letter, computer file, whatever) in this second time and place. (Instructor note: again, invite students to share results and offer suggestions as to what the relationship between these two narratives might be.)

7. Now write the story of how it got there – be as inventive as you can; the laws of physics need not apply! If the first text is unfinished, now you could speculate as to why. Perhaps your second text could discover the circumstances of the person (or thing!) who wrote the first text.

8. Finish this exercise – you might start this in class and continue at home. Bring it to the next class, ready to share.

Works Cited

Betts, Doris, 'Undergraduate Creative Writing Courses', in *Association of Departments of English Bulletin*, 79 (Winter 1984), available at: http://www.ade.org/bulletin/frames_browse.htm [accessed 27 April 2011]

Bloom, Harold, *The Anxiety of Influence: A Theory of Poetry* (New York: Oxford University Press, 1973)

Booker, Christopher, *The Seven Basic Plots: Why We Tell Stories* (London: Continuum, 2004)

Briggs, Julia, *This Stage-Play World: Texts and Contexts, 1580-1625* (Oxford: Oxford University Press, 1997)

Brooke-Rose, Christine, *Four Novels: Out, Such, Between, Thru, The Christine Brooke-Rose Omnibus* (Manchester: Carcanet, 2006)

Brown, J., *et al.*, 'The Short Story in the UK: an overview of the current state and exploration of opportunities for new initiatives' (2004), http://www.theshortstory.org.uk/aboutus/The_Short_Story_in_the_UK_Report.pdf [accessed 27 April 2011]

Calvino, Italo, *If On a Winters Night a Traveller* (London: Vintage Classics, 2007)

Carter, Angela, *The Bloody Chamber* (London: Vintage, 2006)

Danielewski, Mark Z., *House of Leaves* (London: Doubleday, 2000)

Deleuze, Gilles, *Difference and Repetition*, trans. Paul Patton (1968); (New York: Colombia University Press, 1994)

Denham, Holly, *Holly's Inbox* (London: Headline Review, 2007)

Federman, Raymond, 'Four Propositions in Form of an Introduction, in *Surfiction: Fiction Now and Tomorrow*, ed. Raymond Federman (Chicago: Swallow Press, 1975), pp. 5-18

Friedman, Ellen G. and Miriam Fuchs, 'An Interview with Christine Brooke-Rose', *Review of Contemporary Fiction*, 9:3 (Fall 1989), available at: http://www.centerforbookculture.org/interviews/interview_brookerose.html [accessed 18 September, 2008]

Gaarder, Jostein, *Sophie's World* (London: Phoenix, 2006)

King, Stephen, *On Writing: A Memoir of the Craft* (London: New English Library, 2001)

Lively, Penelope, *Making It Up* (London: Viking, 2005)

Nelson, Robin, 'Practice as Research' (2010), available at: http://www.enhancementthemes.ac.uk/themes/SHEECInternat ionalBenchmarking/documents/PaRArtsMediaprofessional.ppt [accessed 27 April, 2011]

Nelson, Robin, 'Set Map Slip = Palimpsest (working title) – "working" because it is provisional and "working" because it is on the move', *Performance Research*, 6:2 (2001), pp. 100-8

Oulipo: *A Primer of Potential Literature*, ed. and trans. Warren F. Motte Jnr. (Lincoln: University of Nebraska Press, 1986)

Robbe-Grillet, Alain, *For a New Novel*, trans. Richard Howard (Evanston: Northwestern University Press, 1989)

Roffe, Jon, 'Gilles Deleuze' (2002) *Internet Encyclopedia of Philosophy*, available at: http://www.iep.utm.edu/deleuze/ [accessed 27 April 2011]

Shrek, dir. Andrew Adamson (Paramount Home Entertainment, 2001)

Thomas, D.M., *The White Hotel* (London: Phoenix, 1999)

Thompson, Craig, *Blankets* (Marietta: Top Shelf Productions, 2003)

University of Salford, 'Writing Fiction: Innovation and Experiment, Module Handbook, 2010

University of Salford, 'Workshop Constitution', 2010. Available in Appendix I

Warner, Marina, 'Plenary Speech, Cross-Gendered Voices Conference', University of Warwick, U.K., 31 May 2008

Wood, Michael, 'The Anxiety of Influence: A Theory of Poetry', New York Review of Books, (17 April 1975), available at: http://prelectur.stanford.edu/lecturers/bloom/reviews.html [accessed 27 April 2011]

APPENDIX I

Writing Fiction: Innovation and Experiment
Collective agreement on scope and parameters of the module

We acknowledge that the terms 'innovation' and 'experiment' present certain difficulties of definition. Definitions or interpretations of these terms may include:

- Challenges norms (but norms change, are fluid, dependent on context, perhaps best defined in contrast to other factors).
- Packaging, branding, presentation; may not look like a conventional 'book'.
- Presents the reader with choices, demands effort on their part. May assume a level of sophistication/cultural knowledge in the reader. Elitist?
- Takes risks, particularly the risk of alienating the reader – it acknowledges that not all readers will respond to the challenges, but it offers something in exchange (e.g. narrative drive compensates for visual interruption).
- Questions the reading process; may offer the reader some help and instruction, or may trust them to work it out for themselves.
- May employ restriction (e.g. following a pattern, not using a particular letter or verb).
- The content may be taboo or push boundaries.
- The label 'innovative' may deter readers, and therefore has commercial implications.
- Innovative or experimental texts take many different guises. They may be conventional in some ways, and experimental in just one respect. Alternatively, they may be experimental in many ways at once.

Manifestations of innovative or experimental activity include:

- Narrative structure (could be fractured, or temporally complex).
- Use of perspective to question morality (e.g. manipulating the reader into sympathising with a morally repugnant character).

- Mechanisms that promote a physical awareness of the reading process.

We acknowledge that the words 'innovation and experiment' have specific implications within the structures of this module. It is hoped that the space provided by this module will be used as a place for experiment, unfettered by commercial implications.

We are wary of innovation for its own sake, which can result in cynical or pretentious work. Therefore we expect that each student on this module will engage with innovation as 'a by-product of a writerly challenge'. Such engagement could be demonstrated by:

- Attempting a technique or genre that is new to the individual writer, even if it would not be identified as 'innovative' by other people.
- Using different mechanisms of composition/working practice (e.g. writing in a particular location, using music as a stimulus, etc.).
- Experimenting with how text is presented (e.g. presenting work on CD-ROM).
- Experimenting with language (e.g. writing in dialect).
- Setting restrictive parameters within which to work (e.g. not using the letter 'e').

We acknowledge that the process of engagement with innovative or experimental practices should be just as important as the end result. We also acknowledge the implications that this statement has for the assessment of work. The following scenarios illustrate these implications:

- A student does not engage seriously with the personal challenge of innovation, but submits a superficially shocking/bizarre/inaccessible piece of work.
- A student grapples with innovation on their own personal terms, and produces a work that is not obviously 'innovative'.
- A student does not attempt to innovate at all, but stays within their comfort zone to produce a piece of competent fiction.
- A student attempts to innovate and produces a work that ultimately fails as a piece of fiction, although its intentions are clear.

We agree that the tutor should seek to reward a genuine engagement with innovation. The tutor may, however, have difficulty in distinguishing between the situations outlined above. Therefore, group members' engagement with innovation can be measured in the following ways:

- Contribution to workshop sessions.
- The sharing of intentions and the sharing of work in progress. Blackboard [our Virtual Learning Environment] would be a good mechanism for recording evidence of such activity.
- In the creative assessment, the three pieces of evidence documenting engagement with innovation (e.g. annotated extracts from drafts, a journal excerpt, notes/exercises done in class, a review of a reading, or an account of a field trip).
- The Writer's Reflection.

In addition, the group understands that the tutor will adopt a positive marking attitude, whereby marks will not be deducted for 'conventional' writing, but students will be rewarded for demonstrating their engagement with innovation. Innovative failure will be treated sympathetically. If a student makes use of the workshop sessions, individual discussions with the tutor, and peer feedback, a safety net is in place to support risk-taking.

This is a collective document, which may be reviewed at any time at the request of any group member.

Creative Writing Creating Community: The Power of the Personal[1]

Deirdre Fagan

My teenaged father[2] attended a poetry workshop with poet Léonie Adams at Columbia University in the middle of the last century. While workshopping a poem one day in class, a fellow student poet recoiled from the criticisms being made about her poem by saying that she could not alter the poem because the alteration would not be true to how the relationship she had written about had been. As my father told the story, which was most certainly altered by memory, Adams had just taken a long drag on a cigarette (smoking in class being common at that time) when my father uttered something to the effect of 'we're not trying to fix the relationship; we're trying to fix the poem' – to which Adams choked out the smoke she had inhaled.

Creative writing workshops must begin with clarity about what criticism is and is about, because student writers, like many writers, are often inevitably married to what they have written and will have to become somewhat unwed if the criticism is going to be noteworthy and impersonal. Unlike other forms of creative writing, when it comes to memoir writing, the personal becomes even more personal, and the criticisms, therefore, must be even less personal.

Just as memoirs have begun to crowd the shelves of neighborhood bookstores, they have appeared more and more in college bookstores. This recent popularity of memoir has led to an increase in memoir reading and writing in the college classroom. One cannot help but note that this interest in memoir has corresponded with the further development of an I-centered, Reality TV culture in which exploring oneself publicly, either on reality and talk shows or through Facebook or Twitter, is a common occurrence. As educators, it would appear that our role would be to work against this popular culture eruption that is frequently deemed solipsistic and self-indulgent, since there are daily reminders that when not kept in check, such self-aggrandizing can lead to destructive individual and collective results. It has become apparent, however, that when carefully

[1] I would like to express my gratitude to the students in my Fall 2008 Creative Writing: Memoir class at Quincy University for their support with this project, and especially to the following students: Shalea Brown, Jake Egelhoff, Amber Epping, Stacy Hankins, Kathryn Seckman, and Kendra Yakle.
[2] Poet Frank Fagan.

and thoughtfully constructed, personal inquiry can lead students not only to profound analysis, but to remarkable written results. Memoir writing can become, then, an analytically productive, as well as creative, endeavor.

In his article on memoir as pedagogy, Steve Simmons, who included memoir in his agriculture and university-wide freshmen courses, argues 'memoir writing is an overlooked but exceptional pedagogy for fostering reflection and student-centered, transformative learning'.[3] The overlooking or dismissal of memoir is often due to prejudices against storytelling, and the impression that creative writing is wholly distinct from academic. But, like Simmons, Carol Schick and Wanda Hurren, in their article on reading autobiographies and memoirs in the social studies classroom, found that 'reading about the lives and times of others in the form of fictionalized history, auto/biography and memoir is an exemplary pedagogical practice', so the practice is not uncommon in a variety of disciplines.[4] Memoir has been a productive resource in teacher education, for example, as Sharon Hollander found that memoirs 'can be used to bridge the gap between general and special education' and to 'promote quality reading and writing, inspire original and insightful responses from students, and foster a sense of community in class'.[5] Memoir can be used to foster intellectual transformations and bridge gaps between the creative and the academic, but ironically, in contrast to these positive claims about the use of memoir from various disciplines, and the overall surge in memoir as a vehicle for education, the personal narrative remains under attack as one advances in school.

Sarah Michaels points out in her article, 'The Dismantling of Narrative', that 'the process of dismantling narrative development is a central part of what it means to become literate in school, to acquire the forms of discourse – description, explanation, justification – that get accorded a privileged status in school and other institutions'.[6] In keeping with this claim, in college English classrooms, as well as in the classrooms of other disciplines, argumentation is widely privileged over narrative. Students are frequently taught to remove the first person from

---

[3] Steve R. Simmons, 'Knowing Our Place and Time: Memoir as Pedagogy', *Journal of Natural Resources & Life Sciences Education* 37 (2008), pp. 1-7.
[4] Carol Schick and Wanda Hurren, 'Reading Autobiographies, Memoirs, and Fictional Accounts in the Classroom: Is it Social Studies?', *Canadian Social Studies* 37.2 (2003). Online.
[5] Sharon R. Hollander, 'Taking It Personally: The Role of Memoirs in Teacher Education', *Electronic Journal for Inclusive Education* 1.4 (2010). Online.
[6] Sarah Michaels, 'The Dismantling of Narrative' in *Developing Narrative Structure*, ed. by Alyssa McCabe and Carole Peterson (1991), p. 303.

their sentences and to adopt a professional or academic discourse. I, too, discourage the unintentional use of 'I' (and also 'you') in my freshmen composition courses, and in arguments of any kind. Indeed, I am even a bit uncomfortable using the first person in this academic essay. But there is a time and a place for 'I' and there are times when its omission is more palpable than its insertion. Its insertion is also not only necessary in certain writing situations, but the interrogation and evaluation of 'I', figuratively and literally, can garner exceptional academic results.

Ardashir Vakil wisely points out:

> Students should be taught how to write essays or respond to texts, to think abstractly and analyse; but the drastic reductions in their opportunities to think and write creatively, that is to write from the unconscious and to get in touch with their own native voice is a sad narrowing of focus, both for the students and teachers.[7]

Vakil urges a restoration of the creative in education. It is clearly arguable that the distinction between creative and academic writing, while commonly perpetuated, need not be so distinct, and there are fruitful bridges to be built with the materials of analysis and creativity; memoir writing is one of them.

We are as a species natural storytellers, so oral narrative often comes easy to most. Indeed, the first written assignment in many basic writing courses is a narrative assignment because students are typically confident when telling their own stories, and the narration can later become a vehicle for developing, or eventually incorporating, more complex forms of discourse. Memoir writing at its best functions in a similar way: the personal narrative becomes a source of and for analysis as well as a product of creativity. Students should be taught not only how to find their academic voice, but also how to think abstractly and analyze their creative writing while identifying their creative voice. Vakil argues that 'Good writing deals with a different part of the brain from good criticism', but he also explains that becoming critics of other people's work allows students to become 'better readers of their own work'.[8] The great leap in creative writing is to make students become as good at criticizing their own work as they are at criticizing others'. While this is always a challenge, it is even more of one when the

---

[7] Ardashir Vakil, 'Teaching Creative Writing', *Changing English* 14.2 (June 2008), pp. 157-65, (p. 165).
[8] Ibid., p. 164.

student is writing directly about her own life, without the veil of fiction. Writing is always a personal vocation, but when the content of that writing is also personal, the creative writing teacher finds herself in an even more precarious position as a critic.

English teachers are often dissuaded from encouraging personal narratives, not only for the purposes of academic voice and a consideration of audience, but because they are reminded that they are not equipped to enter into the sorts of discussions that may arise when delving into the personal. Such discussions, we are often taught, should be left to the school psychologist. Lucia Perillo argues pointedly that 'working on the psychic turmoil must be handled elsewhere', in her *Chronicle of Higher Education* piece, 'When the Classroom Becomes a Confessional', because the English instructor's 'expertise pertains only to [our] students' writing, not their lives'.[9] She also points out, however, that, 'if students can learn to distance themselves enough to make genuine art even out of life's most horrific subjects, then they are cultivating an artistic rigor that they can bring to all of their work'.[10] What becomes most important, then, is not what subjects are tackled in the classroom, but how, and not whether students use first person or not, but when. As Karen Surman Paley concludes in her book, *I-Writing: The Politics and Practice of Teaching First Person Writing*, 'Personal narrative has a significant place in the composition classes of those instructors willing to learn how to teach it'.[11] The same can be said of the creative writing classroom.

Encouraging memoir writing may appear to quickly lend itself to an increasingly difficult to navigate territory for the teacher who opens that can of worms, but teaching memoir does not inevitably lead students to Freudian turns on the couch. When the emphasis is placed on the telling and not on the tale, as in other creative writing classrooms, teaching memoir does not present the teacher as therapist and the students as patients, but the writing classroom as an instrument for the development of sophisticated thinking and writing spurred on by an invested community. Writing, not the content of that writing, must become subject to the criticisms of the class, causing students to boldly take risks as writers and as thinkers, and to hold others equally accountable. While this approach may be necessary in all

---

[9] Lucia Perillo, 'When the Classroom Becomes a Confessional', *Chronicle of Higher Education* (28 November 1997), p. A56.
[10] Ibid., p. 2.
[11] Karen Surman Paley, *I-Writing: The Politics and Practice of Teaching First Person Writing* (2001), p. xii.

writing classrooms, and may become even more significant in the creative writing classroom, in the memoir classroom such distancing is even more paramount, since the 'I' of the piece is so fully centered.

Having taught writing and literature at the university level for nearly 15 years, and having taught three literature and writing courses on the topic of memoir, two of which were identified as creative writing courses, it has become apparent that the genre of memoir does offer distinctive pedagogical results, but the pedagogical methods used to arrive at those results are not so distinctive that they cannot be transferred to other creative, or even academic, writing courses.

In many ways students in any writing classroom consider their writing to be 'about' them and are invested in their products as reflections of themselves. But the student memoirist often has a greater investment in memoir than other forms of academic or creative writing precisely because it is more directly 'about' her, and she also has a stronger investment in accuracy or getting her stories 'right' or 'straight' since she has the capacity to directly implicate others, and because what is written will inevitably become the memory of others, and may even replace the writer's own memories. As I wrote in my article, 'Memory Lost, Memory Regained: The Memoirist's Power in Shaping Truth':

> Due to this great responsibility not perceptible in, say, fiction and poetry, memoir writing seems to make more visible certain aspects of the creative process than other forms of creative writing, even those aspects which are evident in all creative writing classrooms where the integrity of one's words requires deep critical thinking and precise expression – the sort of precision that student writers often dismiss in academic writing. The vulnerability and responsibility of creative writing of any kind naturally develops a sense of ownership, which can facilitate community and a shared governance of the classroom, which is also more difficult to create when students are not as personally invested in the subject matter (as they often are not in relation to their academic work). But while such vulnerability exists in all creative writing classrooms, it is particularly potent in the memoir classroom.

By considering the methodology and outcomes of a 300-level course titled *Creative Writing: Memoir*, which I have taught twice at my home institution, and reviewing student comments generated in and by that course, as well as excerpts from student writing, the particular power the personal has in a creative writing classroom to facilitate critical thinking, generate community, and motivate exemplary writing becomes evident. The practices illuminate that the sort of critical thinking and community building that takes place in a creative writing memoir classroom can be created in other creative writing classrooms as well, when similar pedagogical methods are employed.

The course philosophy and materials

There were nine students registered for the course *Creative Writing: Memoir* – an average number of students for 300-level courses at my institution. The goals of the course were inspired by three philosophies: 1) To write a memoir, one must have read memoirs; 2) In order to write a memoir well, the memoirist must employ the same techniques as in other creative writing; 3) Writers greatly benefit from being critically challenged by a community of readers. We therefore began by reading, analyzing, and critiquing excerpts from published memoirs. The excerpts were selected on the basis of quality and variety, both in voice and subject. Excerpts included but were not limited to those from: Jim Carroll's *The Basketball Diaries*; Frank McCourt's *Angela's Ashes*; James McBride's *The Color of Water*; Mary Karr's *The Liar's Club*; Ruth Reichl's *Tender at the Bone*; Caroline Knapp's *Drinking: A Love Story*; Doris Kearns Goodwin's *Wait Till Next Year*; Azar Nafisi's *Reading Lolita in Tehran*. I chose not to have the students read a memoir in its entirety, since they would be writing roughly 20-25 page memoirs and too much time would be given over to discussing the reading. In the beginning, we spent one period discussing the excerpts and the next doing various creative writing exercises that played with content as well as language. On writing days we wrote our responses to various subjects as broad as fear and compassion; we exposed our faults, both physical and emotional; and we toyed with word choice, structure, voice, and dialogue, among other narrative elements. The students also wrote for homework concise two-page analytical and critical arguments grappling with some aspect or passage of the selected excerpts. As their knowledge of the genre, understanding of the memoir writing process, and critical reading abilities developed, we then began imagining and drafting memoirs.

Fostering trust, community, and student engagement

In order for this class to be successful, a unique community had to be created. This need for community is not as necessary in a literature or even a composition course in which the instructor is the primary source of instruction. But in a creative writing classroom, it is expected that the students will teach each other almost as much as the teacher teaches them. And in a creative writing memoir classroom, community is absolutely necessary because the deeply personal nature of the writing creates atypical vulnerability and a desire for reciprocity.

It may not be difficult to get people to think and write about themselves, but a sense of community and student engagement do not necessarily follow easily from this assumption. Engagement depends on an equal investment in the process, and that investment is built upon the community that is created. Creating community in any line of work is a challenge, since the primary ingredient in any relationship is trust, and creating trust between two people is trying, let alone among many. Doing so in a classroom is particularly challenging given that students typically do not enter a classroom intending to create such relationships, the way they might enter some other sort of situation, and thereby tend to be unprepared for, or even blindsided by, the expectation that such a relationship be formed. In my classroom, even though students had registered for the course, some inevitably entered the classroom with little understanding of memoir. We, therefore, began by discussing the distinction between autobiography and memoir:

1. An autobiography generally seeks to cover an entire life;

2. Memoir tends to focus on a specific time in one's life and also to focus so closely on that period or event that it eschews any information that is not directly related to it (unlike the autobiography that seeks to include all);

3. Unlike autobiographies, memoir tends to be written by ordinary people who have had something extraordinary happen to them, or who can write about the ordinary in an extraordinary way.

As we began discussing the excerpts, we also considered what was accurate in memoir writing and what was fictionalized, what was writer-focused, and what was reader-focused writing. Knowing that creating trust and community was imperative, on the first day students were reminded (as they are in all of my classes) that the course was going to require work, and that they would get out of it what they put into it, but also that I was not solely responsible for the success of the course. Additionally, and more specifically, it was also made clear that the matter involved taking risks and becoming comfortable with discomfort. These warnings were essential because it is common for students to imagine writing about themselves as 'easy'. After all, it is assumed that writing about what one has experienced has to be easier than making stuff up, and one would think, also more difficult to criticize since the instructor clearly does not have more knowledge than the students regarding the subject matter. But with an emphasis on the writing, the students quickly learned this was not the case.

On the first day, I made a point of retelling my father's story (which has served me well in a variety of courses and situations), which he originally began telling me when I was a young writer similarly wed. I also immediately worked toward empowering the students by noting that the course assumed those taking it were interesting and had something to say, even if they did not know what it was yet. I also shared that I had taken a similar course when I was around their age and that at some point in the term, I would share that writing with them – this always engages their curiosity. The second time I taught the course, I was also able to share some of the provocative topics tackled by students the first time. One of those was about a cutter who was intent on explaining why she had harmed herself, and why it was such an addictive behavior. These opening comments about criticism, process, expectations, sharing, and subject matter helped to set the tone of the class.

As the class progressed, several other 'rules' were created in order to allow for trust and community to form. The first was that in order to create trust, students had to be regularly present. While one student may 'disappear' from a typical lecture and discussion course, in the memoir class, students whose attendance is lacking pose a serious threat not only to themselves but to the whole class. In order for community to be created, students need to be equally vulnerable, and this cannot happen when someone is parachuting in and out of discussion, and more important, exposure. This rule was regularly enforced. One student commented that I had kept 'the bond intact when a student or two threatened it by not attending as often as the rest'. The second rule is that the professor cannot be the doctor who administers the medicine but does not take any herself. While the students remained conscious that I was the teacher, in many ways, I became a student. I regularly did the creative writing exercises during class time, and shared the products of those exercises with the class, along with the students. Writing in the moment, sometimes my results were better and sometimes the students' were. This demonstrated that I, too, meet with successes and failures as a writer. And most important, at the appropriate time, which seemed to be roughly halfway through the course (when a bond had been partially formed but before they had to fully expose themselves), I became the most vulnerable of the group by sharing that early memoir. These actions and disclosures placed me, if not on an equal level, at least closer to it. Several students reported that my reading my own memoir was a defining moment. As one said, 'by sharing your own memoir written around a similar age that we were, you included yourself within the circle, and did not stay outside of it as an instructor'. I was, of course, only one member of this community, and therefore did not solely foster it. Actually, as time went on, it was quite the opposite. While I officially led each class, the class eventually began to lead itself, and to challenge each other's writing in various ways. One student reported that he 'was hesitant to share certain stories with a group of strangers initially, but as the semester progressed, [he] bec[a]me more comfortable with others who were diving into themselves in a similar manner. We all shared private things, which inevitably resulted in a trust that we would keep our stories inside the classroom.' The 'all' here is not unintentional. Another recalled, 'It was pretty amazing, shocking really that nobody felt the need to say: Let's take an oath right now that nothing goes outside of this room, or circle of people. We never had to do that.' Again, the 'nobody' includes the instructor. 'There was a sense of respect and responsibility of information in class', another concluded. That respect was created through my leadership; because I respected them and protected the integrity of the class, they respected each other as well as me.

Once the community was established, students became more and more engaged in the course; the work began to occupy students' thoughts outside the classroom and at all hours – a shared hope among teachers that is rarely realized. One student reported, 'I would reflect on my life while driving, listening to music, or right before falling asleep, picking the most pivotal moments in my life to discuss in my story.' Students reported that they had many discussions outside of class, in person, over the phone, and in Facebook chat sessions. Without prompting (although it was an approach discussed in class), students began interviewing family members and friends, seeking validation for their memories. Students also became concerned not only with what stories to tell, but more aware of how to tell them. A student said that being a part of a community of writers helped her to 'delve into memories [...] and become deeply involved in what [she] was writing.' She also said that it 'helped [her] maintain [her] honesty, sometimes brutal, because [she] knew it was expected of [her] since [she] expected it of others.' This brutal honesty is what came to bear importantly on the writing that was produced.

The writing

The critical expectations of the course were born through the criticisms of the published authors read. Since we had begun by reading the writing of established memoirists, the students were at a safe distance when criticizing the style and content of the material. The published pieces also allowed us to begin with a discussion about memory's strengths and weaknesses and about creative writing, fiction, and non-fiction. The students discovered that while memory is important in memoir writing, it is not nearly as important as good storytelling. No matter how truthful the prose, if it is not engaging, it will be not be powerful, meaningful, or memorable to others. If a person wants to tell her story, she must tell it well, otherwise no one will care to hear it. So while we may not be able to 'fix' the relationships of our past, we can certainly 'fix' our writing enough to make those relationships meaningfully understood and significant to others.

A discussion about truth inevitably led to the fluidity of memoir, its unreliability, and to the power of writing. Writing about our lives fixes our memories in our minds. In other words, once a writer drafts or graphs his memories in a particular way, it becomes difficult to undo, and those memories become fixed in the writing, which makes the past less fluid. One of the student's remarks about truth and memoir writing was inevitably born of a discussion about dialogue. Most memoirs include some form of dialogue, however minimal, and some include quite a bit of dialogue. When it comes to memory, students are most skeptical about whether writers can remember any conversations in their pasts word for word. This disbelief lends itself quickly to a discussion of good writing and honesty. One student who used dialogue reported:

> I found that I couldn't recall every conversation with absolute certainty, so I chose to incorporate it as accurately as my memory would allow while making it as effective as possible. I was more concerned with

telling my story in a powerful fashion than with being 100% accurate with every minute detail.

Writing a memoir requires more than writing about oneself, it requires one to employ the same literary techniques as a novelist or short story writer and to be as aware of one's reader. Emphasizing thematic as well as structural elements, voice and the engagement of readers over the content, focused writers on telling the story well. A student wrote, 'Dr Fagan shared her stories and commented on our paper's content, not on the validity of the story. She made it clear from the beginning that her criticisms were not a reflection of our lives and identity, but an effort to help us convey our stories in a more effective manner.' Another student commented that I 'pushed [them] to [their] limits, but only as writers' and that I 'forced [them] to fill in the holes and if [they] couldn't to abandon it all together.' Since I was not there to judge content, the other students were not either; instead the students themselves began to judge the content and validity of their own stories *only*, and to rely on others to remind them they were not writing for themselves. One student said, 'I had other peer writers to count on.' Another wrote that, she 'wanted [her memoir] to be broad and touch many people for many reasons.' Students chose their topics freely, and left the value of their writing and their chosen stylistic and structural elements up to the class to determine.

One student grew fond of the metaphors and similes in the published excerpts we read and felt that employing them would make her memoir 'more tangible for others.' Another reflected on how literature had influenced her life and chose to 'incorporate bits and pieces of stories' she'd read. One attempted to include journal entries and song lyrics in her story but learned they did not work well, and instead chose a 'subtle thread.' That student's thread, as she wrote about her first sexual experience, powerfully likened her to a blow up doll, and became less subtle near the end, as demonstrated in these two excerpted paragraphs. Note that the antagonist is referred to throughout by a pronoun employed as a proper noun:

> Four years later, I still have times when I feel like that blowup doll. In every sexual experience that I have had since Him, I still liken myself to some blonde whore with her mouth wide open – the shape of an O pursed on my lips. In the midst of a man's touch, I defeat myself and lie back and become whomever he wants me to be. It doesn't matter whether I want the

attention; I will let a man do whatever he wants with me because I don't think that what I want matters anyway. I am truly broken, and I have no idea how to fix it. I am not sure if it was Him who broke me, or if this all comes from something from long ago – deep inside. But, I can't seem to stand up for what I want. I just want to give everyone else whatever they want, because I hate to disappoint.

No, I certainly do not think about Him every day anymore, but in a way, I still carry Him with me. I am reminded of Him each time another man reaches over and pulls me closer to him, whispering lies into my ear. He will kiss my lips, but I will never kiss back. His mouth seems to be drawn down my neck, and his hands slip down to touch me and too often up to grab at my breasts – and I say nothing. It is all familiar, it is all the same. But one thing is different: my friends have never left me behind again. They drag me from these situations or prevent me from getting into them at all. I am the inflatable blow up doll; I can easily be carried from place to place, but when it comes time for me to use my legs – get up and walk away, I know that I am merely plastic.

This student's first sexual experience was, in her mind, akin to date rape. But when she first started sharing her writing about it with the class, it was unclear to the rest of us exactly what had happened. With a subject as powerful as date rape, where society often finds the lines drawn quite blurry even when they are not, often to the victimization of one party or the other, the class knew it was treading on tenuous ground when discussing the writing. But as the story was unfolding, it was unclear whether the male perpetrator had been at fault in quite the way the writer believed, because the details emerging from the text did not appear to support her own perspective. Through our criticisms of the text, a painful reality for the writer surfaced: her passivity in the situation had actually contributed to the outcome, even if it should not have. This painful realization led to further realizations about her personality and behavior. The day she arrived at the analogy of a blow up doll, the class and I were astounded. The amount of self-reflection, self-discovery, and self-deprecation involved in the conclusion, as well as the written power of such a comparison, demonstrated a great journey, personally and in writing, had taken place. The student was also aware that her journey was incomplete. She reveals her uncertainty: 'I am not sure if it was Him who broke me, or if this all comes from something from long ago – deep inside.' She demonstrated an understanding that neither the event nor her life could be treated as tidy and complete. This honest recognition is often part of what is appreciated in a successful memoirist.

This excerpt, written by another student, demonstrates attention to detail and mature insight seldom associated with college writing:

> There's no such thing as marital bliss. It's a myth created from Hollywood movies, romance novels, and church officials trying to con people into marrying in order to save them from committing the ultimate sin of sex before marriage, of having sex before God says it's okay to do so. To claw through the myth is to reveal the reality that married couples face once they cross the threshold, and enter the transitional period of sharing a household. Marriage is messy. Married couples do not live under the pretense of bliss. And if they go into it expecting it to be that way, the illusion is quickly broken when they find themselves awkwardly adjusting to a life together rather than the life of frequent intervals of separation and integration that they experienced when dating. They find the idiosyncrasies that they never knew the other possessed: leaving wet towels upon the floor, not cleaning the sink after shaving, leaving dirty dishes to sit in the sink until somebody takes the time to wash them. But it's not just that. Reality lies in the disgusting portion of humanity that is so conveniently left out of fiction: bowel movements, vomiting, scratching, nose-picking, q-tip swabs, tampon wrappers, toe nail clippings found in the waste basket, and toothpaste build-up that's been forgotten in the sink during the rush of the day. These do more to stimulate disgust than any form of romantic intimacy found in books. But you learn to maneuver around these things, to not let them interfere with your marriage, like I learned to do.

This student was in her early twenties, yet the insights evident and details selected demonstrate not only maturity, but a sense of humor about the ordeal of marriage that one would expect from a much older person. The development of her sense of humor about her experience and her ability to convey it were a supreme accomplishment. When her writing began, she was depicting her ex-husband as someone entirely unlikable, loathsome even, as a divorcee is likely to do, but when confronted with such writing about a marriage and a divorce, a primary question of the class quickly turned to the writer: then why did you marry him in the first place? If readers were going to find the text believable and be invested in it, they had to understand the narrator. In the end, this student had to not only recognize the painful fact that she had once loved her ex-husband, but to acknowledge and convey those emotions and her ex husband's positive qualities to her audience. She then had to attempt to figure out exactly when the 'marital bliss' became a marital reality, and then a marital dissolution. The analysis of her own life was difficult but fruitful, because she was eventually actually able to not only see, but to convey the humor inherent in the banalities of a shared daily life to her readers.

The process of writing was challenging for many, but it was not only the process of writing, but of memory:

> Remembering is not something I enjoy. Remembering only makes me furious all over again. The disgust and bitter hatred I have poisons my veins still. You might wonder how one can be so dense, but I believe that we all become blind to venomous engagements, continuously rationalizing our actions to ourselves and others. It usually takes a life-altering, shattering event to smack us awake. For those of you who have the ability to see clearly through your emotions, I admire you. For those of you who actually listen to the valid advice of others, I commend you. You have once found yourself in the situation of abuse, neglect, despair, but rejected it before it consumed you. For the rest of you like me, you have my empathy.

Great storytelling involves honesty, even when the piece is fictional. It involves even more honesty when it's a memoir, but whether fiction or non-fiction, part of what connects readers to the authors they love is recognizing their own flaws and foibles in someone else. While the above excerpt may not demonstrate the same sort of resolution as the first two, it does reveal the reality of the places we are willing to go and the weaknesses that take us there, and those sorts of admissions have the ability to profoundly connect authors to their readers. The best memoirs are no more tidy than the best fiction. Creative writing not only allows authors and their readers to imagine themselves as better people, but it also allows them to embrace their flaws, if not to understand them, then at least wholly to recognize them.

Conclusion

The community created in this creative writing memoir course had a profound effect on student writing. It freed the students to create stories that were important to them, but it also brought them closer to an understanding of the power of writing and the importance of artistry in the development of literature. The genre of memoir was certainly a significant aspect of the course, but so was the approach, which could be adopted in other creative writing classrooms. When the instructor participates as an equal, while at the same time demonstrating what sorts of criticisms are not only acceptable but expected, the class rises to the occasion. Students want to be led, but they also want to lead. If a teacher can lead, but also allow herself to be led, the bond created and the results evidenced will be worth the sacrifice of classroom ownership. This class became a model example of what I hope to achieve in every class, and I not only saw it, others did as well.

The profound impact of the experience was still evident when the class agreed to give a presentation to our university community a semester later. Upon arriving in the presentation room, the students quickly seized control by rearranging the chairs that sat in a row at the front of the room into a semi-circle. After introducing the class, which now sat partly facing each other and a tiered audience of roughly twenty-five, I stepped aside in order to adopt the role of interjecting occasional questions to facilitate discussion (which had also become my position in the class by the end of the previous semester). I asked questions such as: 1) What did you struggle with the most while writing?; 2) How did being a part of a community of writers impact your writing?; 3) How do you think the unspoken oath or circle of trust was created? The students demonstrated for the audience what I had witnessed in the classroom: that creative writing when taught effectively has the power to create the sort of learning environment and the sort of learning that as educators we dream of for every class, but only rarely realize. The remarks of audience members following the presentation revealed their amazement about the bond they had witnessed. The students' bond was not only evident, so was their knowledge of the subject matter, and of themselves; administrators, fellow faculty, parents, and other students responded in an equally positive manner about the students' engagement, learning, and, perhaps most of all, collegiality. One student shared that not only did her writing develop, but that she matured. She added that it 'was the best course [she had] ever taken' and that it was an 'experience that will never be forgotten.' That enthusiasm was conveyed by each participant throughout the presentation. It also was evident the students had not only learned about writing and themselves, but about memory and memoirs generally: 'I don't think people realize, myself included, how fallible memory is until they sit down to try to write a memoir', one student said. 'I think there is always a margin of error in memoirs', said another. And, most profoundly, 'I really think that by writing [my memories] down, I allowed myself to forget them.'

Despite the evident unresolved nature of the writing sampled here, a number of students did describe the experience as 'healing', but the emphasis in the course was not on such, and if healing did occur, that healing was not guided by the classroom or me. Like many English professors, I am not interested in group therapy or group think, I am interested in critical thinking, reasoning, sound analysis, and the powerful execution of all three in writing. If memoir is a source to that end, then the couch can stay, but I will not encourage anyone to lie down on it, any more than I would in any writing classroom. And if the students did not 'make genuine art...out of life's most horrific subjects' then they at least 'cultivat[ed] an artistic rigor that they [could] bring to all of their work'.[12] The pressure I place on student writers to get it right, to 'fix' the poem, essay, or memoir will not be eased, even when the blow by me is shared by spreading it across a community of writers. Perhaps the question is one of physics. When force is exerted in one direction not by one source but by many, the result is even more powerful.

The most telling account of the classroom experience came from a student who explained, 'Very rarely are you given an opportunity to experience a class that touches everyone taking part. It was an experience I never thought I would have encountered in my education...it was truly a magical journey for us all'. I might add that for the teacher, the magic lies in the opportunity to not only witness an individual's journey in writing, but to be a part of the community which engendered it.

---

[12] Perillo.

Writing Exercise: Memory, Perspective and Voice

As mentioned in the article, it was important to me that I reveal myself as a writer who also struggles with various narrative elements in the writing of fiction and non-fiction. One of the early exercises I asked the students to complete stemmed from one of my own struggles about voice. One of the primary decisions any writer has to make is about what sort of voice she wants to adopt. In relation to memoir, it is clear that the voice will be her own, but from what perspective? I have often wondered, when writing about childhood, whether the telling of my story would benefit from the often unreflective, naive, and direct voice of myself as a child, or from the reflective, mature, and often complex voice of my adult self. I wanted the students to consider not only which voice or voices would be best for their own narratives, but to become more aware of the difficulties of staying true to a particular voice. As such, I asked them to each write a paragraph sharing a childhood memory from the perspective they had of the experience initially, when a child, and then write that same paragraph from their current perspective of the experience. Students were to remain aware of the appropriateness of their chosen voice, as well as of content and style. Students not only discovered and grappled with the difficulty of regaining a former perspective and self, but learned about the significance of voice in effective storytelling.

Works Cited

Fagan, Deirdre, 'Memory Lost, Memory Regained: The Memoirist's Power in Shaping 'Truth', *Review Americana* (2 February 2007), not paginated

Hollander, Sharon R., 'Taking It Personally: The Role of Memoirs in Teacher Education', Electronic Journal for Inclusive Education (1 April 2010). Available at: http://www.cehs.wright.edu/~prenick/summer_edition4/fr3.htm

Michaels, Sarah, 'The Dismantling of Narrative', in *Developing Narrative Structure* eds., Alyssa McCabe and Carole Peterson (Hillsdale: Lawrence Erlbaum, 1991), pp. 303-51

Paley, Karen Surman, *I-Writing: The Politics and Practice of Teaching First Person Writing* (Illinois: Southern Illinois University, 2001)

Perillo, Lucia, 'When the Classroom Becomes a Confessional', *Chronicle of Higher Education* (28 November 1997), p. A56

Schick, Carol and Wanda Hurren, 'Reading Autobiographies, Memoirs, and Fictional Accounts in the Classroom: Is it Social Studies?' *Canadian Social Studies* 37.2 (2003). Available at: http://www2.education.ualberta.ca/css/css_37_2/ARreading_autobiographies.htm

Simmons, Steve R., 'Knowing Our Place and Time: Memoir as Pedagogy', *Journal of Natural Resources & Life Sciences Education* 37 (2008), pp. 1-7

Vakil, Ardahir, 'Teaching Creative Writing', *Changing English* 14.2 (June 2008), pp. 157-66

Other Arrangements: The Vital Turn in Poetry Writing Pedagogy

Michael Theune

In 'It Doesn't Work For Me: A Critique of the Workshop Approach to Teaching Poetry Writing and a Suggestion for Revision,' the first chapter of *Teaching Poetry Writing: A Five-Canon Approach*, Tom Hunley offers a vigorous and sustained critique of the workshop method. According to Hunley, while the workshop mode – in which one participant shares a full draft of a poem with other participants in order to garner their critiques of and insights into the poem – may work for 'already polished writers' it generally fails as a pedagogical approach for different kinds of student populations.[1] Hunley states:

> There is no sound theoretical basis for using the traditional workshop model at the undergraduate level, or in most of today's graduate workshops, for that matter. The workshop model was not designed with undergraduates or the ruck of graduate students in mind. It was designed for gifted, elite who needed very little instruction, though they may have benefited from criticism on their manuscripts.[2]

Hunley argues that there are a variety of reasons why the workshop approach is ineffective for so many of those who now participate in – or are subjected to – it. He notes that 'the traditional workshop model is perfectly suited to the [...] insidious practice of punishing necessary risk-taking, rewarding safety and conformity, and routinely putting writers on the defensive'.[3] Additionally, referencing Peter Elbow's critique of the workshop model, Hunley observes that the workshop focuses 'on critique of drafts at the expense of all other aspects of the writing process.'[4] Hunley clarifies:

> While the traditional workshop model affords student writers the opportunity to hear a multitude of suggestions about changes that they might make to their work, it makes no serious attempts to endow

---

[1] Tom C. Hunley, *Teaching Poetry Writing: A Five-Canon Approach* (2007), p. 4.
[2] Ibid., p. 3.
[3] Ibid., p. 8.
[4] Ibid., p. 9.

them with the revision strategies that could enable them to make those changes.[5]

And Hunley also charges that students who 'often lack the terminology needed to intelligently critique each other's writing, even after participating in several different workshops', often simply are not equipped to participate meaningfully in a workshop.[6] And yet, for a variety of reasons – including the tendency to follow the models provided by mentors, 'the lack of attention to teacher training and pedagogical theory within MFA programs', and the workshop's general convenience for instructors (at the cost of effective instruction) – the problematic workshop approach remains a central approach for teaching poetry writing.[7]

Clearly recognizing the need to supply an alternative to the workshop model, Hunley suggests what he calls 'the computer-assisted five-canon approach'.[8] In this approach, discussions of students' poems occur in online discussion threads and occasional conferences with the teacher, and this provides the opportunity to use class time to apply 'the five canons of classical rhetoric – invention, arrangement, style, memory, and delivery – to poetry writing.'[9] According to Hunley:

> This five-canon process was extrapolated by ancient Greek and Roman scholars from Aristotle's *Rhetoric* and used in handbooks devoted to teaching students to compose speeches. It is easily adaptable to poetry writing instruction and it is in fact a perfect model for teachers of undergraduate poets.[10]

In the second chapter of *Teaching Poetry Writing*, 'Rhetorical Theory as a Basis for Poetry Writing Pedagogy', Hunley further makes the case for using rhetorical theory to teach poetry writing, arguing that 'using the five canons of rhetoric in poetry writing classrooms [...] can make instruction more systematic, less haphazard', and that, additionally, 'rhetoric-based poetry writing instruction [...] provides students with a greater arsenal of figures and tropes (which are bread and butter to poets) [...] aids the construction of a speaking persona, and [...] helps student poets gain awareness of their audience'.[11] In the rest of

---

[5] Ibid.
[6] Ibid.
[7] Ibid., pp .5-6.
[8] Ibid., p. 10.
[9] Ibid.
[10] Ibid., p. 11.
[11] Ibid., pp. 28-9.

his book, Hunley describes each of the five canons and makes clear how they relate to teaching poetry writing.

Whether or not it is the 'perfect' model, Hunley's five-canon approach certainly offers a well-developed and viable alternative to the workshop model.[12] In part inspired by my own felt dissatisfaction in using the workshop method to teach undergraduates and in part encouraged by Hunley's arguments, I have taken steps to revise my approach to teaching poetry writing, and the result has been poetry writing classes that emphasize the first three canons – invention, arrangement, and style. (Memory and delivery are major components of a literature course I teach called 'Poetry through Performance'.) Overall, I am quite pleased with the changes brought about by this new focus. Having engaged in invention strategies, the work students share often is far more advanced than it would be otherwise. And having engaged in imitation, students become more attuned to the range of possibilities for their own poetic style. However, having students think in conscious ways about arrangement perhaps has provided what I believe is the greatest boon to my pedagogy – little has assisted my teaching or my students' writing as much.

My approach to arrangement differs, however, in some significant ways from Hunley's. According to Hunley, arrangement *can* mean the ordering and organization of a poem's content; he opens his chapter on arrangement – chapter four, 'Some Specifics about the General: Arrangement' – quoting the *Encyclopedia of Rhetoric and Composition*, stating, 'Rhetoric's second canon, arrangement (Greek *taxis*, Latin *disposition*) is "the art of dividing a discourse into its parts and the inclusion, omission, or ordering of those parts according to the rhetor's needs and situation and constraints of the chosen genre."'[13] However, by arrangement, Hunley mainly means *formal* arrangement. He states, 'form is indeed the term poets use that most closely corresponds with arrangement.'[14] And when Hunley discusses different poetic arrangements, he discusses poetic forms, such as the sestina.[15] Additionally, a large portion of the chapter devoted to arrangement consists of a discussion about the debates regarding the relative merits of formal and free verse.[16]

However, form – including the formal consideration of

---

[12] Those intrigued by the five-canon approach also should examine Hunley's *The Poetry Gymnasium* (2011), which offers practical writing exercises related to each of the five canons.

[13] Hunley, p. 57.

[14] Ibid., p. 58.

[15] Ibid., p. 15.

[16] Ibid., pp. 64-75.

aspects of free verse poems, including line-lengths and –breaks – is not the only significant way, or even the primary way, to arrange poems. As I have argued elsewhere, poems also are composed via specifically *structural* arrangement, and by structure, I specifically mean the pattern of a poem's turning.[17] In what follows, I will offer an overview of poetic structure and provide reasons for why it should be an important component in teaching poetry writing – that *at least* it should be a part of arrangement in the five-canon approach to teaching poetry writing. Additionally, I will offer some thoughts about how to incorporate lessons about specifically structural arrangement in the poetry writing classroom.

A poetic turn is a major shift in a poem's rhetorical and/or dramatic trajectory. Randall Jarrell states, 'A successful poem starts from one position and ends at a very different one, often a contradictory or opposite one; yet there has been no break in the unity of the poem.'[18] The movement from one position to another in a poem is marked and created by a turn, or turns. Though most famously a feature of the sonnet tradition, where a turn often is referred to as a *volta*, turns actually are a significant part of all kinds of significant poetry, formal and free. As the poet-critic Ellen Bryant Voigt notes: 'The sonnet's volta, or "turn" [...] has become an inherent expectation for most short lyric poems.'[19] And Voigt echoes the insight of an earlier poet-critic who made an even greater claim; T. S. Eliot calls the turn 'one of the most important means of poetic effect since Homer'.[20]

Much excellent criticism has been written on non-formal structure and the turn, including essays by poet-critics, including John Ciardi, Carl Dennis, Stephen Dobyns, Jorie Graham, Jane Hirshfield, Hank Lazer, Peter Sacks, and Ellen Bryant Voigt, and literary scholars, including M. H. Abrams.[21] Additionally, poets

---

[17] See Michael Theune, *Structure & Surprise: Engaging Poetic Turns* (2007), online, and 'Poetic Structure and Poetic Form: The Necessary Differentiation', *American Poet: The Journal of the Academy of American Poets* 32 (Spring 2007), pp. 9-12.

[18] Randall Jarrell, 'Levels and Opposites: Structure in Poetry', *Georgia Review* 50.4 (Winter 1996), pp. 697-713, (p. 699).

[19] Ellen Bryant Voigt, *The Art of Syntax: Rhythm of Thought, Rhythm of Song* (2009), p. 164.

[20] T.S. Eliot, 'Andrew Marvell', *Selected Essays, 1917-1932* (), p. 254.

[21] John Ciardi, 'The Poem in Countermotion', *How Does a Poem Mean?* (1959), pp. 994-1022; Carl Dennis, 'The Temporal Lyric,', in *Poet's Work, Poet's Play: Essays on the Practice and the Art* ed. Daniel Tobin and Pimone Triplett (2008) pp. 236-49; Stephen Dobyns, 'Writing the Reader's Life', in *Best Words, Best Order: Essays on Poetry* (1996), pp. 35-52; Jorie Graham, 'Introduction: Something of Moment', *Ploughshares* 27.4 (Winter 2001-2), pp. 7-9; Jane Hirshfield, 'Close Reading: Windows', *The Writer's Chronicle* 43.4 (Feb. 2011), pp. 22-30; Hank Lazer, 'Lyricism of the Swerve: The Poetry of Rae Armantrout', *Lyric & Spirit: Selected Essays, 1996-2008* (2008), pp. 95-126; Peter Sacks, *You Only Guide Me by Surprise: Poetry and the Dolphin's Turn* (2007); Ellen Bryant Voigt, 'The Flexible

often think about the turn *in* poems. Not only are turns enacted but they are pointed to, highlighted, commented upon in poems that self-reflexively mention the turn as a turn is being taken. For example, as Carl Sandburg's 'Chicago' turns from the initial concessions the poems make about Chicago to singing the praises of that city, Sandburg writes, '[s]o I turn once more to those who sneer at this my city, and I give them back the sneer and say to them [...]'.[22] This excellent thinking, however, so far has been largely scattered in various publications, essays and poems, and so has not had the effect it might have if seen *en masse* and understood as contributing to a larger, significant conversation.

However, it is possible to begin to delineate and define this conversation. Beyond revealing the significance of non-formal structure, the conversation suggests that a taxonomy of turns is possible. Just as poets, critics, editors, and teachers have managed to create a useful taxonomy of verse forms from out of what in fact are the infinite varieties of poetic form, it is possible to begin to create a robust and helpful taxonomy of kinds of turns. Poems turn in a variety of ways. They inscribe the transitions from one emotional state to another – for example, as in Shakespeare's 'When in disgrace with fortune and men's eyes' and Thomas Hardy's 'The Darkling Thrush' (in which the emotional transition does not quite take place), from dejection to elation. They inscribe the transition from one mental state to another – for example, as in Ella Higginson's 'Dawn' and Keats's 'Ode to a Nightingale', from dream to waking. They turn in the ways that arguments turn. Poems such as Jane Hirshfield's 'Those Who Cannot Act' and Zbigniew Herbert's 'I Would Like to Describe' employ the summary-and-response structure that, as Gerald Graff says, 'represents the deep structure of most written argument.'[23] Other poems, such as Shakespeare's 'My mistress's eyes are nothing like the sun' and Carl Sandburg's 'Chicago' employ concessions before turning to make their central point. Poems such as Sidney's 'Who will in fairest book of nature know,' Dorothy Parker's 'Comment,' and John Ashbery's 'The Cathedral Is' turn like jokes, from set-up to punch line. Such a taxonomy is important in that it will introduce students to important aspects and details of poetry and poetic tradition. But it is perhaps even more important as a sign of the general

Lyric' in *The Flexible Lyric* (1999), pp. 114-71; M.H. Abrams, 'Structure and Style in the Greater Romantic Lyric', in *Romanticism and Consciousness: Essays in Criticism*, ed. Harold Bloom (1970), pp. 201-29.
[22] Carl Sandburg, 'Chicago,' *The Complete Poems of Carl Sandburg* (1950), pp. 3-4. See also 'The Self-Reflexive Turn,' online.
[23] Gerald Graff, *Clueless in Academe: How Schooling Obscures the Life of the Mind* (2004), p. 156.

significance of the turn, as a statement, a demonstration, that structure is at least as significant as form.

And it is important that students be familiar with the poetic turn. The turn offers much, providing students with an accurate yet complex, accessible yet demanding vision of what poems are and do. Extending Hunley's idea that students often lack the terminology necessary to discuss poems, I might add that students do not always lack terminology but often employ *mistaken* terminology, which leads to mistaken conceptual-izations of poetry, misreading, and unhelpful feedback. For example, students often approach a poem expecting that, like other kinds of literature they have encountered, it will either tell a story, or else it will be, in Wordsworth's famous formulation, 'the spontaneous overflow of powerful feelings'.[24] But neither of these understandings is really accurate or helpful. Certainly, some poems tell stories, and some employ narrative elements, but not all do. And it is very rare to find a good poem that actually is simply the expressive flow of one inner feeling; much more often, poems capture and orchestrate the movement from one feeling to another. However, it is quite accurate to claim that virtually all poems turn – it is very rare to find a good, not to mention a *great*, poem (including both the narrative and the expressive) that does not include a significant, often surprising turn. In this way, introducing the turn necessarily complicates a student's picture of what poems are and do, but also makes that picture more accurate.

However, attaining this new level of understanding of poems is not difficult – if anything, considering turns in poems makes poems more accessible. Poems thus are no longer some strange, foreign linguistic objects separate from other language acts – as they can seem when form is emphasized (nobody speaks or thinks in, say, villanelles or sestinas) – but rather become more familiar, come to seem connected to the student's own language use. With minimal effort, a student can come to see how they incorporate turns in their thinking and speech all the time. Introducing students to turns is less introducing students to something radically new and more a matter of waking them up to features of their own experience, thought, and speech – all of the kinds of turning mentioned above are familiar patterns. Additionally, the retrospective-prospective structure, which turns from consideration of the past to thinking about the future, is not foreign to anyone who has, as in confession, given an account of past deeds to make resolutions about future behavior. And a poem that moves from offering a metaphor to supplying

---

[24] William Wordsworth, 'Preface to the Second Edition of *Lyrical Ballads* (1800)', *Selected Poems and Prefaces*, ed. Jack Stillinger (1965), p. 447.

the meaning of that metaphor is not unfamiliar to anyone who has ever told or heard a story with an explanation, or a moral, attached to it. While, initially, it may seem somewhat new to apply structures when encountering poetry, the structures, and their connections with poems, readily become apparent to students. The turn offers much to students with regard to their reading and understanding of poems.

And this is good, because students also will be challenged by turns in their writing. Once a student is acquainted with turns and sees the turn's prominence in poetry and poetics, the turn no longer is some kind of feature that one simply does or does not decide to put into a poem – it is a requirement. The turn stands as a kind of challenge to, making demands on, any kind of poem a student is working on. Unlike form, which does not necessarily make this kind of demand, the turn requires that the poem go somewhere, that it do something. Ezra Pound famously says that '[p]oetry must be as well written as prose'.[25] The turn helps to make the connection between poetry and prose, raising the stakes of what can be done with prose, and in the process raising the stakes of what can, and perhaps should, be done in a poem.

The kind of challenge the turn offers to students relatively new to poetry is the kind of challenge needed today: one that offers both a significant introduction to rhetoric and an encouragement for students to take risks, to aim to do something new and surprising in the poem. In an essay that first appeared in the mid-1980s, poet-critic Mary Kinzie already noted that '[t]he current generations of writers in America have less command over, because [of] less acquaintance with, the reasoning, the rhetoric, and the distinctions that were basic equipment for poets in the great ages of prose [...]'.[26] And Hunley clearly agrees with Kinzie that rhetoric should be a vital component for, and part of the basic equipment of, what we teach poets today. Hunley begins chapter two, 'Rhetorical Theory as a Basis for Poetry Writing Pedagogy,' with a quote from the *Princeton Encyclopedia of Poetry and Poetics* which states, '[T]hroughout most of the history of Western civilization, poetry was written and read by people for whom rhetoric was the major craft of composition.'[27] However, it's interesting to see where Kinzie goes with rhetoric, how she defines its aim; according to Kinzie, this lack of 'basic equipment,' which was embodied and revealed in 'the reduction of poetic possibility to the brief

---

[25] Ezra Pound, Letter to Harriet Monroe, January 1915, *The Selected Letters of Ezra Pound, 1907-1941*, ed. D. D. Paige (1950), p. 48.
[26] Mary Kinzie, 'The Rhapsodic Fallacy', in *The Cure of Poetry in an Age of Prose: Moral Essays on the Poet's Calling* (1993), p. 4.
[27] Quoted in Hunley, p. 22.

compass of the free-verse lyric, entails the loss (and I mean the literary *and* cultural loss) of the very keystone of logic, namely, the art of making the transition – the art of inference and connection, the art of modulation and (hence) surprise'.[28] For Kinzie, the proper end, the goal, of rhetoric – which, with its emphasis on transition, connection, and modulation, is clearly related to the turn – is the creation of surprise.

And because structural arrangement's turn focuses on making surprise, a powerful effect students often want to create themselves, students want to learn and practice it. Poetic structure and the turn ask for effort and risk: the effort is necessary to orchestrate the poem's risky leaps, turns, and surprises, but the risk makes the effort worth it. This is one of the chief effects of the turn in pedagogy: once students are introduced to turns and feel their power, their potential, they want to emulate them. It is just this transference of reading to writing that Kate Light captures in her sonnet *And Then There Is That Incredible Moment*:

> when you realize what you're reading,
> what's being revealed to you, how it is not
> what you expected, what you thought
> you were reading, where you thought you were
> heading.
> Then there is that incredible knowing
> that surges up in you, speeding
> your heart; and you swear you will keep on reading,
> keep on writing until you find another not going
> where you thought—and until *you* have taken
> someone on that ride, so that *they* take in
> their breath, so that *they* let out their
> sigh, so that they will swear
> they will not rest until they too
> have taken someone the way they were taken by
> you.[29]

Incorporating the turn into teaching poetry, writing need not be difficult. The turn at least can be incorporated in every way that form is in Hunley's five-canon approach. For example, for a class period devoted to arrangement, Hunley provides the following imagined outline: 'Students will learn how to appreciate and write sestinas. First, the instructor can read the class a sample of a sestina [....] The instructor could then provide

---

[28] Kinzie, p. 4.
[29] Kate Light, *The Laws of Falling Bodies* (1997), p. 52. The poem is dedicated to Agha Shahid Ali.

a little history of the form [....] The instructor could then explain the [sestina's] simple pattern [...]'.[30] Hunley even suggests that the writing could become 'a collaborative exercise.'[31] The exact same pattern of activities could be used to teach a poetic structure. For example, for a day devoted to arrangement, students could learn how to appreciate and write poems employing the dialectical argument structure. The instructor could read an example of a dialectical argument poem, provide a little history of the form in philosophy and poetry, and then explain its relative pattern of thesis / antithesis / synthesis. The instructor could even lead the class in a collaborative exercise.[32]

Hunley also notes that, '[g]iven the interrelatedness of the five canons and the importance of invention and style [...]', arrangement often interacts with the other canons.[33] And, indeed, structural arrangement certainly could assist with invention. Hunley writes:

> Skilled writers invent assignments for themselves. This staves off writer's block and helps writers push forward into new realms of the imagination [....] An art of poetic invention [...] should come from inductive study of poets' practice. I frequently invent writing exercises for my students based on what I see happening in finished, published poems.[34]

The turn, of course, is a big part of what happens in 'finished, published poems', and assignments that feature the turn can and should be developed.

'The Filibuster Poem' is an assignment I developed using a method like Hunley's. I first had an inkling of this assignment when I first read Courtney Queeney's 'Filibuster to Delay a Kiss':

> I invoked the dictionary's authority – *Incidental* to *Incompatible*,
> *Juvenile Hormone* to *Kangaroo*, *Keeper* to *Ketchup*,
> *Plain People* to *Planned Parenthood*, *Yokel* to *Yuck* –

---

[30] Hunley, p. 15.
[31] Ibid.
[32] For information on the dialectical argument structure, see John Beer, 'The Dialectical Argument Structure,' in *Structure & Surprise: Engaging Poetic Turns*, ed. Michael Theune (2007), pp. 99-121. For a collaborative exercise related to the dialectical argument structure, see 'Teaching Collaborative, Dialectical Argument Poems,' online.
[33] Hunley, p. 57.
[34] Hunley, *Teaching Poetry Writing*, pp. 44-5.

Then segued into ingredients from a cereal box side
panel,
The noble gases: helium, neon. When I forgot my
own chemistry,
I rattle off one page of the phone book, Smith to
Smith,
Then argued against drilling for oil in the Arctic,
Then shut my eyes to describe the windshield's
panopticon from memory,
Then opened them and fugued lyrically on ocean
reeds –
All so he'd lose interest and wander off – I recited
Woolf's last letter,
Floundered through Hamlet's *To be or not to be*,
mustered
Synonyms for *alone, insulated, aloof*, because at any
break
I knew there'd be the hand over my mouth.
There'd be his mouth.[35]

I was taken by the delay/reveal structure of this poem, how
the speaker of this sonnet goes to great lengths all in the hope
that a certain 'he' might 'lose interest, wander off', as a way to
avoid a kiss, and, one imagines, all the entanglements that love
so often entails. The glossary of the U.S. Senate's website defines
'filibuster' as an '[i]nformal term for any attempt to block or
delay Senate action on a bill or other matter by debating it at
length, by offering numerous procedural motions, or by any
other delaying or obstructive actions.[36] However, in 'Filibuster to
Delay a Kiss', and in other poems I've read that seem to
exemplify this structure, the filibuster is a personal delay
strategy, a tactic for putting off something one does not want to
admit or face up to, though, inevitably, the filibuster poem
finally does reveal what it was trying to avoid.

I noticed a similar structure in Austin Smith's 'Instructions for
How to Put an Old Horse Down', which offers a list of desperate,
heartbreaking avoidance strategies before arriving at its
devastating conclusion:

This is what you need to do:
wait for one of those mornings
that seems as if it will never come,

[35] Courtney Queeney, 'Filibuster to Delay a Kiss,' in *Filibuster to Delay a Kiss*
(2007), p. 38.
[36] Available at:
http://www.senate.gov/reference/glossary_term/filibuster.htm.

and when it comes, wait for evening.
While waiting for evening,
do as little as possible,
and don't visit the horse:
you'll only lose heart.

Remind yourself that she
is suffering and that
her time has come.
One thing you can do
is find a length of rope
hanging in the shape
of a racetrack in the barn:
you won't need it
but it's a good thing to find.

If you have kids, tell them
what's going to happen
sometime in the afternoon.
They'll understand.
If you wait and tell them
afterwards what you've done,
they'll never forgive you.

Finally, in that hour when
you usually visit her,
walk into the field with oats
in your pockets.
Let her eat them
out of your hand
until they're gone,
then lead her in.

Then lead her in.[37]

On the basis of Queeney's and Smith's poems, I developed the idea of a 'filibuster poem', which consists of a two-part structure: an extended transcript or a record of the delay, followed by the ultimate delivery of the material the poem's speaker had wanted to avert or elude. I introduced this structure to a group of students and got many interesting and powerful results. Here's one, Alicia Vallarta's 'Filibuster for Life':

---

[37] Austin Smith, 'Instructions for How To Put an Old Horse Down,' in *Instructions for How To Put an Old Horse Down* (2009), not paginated.

Sweet potato fries are always presented as
the healthy fry. They are the gardenburger of
the Rasta hat and hair costume.
I just got offered coke by a strung-out pilot but
fatherhood involves many sacrifices and
Peter Pan does not stand a chance.
He's far too high to try and explain
daylight savings time.

I remember we said the Lord's Prayer before
we went out last night but
it was all downhill after the free Blackjack taco.
They promote it like it's the second coming

and to most of Wisconsin it's scarier.
Currently in a meeting and I am playing
the not-throw-up game.
God I hope I don't lose

always feels a little racist.
I washed my feet in the bathroom between classes
and I have before 2 a.m. pics and after 2 a.m. pics...
which ones do you want to see first?

Four girls totally judged me.
Neighbors thought I was a lawn decoration but
I'm not homeless, I just graduated early.
I guess that's what happens when you find your
girlfriend at the zoo.

I'm naming my child 'Velociraptor' and you can
be part of its life if you want but that's its name
because I have the vagina and
every boy wants to be the hero.

It's either this or feel my feelings.

Alicia created this poem using invention methods derived
from Flarf approaches to poetry. She used material gathered
through various web browsing methods – bits from 'Texts from
Last Night' and friends' Facebook status updates – and she
collaged them into this poem. The poem is funny throughout,
and its humor largely derives from its wild, surprising turns
throughout, but the poem's power comes, as tends to be the case
with this kind of poem, at the end, where Alicia's last line takes a
turn and reveals what all of the silliness, all of the playing

around, is a delay tactic for: actually feeling one's feelings. In this instance, this exercise led to a strong, startling maneuver in a poem that, at its conclusion, becomes truly urgent and thrilling. In general, I believe the filibuster poem assignment can assist any poetry-writing instructor who wants to teach their students – who may wonder about poems *Why doesn't the poet just say what she means? Why take so much time to get to the point?* – not only about turns but also, more specifically, about the significance of delay and even expansive digression, and the relationship between suspense and surprise in powerful, moving poems.

Attention to turns, to poetic structure, clearly has much to offer as the teaching of poetry writing moves beyond the workshop. Certainly, learning the kinds of moves poems make is another way to be introduced to the terminology of poetry, and this will generally contribute much to the reading and understanding of poetry whenever students encounter it, and thus will offer new ways to respond to the work produced in poetry writing classes. In conferences or online, at some point, commentators should look for turns, and determine where they might be and how they might be made more effectively. Additionally, structure offers pedagogical methods and exercises that are at once new and revelatory, capable of capturing and conveying to new audiences a significant aspect of what poems are and do. A new focus on poetic structure also will raise important questions and encourage conversation: *How best to introduce turns to students? How to teach structure in conjunction with form? What other kinds of turns are there?*

But, whatever the exact approaches, questions, and answers that emerge, it is time for this conversation. Two decades ago, Dana Gioia wrote:

> I suspect that ten years from now the real debate among poets and concerned critics will not be about poetic form in the narrow technical sense of metrical versus nonmetrical verse. That is already a tired argument, and only the uninformed or biased can fail to recognize that genuine poetry can be created in both modes. How obvious it should be that no technique precludes poetic achievement, just as none automatically assures it (though admittedly some techniques may be more difficult to use at certain moments in history). Soon, I believe, the central debate will focus on form in the wider, more elusive sense of poetic structure. How does a poet best shape words, images, and ideas into meaning? How much

compression is needed to transform versified lines – be they metrical or free – into genuine poetry? The important arguments will not be about technique in isolation but about the fundamental aesthetic assumptions of writing and judging poetry.[38]

Hunley undoubtedly was correct to emphasize the importance of training in poetic form for students of poetry, and even in introducing the formal and free verse debate as part of his five-canon approach – students need to be aware of this issue. Yet it is also clearly time for a shift in poetry writing pedagogy, time to think in new ways about how poets might 'best shape words, images, and ideas into meaning,' time to make 'the wider, more elusive sense of poetic structure' more tangible so that those of us who teach poetry writing can better transmit to our students a more accurate account of what we are taken by in the poems that we love.   As we begin the turn away from the workshop approach, we must find ways to incorporate the turn into that process.

---

[38] Dana Gioia, 'Notes on the New Formalism', in *Can Poetry Matter?: Essays on Poetry and American Culture* (1992), pp. 29-41, (p. 41).

Writing Exercise

Write your own filibuster poem. Begin with invention: brainstorm ideas for your poem. Make a list of tasks that are psychologically difficult for you, or people you know: saying goodbye; leaving home or leaving your friends; giving somebody bad news; admitting you're wrong; asking for help; writing a poem. Select a topic that you think might be productive for you to write about. Then, brainstorm ways that you, or people you know, have avoided, or could imagine avoiding, undertaking this difficult job. Write each thing on a separate sheet of paper. Be playful. Delve. Make a long list. Push yourself – try to list, say, twenty things.

Don't worry about what will work and what won't – that will come later. Instead, the key here is to be as detailed as possible – look over the filibuster poems in this essay, especially Courtney Queeney's, and consider all the detailed items you could include in your own filibuster poem: lines from books; specific bits of advice others have given you; details from current events; riffs on the contents of your own memory, or whatever happens to be right around you. Or you might, as Alicia Vallarta does, actually undertake the delay strategy: if being online is one way that you, say, put off writing poems, actually go online – just be sure to take notes about what you're reading and seeing, and, perhaps, imagining and dreaming.

Next, arrange your list. Be playful and experiment with lots of possibilities. As you move your sheets of paper around your desk or on the floor, consider: *what items go together? where you can make interesting breaks and leaps? are any funny or poignant transitions possible?* If each of the items from your brainstorming session fits your poem, that's fine – but there's no need to include them all. In fact, to challenge yourself to only include the interesting writing, consider cutting *at least* a quarter of the items from your draft. You also might think of great new ideas as you're arranging your list. Feel free to include those.

The final step of arrangement is to include some mention of what all this delay was for. Notice, though, how Queeney and Austin Smith develop slightly other ways to say 'kiss' and 'put down' (that is, 'kill'). You, too, might think of a slightly different way to say what you have tried to avoid doing. For example, if you were avoiding saying goodbye to someone, you might, instead of actually saying 'goodbye', finish your poem with a gesture of waving.

One more step remains: consider your style. Do you want your poem to be written, like Queeney's poem, as an account of something that happened? Or do you want your poem to be written, like Smith's poem, as a set of instructions? Or do you want your poem to be as seemingly random yet shockingly surprising as Vallarta's? Take some time to style your poem in a way that you find powerful – just keep in mind that power can be subtle, understated.

By this point, you could have a draft of a poem that you like enough to share with other people – friends, fellow poets, a mentor. Show them your poem. Get their feedback. Try out some of their ideas. Memorize your finished poem. Deliver it at your local slam or open poetry reading.

If this process was productive, begin again anew. No excuses.

Works Cited

Abrams, M. H., 'Structure and Style in the Greater Romantic Lyric', in *Romanticism and Consciousness: Essays in Criticism*, ed. Harold Bloom (New York: Norton, 1970), pp. 201-29

Beer, John, 'The Dialectical Argument Structure', in *Structure & Surprise: Engaging Poetic Turns*, ed. Michael Theune (New York: Teachers & Writers, 2007), pp. 99-121

Ciardi, John, 'The Poem in Countermotion', in *How Does a Poem Mean?* (Boston: Houghton Mifflin, 1959), pp. 994-1022

Dennis, Carl, 'The Temporal Lyric', in *Poet's Work, Poet's Play: Essays on the Practice and the Art*, eds. Daniel Tobin and Pimone Triplett (Ann Arbor: University of Michigan Press, 2008), pp. 236-49

Dobyns, Stephen, 'Writing the Reader's Life', in *Best Words, Best Order: Essays on Poetry* (New York: St. Martin's, 1996), pp. 35-52

Eliot, T. S., 'Andrew Marvell' in *Selected Essays, 1917-1932* (New York: Harcourt, Brace, 1932), pp. 251-63

Gioia, Dana, 'Notes on the New Formalism', in *Can Poetry Matter? Essays on Poetry and American Culture* (St Paul, Minneapolis: Graywolf Press, 1992), pp. 29-41

Graff, Gerald, *Clueless in Academe: How Schooling Obscures the Life of the Mind* (New Haven, Connecticut: Yale University Press, 2004)

Graham, Jorie, 'Introduction: Something of Moment', *Ploughshares* 27.4 (Winter 2001-2), pp. 7-9

Hirshfield, Jane, 'Close Reading: Windows', *The Writer's Chronicle* 43.4 (February 2011), pp. 22-30

Hunley, Tom C., *The Poetry Gymnasium* (Jefferson, North Carolina: McFarland, 2011)

Hunley, Tom C., *Teaching Poetry Writing: A Five-Canon Approach* (Clevedon: Multilingual Matters, 2007)

Jarrell, Randall, 'Levels and Opposites: Structure in Poetry', *Georgia Review* 50.4 (Winter 1996), pp. 697-713

Kinzie, Mary, 'The Rhapsodic Fallacy', in *The Cure of Poetry in an Age of Prose: Moral Essays on the Poet's Calling* (Chicago: University of Chicago Press, 1993), pp. 1-26

Lazer, Hank, 'Lyricism of the Swerve: The Poetry of Rae Armantrout', in *Lyric & Spirit: Selected Essays, 1996-2008* (Richmond, California: Omnidawn, 2008), pp. 95-126

Light, Kate, 'And Then There Is That Incredible Moment', in *The Laws of Falling Bodies* (Brownsville, Oregon: Story Line Press, 1997)

Pound, Ezra, Letter to Harriet Monroe, January 1915, *The Selected Letters of Ezra Pound, 1907-1941*, ed. D. D. Paige (New York: Harcourt, Brace, 1950)

Queeney, Courtney, 'Filibuster to Delay a Kiss', in *Filibuster to Delay a Kiss* (New York: Random House, 2007)

Sacks, Peter, *You Only Guide Me by Surprise: Poetry and the Dolphin's Turn* (Berkeley, California: The Bancroft Library at The University of California, Berkeley, 2007)

Sandburg, Carl, 'Chicago', in *The Complete Poems of Carl Sandburg* (New York: Harcourt, Brace, & World, 1950), pp. 3-4

Smith, Austin, 'Instructions for How to Put an Old Horse Down', in *Instructions for How to Put an Old Horse Down* (Green River, Vermont: Longhouse, 2009), not paginated

Theune, Michael, 'Poetic Structure and Poetic Form: The Necessary Differentiation', *American Poet: The Journal of the Academy of American Poets* 32 (Spring 2007), pp. 9-12

Theune, Michael, 'The Self-Reflexive Turn', available at:
http://structureandsurprise.wordpress.com/theory-
criticism/the-self-conscious-turn/

Theune, Michael, *Structure & Surprise: Engaging Poetic Turns*
(New York: Teachers & Writers, 2007)

Theune, Michael, http://structureandsurprise.wordpress.com

Theune, Michael, 'Teaching Collaborative, Dialectical Argument
Poems', available at:
http://structureandsurprise.wordpress.com/pedagogy/teachin
g-collaborative-dialectical-argument-poems/

Vallarta, Alicia, 'Filibuster for Life', unpublished poem

Voigt, Ellen Bryant, *The Art of Syntax: Rhythm of Thought, Rhythm
of Song* (St Paul, Minneapolis: Graywolf Press, 2009)

Voigt, Ellen Bryant, 'The Flexible Lyric' (Athens, Georgia:
University of Georgia Press, 1999), pp. 114-71

Wordsworth, William, 'Preface to the Second Edition of *Lyrical
Ballads* (1800)', in *Selected Poems and Prefaces*, ed. Jack Stillinger
(Boston: Houghton Mifflin, 1965), pp. 445-64

Making the Writing Process Strange: New (and Recycled) Approaches to Teaching Creative Writing

Jenny Dunning

The longer I teach, the more convinced I am that our primary task in the creative writing classroom is to facilitate for our students a radical encounter with the writing process. We need to make language and the act of writing strange for them. This project has multiple fronts: to inculcate a variable and complex creative process across the spectrum of composition – from generation through development and revision; to provide students with tools in the form of diverse strategies to build literature; to set up opportunities for feedback including, but not limited to, the workshop; and to practice the art of reading as a writer. These fronts are not distinct but are all part of the same project that overlap in interesting, productive ways.

I describe the project as a radical encounter because it goes against the grain of much of students' prior writing education. The need to approach the writing project as a wholly new endeavor is particularly critical in the United States where the predominance of the workshop as handed-down from graduate creative writing has distorted our understanding of what we teach and how we teach it. We have narrowed our scope, focusing on technique, conventions and end product rather than teaching the creative process as it applies to creative writing.

In the ten years or so I've been teaching, I have moved from teaching as I was taught – spending at least two-thirds of my class time in workshops – to a very different classroom practice; a practice that aims to instill a composition process similar to the varied processes of successful contemporary writers. In rethinking creative writing pedagogy, I've turned to the studio art classroom as a model. I've shifted the balance of how class-time hours are spent – doing no workshops in introductory classes and fewer in intermediate and advanced classes so as to leave more time for small-group peer review, invention exercises, opportunities to practise specific strategies, revision activities, exercise in reading as a writer, guest visits by writers, and more. Not only am I more satisfied with the writing my students are doing at all levels, I am confident that they are developing a much more realistic composition process, one that will sustain them in their future projects, as well as being valuable training in creativity in its own right.

The workshop works against creative composing strategies

Issues of authority have historically plagued the writing workshop – the tendency toward orthodoxy (what Brent Royster refers to as 'particular, validated modes of writing') and overplay of the teacher's aesthetic and influence generally.[1] These critiques have merit. Because students submit completed drafts of poems, stories and essays for workshops, we eliminate the opportunity to mediate the actual composition process. Recently, there has been a call to consider what we've given up by doing so. Steve Healey, for instance, suggests that 'a new pedagogy could *front-load* classes with interventions in the writing process before it begins and while it's happening, instead of the more traditional *back-loading* – that is, intervening after a written product already exists'.[2] I embrace this challenge in my rethinking of creative writing pedagogy.

The workshop's emphasis on product has another consequence: it reinforces students' assumption that creative writing works like academic writing. With academic papers, they typically write as few drafts as possible. They begin with a pre-determined thesis. They outline. They make their ideas explicit. They write papers in straight lines, no digressions. The most successful students use their time efficiently, minimizing false starts and wrong turns by writing what they already know they want to say. In other words, they trade exploration for efficiency. In the years since I was an undergraduate, academic writing has become increasingly focused on developing an argument. While the issue lies outside the scope of this essay, I'm not convinced that this approach results in students producing their best work in academic subjects. But in the creative writing classroom, I *know* these strategies are counter-productive.

My own formal education in creative writing set up unrealistic expectations in regard to the composition process. It took me years to unlearn the habits of writing for a workshop deadline; to learn to start over again and again, to feel for the voice, the character, where the story comes from; to let a story tell me how to tell it. I don't want my students to have the same experience – but I also don't want to impose my composing process on them. As an experiment, I leafed through the 'Contributors' Notes' sections of the 2010 *Best American Poetry*

---

[1] Brent Royster, 'Inspiration, Creativity and Crisis: The Romantic Myth of the Writer Meets the Contemporary Classroom', in *Power and Identity in the Creative Writing Classroom*, ed. Anna Leahy (2005), p. 35.
[2] Steve Healey, 'The Rise of Creative Writing & the New Value of Creativity', in *The Writer's Chronicle* (February 2009), pp. 30-38, (p. 38).

and *Short Stories* anthologies. The results were eye opening. Here's a partial list of the 'triggers' for the stories and poems included in the anthology: photos, an image from a film, memories, random conversations, a book title, a musical performance, a prison diary, a newspaper clipping, other poems, a misread line from a student poem, an idea, a dream, a person's name, the lives of real people, actual events, an anecdote borrowed from a classic story, the word *valetudinarian*, a writing prompt, research, a cross-country drive. Both poets and fiction writers referred to long gestation periods, drafts revised over many years, drafts rediscovered after, in two cases, twenty years, as well as drafts that came surprisingly quickly. A selection of gems about the varied writing processes follows:

- 'My creative process has taught me to accept failure (all forms of it), to try again and try again and try again [....]'[3]

- 'I am generally quite a slow writer, and it often takes many years for me to arrive at the mature version of a poem – this one went through half a dozen iterations over almost fifteen years, and bears almost no discernible relationship to its original draft.'[4]

- 'I finished the whole sequence in less than a month, which is unusual for me. I'm a very slow writer. It was as if I'd been possessed. I certainly didn't have a plan, which is obvious when you look at the subject matter of the poems.'[5]

- 'It's really awe inspiring [...] to see the end of a poem coming, visible and invisible, no words there yet, but a clear sense that there are no more than three or four lines to go, and you better get ready for that. The pressure is a bracing, galvanizing, thrilling problem, and before you know it, that's that. It's done. And then it's time to go looking for the next poem.'[6]

- 'The piece became a way of exploring, obliquely, some of the deep reasons for [the] tragedy.'[7]

- 'That's how I write a story, bit by bit, with sustained and single-minded focus that's relinquished only after a final draft – in this case, thirteen weeks of work.'[8]

---

[3] Thomas Sayers Ellis in *Best American Poetry 2010*, ed. David Lehman (2010), p. 185.
[4] Amy Glynn Greacen, ibid, p. 189.
[5] Barbara Hamby, ibid, pp. 192-3.
[6] J. E. Wei, ibid, p.216.
[7] Jennifer Egan in *Best American Short Stories 2010*, ed. Heidi Pitlor (2010), p. 394.
[8] Joshua Ferris, ibid, p. 395.

- 'The heat and pressure of years of writing temper my characters and turn them into people quite different from those who first capture my interest.'[9]
- 'My writing unfolds like a connect-the-dots exercise. Anecdotes and images pop into my head and my job is to figure out how they all tie together.'[10]
- 'I felt myself to be in the presence of intensely powerful and nearly equal conflicting values and/or feelings: always a good sign, in terms of the production of literary fiction, as far as I'm concerned.'[11]

What can we take away from these insights into the composition process, as well as the fuller comments in the 'Notes'? First, that the process is variable for each individual and each piece. The process is an intuitive one – not the know-what-you-want-to-say-before-you-write sort so many students employ for academic writing. Inspiration comes in the middle of the night, or when doing activities other than writing. Discovery, the need to understand something, drives the process. The writer doesn't control the process and is genuinely surprised at the outcome. The process can take twenty years or more. Or it can happen very quickly. False starts and unexpected turns are how to get where one is going. Sometimes, a friend's or editor's suggestion propels a piece in a new direction.

We need to help students feel comfortable with the entire spectrum of the composing process, from recognizing triggers to feeling their way to the deeper subject of a piece. We need to encourage students to cultivate inspiration, to let images, characters, ideas simmer while they go about their everyday activities. One way to 'teach' the spectrum of the composing process is to ensure that students read about and hear about many different writers' experiences. Students can talk to writers in person, find interviews with writers, read essays about the composition process in some of the anthologies now available that include essays by the authors.[12] All of these are worthwhile. But when it comes to setting up students to have these experiences themselves, I've found inspiration in the studio art classroom.

---

[9]   Lauren Groff, ibid., p. 395.
[10]   Lori Ostlund, ibid., p. 401.
[11]   Jim Shepard, ibid., p. 403.
[12]   For example, *Contemporary American Poetry: Behind the Scenes*, ed. Ryan Van Cleave (2002) and *The Story Behind the Story*, eds. Peter Turchi and Andrea Barrett (2004).

What we can learn from the art classroom

I had been teaching at St Olaf College for a couple of years, and was frustrated with the results of the traditional approach to teaching creative writing. My students were too invested in their drafts and approached revision as a one-time fix-it process. Too many of them put their time into polishing drafts that should have been stepping stones in their learning process. Furthermore our workshop discussions were often unproductive because students hadn't read widely enough or done enough writing to be truly insightful about each others' work. But I wasn't sure how to restructure my classes to address the problems. I was wary of shifting too much class time to in-class writing prompts because that wouldn't help students with their writing when the class was over. I wanted students to practice the trial-and-error, slow-growth composing process more similar to the processes of contemporary writers. How could I do that?

I began to find my answer when I attended a multi-disciplinary faculty luncheon discussion on creativity. The chair of our Art Department, Irve Dell, presented a list of strategies, culled from suggestions by his faculty, that 'promote creative outcomes'. I realized that these are all strategies we can apply in creative writing, though in different ways. Here's the list:

- never tell students their work is bad
- inspire, model and provide opportunities for active observation
- let students help shape an idea or assignment
- give assignments that limit variables and allow students to discover that creativity can blossom when it has constraints to flex against
- reinforce the practice of the creative process – do and redo; react and allow for change; be pulled by the work; collaborate with your material; don't begin by visualizing the final product; seize the accident along the way
- ask students what their passions are and encourage them to incorporate those in their work
- encourage and reward risk-taking; make grading practices reflect the value of risk-taking
- journal
- makes series or repetitions – 100 'drawings' of the same subject, for instance
- use unorthodox material
- change scale

- explore the power of juxtaposition
- present case studies
- destroy and rebuild
- de-emphasize end products, at least some of the time – give more smaller, lower-stakes assignments
- assign collaborative work (lowers risk)
- ask students to take a walk or play in the 'sandbox'

What stands out here is the importance of low-stakes assignments and encouraging students to take risks, experiment and play. Foster a recursive process, a process in which students develop the same material in different ways. In writing this might mean experimenting with various poetic forms and schema, trying out different points of view and/or voices, changing tenses, trying out different organizational patterns (the list, the braid, abecedarian order, fractured narrative structure, etc.). Incorporate chance into invention and even revision exercises. Do some collaborative projects. Play in the (metaphorical) sandbox.

For the last few years, I've offered a multi-genre 'Fundamentals of Creative Writing' course at St Olaf which focuses on the creative process itself. For three-quarters of the semester, we consider various strategies used in creative writing, such as building tension, heightening energy, using metaphor, making patterns. Each week students choose from a list of low-stakes prompts that practice particular strategies. Often the prompts ask students to recycle material from earlier in the semester, developing it differently. In addition to the weekly prompts, students record 'germs' – images, quick thoughts, very brief ideas that they might develop into a piece of writing at a later time: practice in the habit of finding inspiration. They also do weekly sets of 'observations' – concrete descriptions of a specific object, scene, moment, built detail by detail, without evaluation, explanation or judgment, that end with a simile. At first, these are hard for students to do. They want to say what the object, scene, moment means. But over the semester, they learn to let the concrete details and the simile communicate meaning to them and their readers, a critical skill in creative writing. As with art students, writing education should provide an apprenticeship that gives students practice in a variety of strategies.

Students meet weekly in small-group peer review sessions. These are not workshops. Following the recommendations of Peter Elbow in *Writing Without Teachers*, students mirror back to the writer their reading experience by identifying words, images or moments in a piece of writing that are striking, moving, funny, exciting, etc., as well as moments that are confusing or distracting. They talk about what interests them most about the piece, what Elbow refers to as 'centers of gravity'.[13] Each week I suggest a question or two that focus on the strategies we're practicing that week. In the last quarter of the course, students develop favorite pieces for a portfolio. Another key component of the course is lots of practice reading as a writer, as discussed below.

While 'Fundamentals' actually focuses on the creative process as it applies to creative writing, I've incorporated many of these strategies into intermediate and advanced courses as well. Before students turn in a complete draft of a story, they write 'story starts,' three-to-four page explorations into character/world/story. Sometimes I ask students to focus on a specific aspect of writing in a start: develop a complex character, get across the illusion of the fictional world, try out a particular point of view and such – starts serve as a convenient place to practice specific skills. Students share 'starts' in small peer review groups so that they understand how others experience their work. And I devote class time to visits by writers, exploring literary journals, and 'craft talks', student presentations based on their own research into particular craft issues.

Revision can be taught

When I started writing seriously, my teachers commented that my revisions weren't much different from my drafts. Looking back, I realize that I needed to learn how to revise. I had no trouble making editorial changes, but I was reluctant to re-imagine a story. It never occurred to me to start over. But starting over is exactly what real writers do, what I do now. In a recent *Writer's Chronicle* interview, poet Nikki Giovanni says exactly that: 'No, I don't revise. I start all over again'.[14]

My students are no different. They don't know how to take on true revision. In the conventional writing paradigm, to start over is to waste one's hard work; it's inefficient. Further, revision is perceived as a process distinct from the composing process. But, as my perusal of the 'Contributors' Notes' of the Best American anthologies shows, revision is an integral part of the writing process from the beginning, and failure is how many eventually succeed. Of course, in a semester-long class, students don't have

---

[13] Peter Elbow, *Writers Without Teachers* (1973), p. 86.
[14] Chapman Hood Frazier, 'A Conversation with Nikki Giovanni', in *The Writer's Chronicle* (March/April 2011), p. 10.

ten or 20 years to let a piece gestate and evolve. However, revision exercises can foster a more realistic development process. For example, students might write three different versions of the same piece and then revise again, using what worked best. Or they might choose between possible tactics such as extracting a line from a piece and starting over; inserting an arbitrary sentence into the middle of a piece and redirecting it; translating the central idea of a piece into a single sentence and then revising with that in mind; combining two different pieces. Grades reflect students' willingness to experiment and move away from their initial drafts. Students include drafts in their portfolios as well as a course reflection in which they discuss their process. Not only does this encourage them to think about process in a complicated way – it allows me insight into their process for grading purposes.

In intermediate and advanced courses, I devote even more time to revision. I assign students 'radical revisions', revisions which require them to start over with at least one 'radical' difference in approach.[15] This project often results in the best writing students do during the semester. They are required to research their radical approach: explore a particular author or style – Ray Carver's minimalism, for instance – or consult articles on alternative grammars and structures, or essays about writing from a so-called 'female aesthetic'.[16] The point is not for students to write a minimalist or a collage story, or to write 'close to the body' – it's for them to approach their material in an unfamiliar way. I challenge students to risk failure in these stories. This is not a 'final' revision – students revise again for their final portfolio, drawing on what they learned from both versions of the story. Again, willingness to experiment matters more in grading than polish.

---

[15] Adapted from Wendy Bishop, 'Contracts, Radical Revision, Portfolios, and the Risks of Writing', in *Power and Identity in the Creative Wrting Classroom*, ed. Anna Leahy (2005), pp. 109-20.

[16] Articles about alternative grammars and structures can be found in *Elements of Alternate Style*, ed. Wendy Bishop (1997). For ideas about a female aesthetic, I suggest Hélène Cixous's 'Laugh of the Medusa' in *French Feminism Reader*, ed. Kelly Oliver, pp. 257-75; Rachel Blau DuPlessis's 'For the Etruscans' in *The Pink Guitar: Writing as Feminist Practice* (1990), pp. 1-19; and Lillian Bridwell-Bowles's 'Discourse and Diversity: Experimental Writing within the Academy' in *College Composition and Communication* 43.3 (1992), pp. 349-68.

Reading as a writer: Writing as an experience

Learning to read as a writer is an essential part of helping students to encounter the writing process in a new way. 'Reading as a writer' – it's a much-used phrase that has recently become a subject of critical discussion: what is it? Is it truly different from critical reading? What is its role in the creative writing classroom? In *Creative Writing and the New Humanities*, Paul Dawson documents the history of the concept, tracing it back to an 1884 Walter Besant essay. Dawson claims that the distinction writers over the years have maintained between reading as a writer and literary criticism does not hold up, that the strategy boils down to a version of the formalist critic's close reading which creative writing classes have '"naturalized" as a writer's perspective in opposition to a critic's'.[17] While the approach is formalist, I believe that Dawson misses the spirit of the exercise of reading as a writer, misses the artful nature of the practice that distinguishes it from the critic's project.

The American novelist Francine Prose devotes an entire book, *Reading Like a Writer*, to demonstrating the strategy. She better captures the artfulness of the approach, which she describes as involving 'a sort of osmosis'.[18] She likens the process of close reading – word by word, sentence by sentence (her chapter topics move from words to sentences to paragraphs to narration, character, and so on) – to 'private lessons in the art of fiction'.[19] From her demonstrations, we can see that the approach involves paying close attention to an author's choices and how those choices affect the reader's experience of the work, as well as cultivating an appreciation for good writing, all of it happening at both a conscious and a more intuitive level.

But what's really different from reading as a writer and critical reading is that the critic accrues evidence for a particular interpretation of a work, for what it means, even if that meaning is understood to be one of a number of valid readings. There's no such unifying trend in the practice of reading as a writer. Indeed, to the extent that we want students' reading to serve as internalized models for writing (Prose's 'osmosis'), it's key that students *don't* read for meaning. The writing process we want to inculcate involves allowing meaning to emerge from the raw material of the words, images, characters, story, instead of being preconceived and imposed on the material. For most students, schooled to read for meaning – and most practiced in the

---

[17] Paul Dawson, *Creative Writing and the New Humanities* (2005), p. 98.
[18] Francine Prose, *Reading Like a Writer* (2006), p. 3.
[19] Ibid.

symbolic decoding of modernist works – this entails a paradigm change that reading for how it works can facilitate.

In creative writing, we don't communicate a message so much as create an experience, hence the maxim 'show don't tell'. It's critical that students understand the difference. Before taking creative writing, many students equate creative writing with journaling. However, journaling involves writing *about* experiences and emotions rather than creating them for a reader. The audience is the self. For these students, learning to read as a writer can help them negotiate the new orientation.

When we read as a writer, we focus on the experience created by the piece of writing. Students need opportunities in a range of settings – small groups and whole class, internet forums and individual writing responses – to mirror back their reading experience, much as they do with each others' work in small peer review groups. Students also need to explore how specific strategies contribute to that experience, thus overlapping with the development of their creative writing toolbox. I'm referring to strategies such as sound effects, compression, jumps, associative shifts, repetition and variation. Students can become aware of how opposition and imagery can create an 'image narrative' below the surface of a piece. And students can explore how form and structure work in a particular piece, how the final moment in a poem, story, essay weights the experience. All of this becomes part of the way we learn to listen to the words, images, ideas, characters, narrative, form that is, analogous to a sculptor's clay, the material of creative writing.

We need to be more innovative about the ways we ask students to interact with literature. In 'Let Stones Speak: New Media Remediation in the Poetry Writing Classroom', Jake Adam York discusses having students use graphic editing software to translate words into waves, allowing them to perceive sound as the continuous stream it is. They look at the patterns of various sounds together, learn what makes for smooth transitions, what for rough. And they take this new way of encountering language back to the writing classroom.[20] I'm fascinated. In my classroom, I have asked students to 'translate' short pieces of literature into other media – film, music, visual art. Students enjoy these activities and they gain a real appreciation for the power of the image narrative. These types of projects work well as collaborative assignments. We need to get creative about finding ways to create these sorts of encounters.

---

[20] Jake Adam York, 'Let Stones Speak', in *Creative Writing Studies*, eds. Graeme Harper and Jeri Kroll (2008).

A limited role for the writing workshop

There is, I believe, a place for workshop in the undergraduate creative writing classroom. My students at the intermediate and advanced levels expect to do some workshopping and would be disappointed if we didn't. For one, students appreciate having an audience for their writing. Workshop, in effect, serves as a place for students to 'publish' their work. Furthermore, the 'group therapy effect' comes into play: students can recognize problems in the work of others that their defenses don't let them see yet in their own.

However, it's critical that we establish a 'draft culture' in workshops. Discussion proceeds very differently when we're talking about a stage along the way to a finished piece, which has gifts as well as missed opportunities, than if we use a 'fix-it' approach. Peer review of low-stakes work and 'starts' help establish this draft culture. It also helps to postpone workshops to the second half of a course, allowing plenty of time to set the tone. I begin workshops by enumerating a piece's gifts, insisting that students hold off on critique until after we've generated a list of positives (students are often better at this than I am). And I encourage students to be open to reassessing a piece during our discussion – I share my own changes of heart with them.

To address the authority problem inherent in the workshop, I assign student facilitators to lead discussions. Students introduce a primary gift of the story, giving an example from our course reading of a similar gift. Likewise when we move onto critique, the facilitator identifies an aspect of the story that doesn't satisfy, and gives an example of a how a published writer handles a similar situation. There are times where my experience provides needed insight in a discussion, but I try to avoid falling into the 'final say' pattern of closing a workshop with a summary assessment.

However, we need to guard against workshops taking up the majority of class time. The Associated Writing Programs recommends that writing workshops be limited to 12 students and not exceed 15, but many of us don't have that luxury in our classrooms.[21] One writing cycle can take several weeks to get through in a larger class, and often workshops of individual pieces are hurried and brief. Furthermore, as I've been discussing, there is just so much else we need to do in our classes. In 'Workshopping the Workshop and Teaching the Unteachable', Kevin Brophy suggests ways for students to get feedback on their work that can supplement whole-class

---

[21] 'The AWP Director's Handbook', online.

workshop: workshops in pairs or smaller groups, workshops via internet forums, peer review meetings outside of class, asking students to talk about a writing project without showing it, and public readings.[22] I would add to this, publishing class anthologies, either in print or on the web.

The value of creativity

At a presentation by comic artist Chris Monroe recently, I was struck by a photo she shared of a brainstorming activity that helped her generate new ideas for her comic strip: a list of associations and word play related to the phrase 'back to school'. The strategy, she said, came from a class she took in art school on creative thinking. A class on creative thinking? I was intrigued. It's been some years since Monroe attended the Minneapolis College of Art and Design. Nevertheless, I contacted the school to see if they still offer the class. Now it's titled 'Creative and Critical Thinking'. Jerry Allan's syllabus for the course includes units on techniques for mental fluency, the nature of problems, procrastination versus incubation, invention techniques, creativity and collaboration, and more. At the end of the course, students present a review of a personal project from the perspective of creativity. Maybe we should include such 'Creative Thinking' courses in our creative writing curricula.

Increasingly, teaching creativity is perceived as valuable in its own right.[23] I bring this up because it's important to remind ourselves that the majority of our undergraduate students will not go on to publish their work or to pursue graduate study in creative writing. For these students, the value of a class in which new paradigms are introduced, in which language and the act of writing are made strange, is just that: a new experience with language and immersion in the creative process.

---

[22] Kevin Brophy, 'Workshopping the Workshop and Teaching the Unteachable', in *Creative Writing Studies: Practice, Research and Pedagogy*, eds. Graeme Harper and Jeri Kroll (2008), pp. 75-87, (pp. 80-1).
[23] See, for instance, Healey, 'The Rise of Creative Writing & the New Value of Creativity'.

Writing Exercise – A Process-Based Fiction Prompt

Writers tune into the world at particular frequencies. We notice what others don't. Zero in on a person who has caught your attention in some way, a person you don't know personally. Maybe you overheard a striking line of dialogue. Or noted an unusual mannerism. Or a detail that seemed out of place. Fiction writer Charles Baxter refers to these as widowed images, images that stick with us long after the context disappears.[24] Beginning with the dialogue, mannerism, detail that caught your attention, describe a character who says, does, or has this. Use only concrete details to describe this character – don't overthink; you want this character to tell you who she is, who he is (about a page). Now look back at what you've written. Let the details you've chosen tell you what this character wants. Writing now from the character's point of view (use either first or third person), let this desire drive the story forward without knowing where it's going. Remember that often our desires trip us up – don't be afraid to get this character in trouble.

---

[24] Personal communication with the author.

Works Cited

Bridwell-Bowles, Lillian, Discourse and Diversity: Experimental Writing within the Academy, *College Composition and Communication* 43.3 (1992), pp. 349-68

Brophy, Kevin, 'Workshopping the Workshop and Teaching the Unteachable' in *Creative Writing Studies: Practice, Research and Pedagogy*, eds. Graeme Harper and Jeri Kroll (Clevedon: Multilingual Matters, 2008), pp. 75-87

Cixous, Hélène, 'Laugh of the Medusa', in *French Feminism Reader*, ed. Kelly Oliver (Lanham, Maryland: Rowman & Littlefield Publishers, 2000)

Cleave, Ryan Van, ed., *Contemporary American Poetry: Behind the Scenes*, (New York: Longman, 2002)

Dawson, Paul, *Creative Writing and the New Humanities* (London: Routledge, 2005)

DuPlessis, Rachel Blau, 'For the Etruscans', in *The Pink Guitar: Writing as Feminist Practice* (New York: Routledge, 1990)

Elbow, Peter, *Writers Without Teachers* (New York: Oxford University Press, 1973)

Healey, Steve 'The Rise of Creative Writing & the New Value of Creativity', *The Writer's Chronicle* (February 2009)

Leahy, Anna, ed., *Power and Identity in the Creative Writing Classroom* (Clevedon: Multilingual Matters, 2005)

Lehman, David, ed., *Best American Poetry 2010* (New York: Scribner, 2010)

Pitlor, Heidi, ed., *Best American Short Stories 2010* (Boston: Mariner, 2010)

Prose, Francine, *Reading Like a Writer* (New York: Harper, 2006)
Turchi, Peter, and Andrea Barrett, eds., *The Story Behind the Story* (New York: Norton, 2004)

York, Jake Adam, 'Let Stones Speak: New Media Remediation in the Poetry Writing Classroom', in *Creative Writing Studies: Practice, Research and Pedagogy*, eds., Graeme Harper and Jeri Kroll (Clevedon: Multilingual Matters, 2008), pp. 21-35

A Whole New Creative Writing Classroom: Daniel Pink, Digital Culture and the Twenty-First Century Workshop

Stephanie Vanderslice

In *A Whole New Mind: Why Right Brainers Will Rule the Future*, Daniel Pink invokes six 'abilities' critical to surviving and flourishing in twenty-first century culture: Design, Story, Symphony, Empathy, Play and Meaning.[1] Two of these, Story and Empathy, are directly linked to skills nurtured by students in creative writing classes (although arguably these courses also involve the other four indirectly). But as creative writing teachers, is it enough just to pat ourselves on the back over the fact that we just happen to be swimming with the new millennial tide, or should we be doing more? Should we be altering the forms that creative content takes in our courses in order to show students how these intuitive 'abilities' tap into twenty-first century culture? Should the twenty-first century creative writing course look radically different from its twentieth century counterpart? In recent years, as I have observed the ubiquitous influence of New Media in my students' lives and that of my own children, I have become convinced that the answer to this question should be an unequivocal 'yes'.

In addition to calling my students' attention to Pink's influential work and the reasons why the skills they are cultivating in creative writing courses *matter*, I also include, on every course syllabus, a list of Ten Digital Competencies for Every Graduate, taken directly from a technology blog on the Inside Higher Education Website.[2] They are as follows:

Ten digital competencies for every graduate

Graduates should be able to:

1. Start a Blog
2. Buy an Audio Recorder and Learn to Use It
3. Start Editing Audio

---

[1] Daniel Pink, *A Whole New Mind: Why Right Brainers Will Rule the Future* (2006): Pink employs the terms 'abilities' and 'senses' in reference to these categories of Design, Story, Symphony, Empathy, Play and Meaning.
[2] Inside Higher Education website. Online

4. Post an Interview (or Podcast) on Your Blog
5. Learn How to Shoot, Crop, Tone, and Optimize Photos (And Add Them to Your Blog)
6. Learn to Create Effective Voice-Over Presentations with Rapid Authoring Software
7. Tell a Good Story with Images and Sound
8. Learn to Shoot Video
9. Edit Your Video with iMovie, Windows Movie Maker or Windows Storyteller
10. Publish Your Video on Your Blog.

Beyond directing my students to a few online tutorials, I do not actually teach these competencies – rather my course assignments expect that students will *utilize* some of these competencies in determining the form for the course's creative content. For example, in every class, students create individual blogs where they respond to course readings and other course content. More than just a digital course journal, they are expected to use these blogs to connect to other relevant subject matter, online content, photos, videos, podcasts and the like. In addition, most of my courses involve reading and presenting on a free-choice book related to the subject matter; all of these presentations must now be in digital format, such as Prezi or Glogster. Finally, my teaching creative writing course formerly ended with a creative writing literacy narrative that incorporated sources we'd read that semester; now students study and create digital literacy narratives that achieve the same end. What's more, since I'm teaching future teachers in the later course, I'm also modeling good pedagogy.

The majority of my students are undergraduate writing majors – some of who will succeed as writers and others who will find success in related fields – but all of them have an earnest desire to work in a world of words. I take seriously the responsibility of not only teaching them critical transferable skills (story, empathy), but also of showing them how these skills can be foundational to their careers. Indeed, it is my responsibility to stay abreast of trends in these foundational skills. In addition to following Pink's writing, I also read *Fast Company*, *Inside Higher Education* and *Education Week*, just a few of the media sources that give me a sense of the kind of changing world my students will be entering. I know what it feels like to have a satisfying career and want that satisfaction for my students, but I recognize that the playing field continues to change. In order to meet my goals as a teacher, I must change with it.

Of course, as creative writing teachers, we still teach the writing of fiction, poetry, creative nonfiction and drama – the genres that are the heart of our field. All of these genres are currently in flux, however, as they have always been, only now, with the dawn of the digital age, more rapidly and dramatically. We must teach our students that the ability to convey information through story is a foundational human instinct, but one whose frontiers continue to shift from the oral storytellers of ancient times, to Shakespeare, to the novel, to the modern role-player video game which is deeply anchored in narrative. Creative writing students are poised to dominate this new creative culture, amorphous as its shape may seem to us right now. With our encouragement and willingness to teach from the evolving digital culture in which they live, they will determine its form and trajectory.

Transcending the traditional

The traditional writing workshop in its most basic form features a lead teacher and a group of students joining together to bring their knowledge and experience to bear on student work in the featured genre, serving as a writer's early audience, if you will. I would like to argue that the twenty-first century writing workshop, led by a reflective teacher who is cognizant of twenty-first century culture, can and should do more than that. Indeed, a reflective teacher who is teaching creative writing responsibly is not only teaching craft, but is also modeling the kind of meta-cognition and cultural awareness that can help future writers to make nimble transitions as the culture of the written word shifts over the course of their careers.

She can do this by not only teaching the elements of craft, the core of the course, but by placing these elements of the course in the context of current ideas about creativity and culture. By staying abreast of these ideas, I am able, for example, to refer to them in the classroom as we discuss student work as well as issues in writing and publishing. As we talk about the process of writing a poem or a prose piece, we might talk about 'flow', for example, the well-known optimal state of mind Daniel Golman describes as a 'feeling of spontaneous joy, even rapture, while performing a task',[3] something most artists strive to achieve while creating, and refer students to Mihaly Csikszentmihalyi's famous work on the subject as potentially useful for helping them understand their own creative processes.[4] We might also

---

[3] Daniel Golman, *Emotional Intelligence: Why it Can Matter More than IQ* (2006).
[4] Mihaly Csikszentmihalyi, *Creativity: Flow and the Psychology of Discovery and*

talk about flow in terms of the optimal experience we hope to create for the readers of our work. Or, we might talk about current theories on gaming culture and flow. If the challenge of a 'game' brings about 'flow', how might we use games to spur our own writing process (I would argue that National Novel Writing Month, or NaNoWriMo[5] uses many 'game' features – community, challenge, leveling – to encourage flow and encourage writers to meet their novel–in–a–month goals) or how might we use 'gaming' principles to optimize the experience for readers so they experience 'flow' while reading.

What I'm modeling here is the kind of curiosity and initiative that can help a writer broaden his understanding of his creative process, his writing and its place in a rapidly evolving literary culture. At the beginning of my writers' workshops I ask students to choose a book from a list of 'writing life' books to read and report on, as a means of expanding his sense of the many forms and paths a writer's life might take. In more advanced workshops, however, I have begun asking students to choose a book from a list of what I call 'creative culture' books, books that can help them to see how their development as a writer fits into literary culture writ large – the current atmosphere of blogging, remixing, gaming, digital media and so forth (a suggested list is included at the end of this essay). By allowing them to choose a book from the list that speaks to them and not insisting that the entire class read one book dictated by my current interests, my hope is that the book they choose will so excite them that they will not stop there but will be set on a path that will lead them to many other books on creativity and culture.

In effect, what I am hoping to do is to make my workshop environment one that not only develops students as writers but also, as Anna Leahy describes it, encourages them to be 'nerds', to 'practice the habits of mind, especially curiosity, that lead to creativity'.[6] In 'Who Wants to be a Nerd? Or How Cognitive Science Changed My Teaching', Leahy effectively argues that by pushing students to broaden their horizons outside the craft of writing into other areas, like creativity, culture, or even cognitive science, we set the stage for a kind of divergent thinking that can help them look at their writing in new ways that can even help them solve problems in the process. Moreover, like Leahy, I want to remind my students that no one makes art in a vacuum, that

---

Invention (2008); *Flow: The Psychology of Optimal Experience* (2008).
[5] www.nanowrimo.com.
[6] Anna Leahy, 'Who Wants to Be a Nerd: Or, How Cognitive Science Changed My Teaching', *New Writing: The International Journal for the Practice and Theory of Creative Writing* 7.1 (2010), pp. 45-52, (p. 45).

'What we do in creative writing courses is connected with what it means to be human. We are all in this life adventure together'.[7]

Story and empathy

While I try not to force my own interests on my students but to encourage their own, I do feel they need to be aware of major ideas influencing the culture they write in and to be able to connect those ideas to their own work. The reasons why Pink's *A Whole New Mind: Why Right Brainers Will Rule the Future* is a critical book for any creative person working in the twenty-first century are right there in the title, for, as Pink notes in his introduction, 'The future belongs to a very different kind of person with a very different kind of mind – creators and empathizers, pattern recognizers and meaning makers. These people – artists, inventors, designers, storytellers, caregivers, consolers, big picture thinkers – will now reap society's richest rewards and share its greatest joys'.[8] It is not enough to tell students this, however, and exhort them to go read the book. We need to talk about the arguments Pink makes and *what this means for writers*. This understanding is critical if students are to understand that it is not simply enough for the kind of knowledge Pink advocates to exist, they must each decide what it means for them and act on that knowledge. Otherwise they will only comprehend these or other 'game changing' books on a surface level, parroting 'right brain skills are valuable', without understanding *how* to translate these skills into success in contemporary culture. Otherwise they will be left in a cubicle somewhere or worse, behind a fast food counter making change and thinking, 'yeah right, right brain skills are valuable'.

In a way, promoting the value of 'right brain' skills is something the workshop has been doing for years. Unfortunately, as I note in my book, *Rethinking Creative Writing*, M.F.A. programs and the workshops they promote have been trying to have it both ways.[9] In one essay on the M.F.A., for example, D.W. Fenza notes that 'no advanced degree necessarily secures jobs for artists', and then adds a few sentences later that 'study in the arts is applicable to many types of employment outside academe'.[10] My argument is that programs in the arts *can*

---

[7] Ibid., p. 47.
[8] Pink, p. 1.
[9] Stephanie Vanderslice, *Rethinking Creative Writing* (2011).
[10] D.W. Fenza, 'Creative Writing and Its Discontents', *The AWP Chronicle* (2001), online.

produce graduates who are able not only to adapt to changes in culture but flourish in them, but in order to do so, they must be very conscious of their efforts and how they translate into the curricula. To appropriate an oft-invoked workshop phrase, they can't just *tell* students the skills they are gaining are valuable, they must also *show* them that they are.

I believe that all of the six important 'senses' Pink addresses in his book – Design, Story, Symphony, Empathy, Play and Meaning – relate in some way to what students learn in the workshop, but the two most obvious connections to be made are with story and meaning. In terms of story, Pink reminds us that 'the essence of persuasion, communication and self-understanding has become the ability also to fashion a compelling narrative'.[11] We don't remember facts, we remember stories, and as facts threaten to overwhelm us in their ubiquity, stories become even more important. Fortunately, the writing workshop, whether its focus is prose or poetry, is inherently about narrative design. We need to remind students that while they are studying an essential element of craft, what makes a good story, they are also learning something that naturally attracts humans in all disciplines and walks of life and cultivating a skill that other fields covet. According to Pink, 'the clearest example is a nascent movement called "organizational storytelling" which aims to make organizations aware of the stories that exist within their walls – and then to use those stories in pursuit of organizational goals'.[12] Likewise, Robert McKee's Story Seminar has attracted a following among not only the screenwriters for whom it was intended but also 'the executives, entrepreneurs, and workers of transitional business'.[13] McKee describes the unintended phenomenon this way: 'If a businessperson understands that his or her own mind naturally wants to frame experience in a story, the key to moving the audience is not to resist this impulse but to embrace it'.[14] Moreover, story has become important not only in business but also in marketing and in medicine, something Robert Coles first identified many years ago in his book, *The Call of Stories: Teaching and the Moral Imagination*,[15] but has since evolved into a movement toward narrative medicine. In fact, today, at Columbia University Medical School 'all second-year medical students take a seminar in narrative medicine in addition to their hard-core science classes. There they learn to listen more

---

[11] Pink, p. 102.
[12] Ibid., p. 107.
[13] Ibid., p. 106.
[14] Quoted in Pink, pp. 106-7.
[15] Robert Coles, *The Call of Stories: Teaching and the Moral Imagination* (1990).

empathically to the stories their patients tell and to "read" those stories with greater acuity'.[16]

In order to help students in a workshop understand the universality of story and how they can use it regardless of whether they become writers or whether they go into a related – or even unrelated – field, we need to teach them that stories are everywhere around them, not just in the content of the workshop; in fact we need to teach them to look for stories outside the workshop as much as inside. In the classroom, this translates into encouraging students to also look for the many ways that exist to *tell* a story, whether through digital media or collage, music or comics and to try them out and see what they learn from them. It also means repeatedly returning to the elements of storytelling – as a sort of scaffolding – in the genres the workshop emphasizes – what makes a good first line of a short story or a novel? What makes a good first line – or last line of a poem? Why?

Another 'sense' Pink describes as critical to the twenty-first century and which features prominently in the writing workshop is 'empathy', the 'ability to imagine yourself in someone else's position and to intuit what that person is feeling […] sensing what it would be like to be that person'.[17] Arguably, beyond understanding the elements of a good story and a perfect line or sentence, writers need to score highly on the empathy quotient if they are to write for a reader, someone who is not the self, and if they are to create three-dimensional characters. Empathy is not just increasingly important in the writing workshop however, but in the increasingly technological, global world in which we live, for as Pink tells us, it is the 'one aptitude that's proven impossible for computers to reproduce and very difficult for faraway workers connected by electrons to match'.[18] In fact, one of the ways Pink encourages his readers to develop their sense of empathy is to eavesdrop on conversations, something most writers do, and then to take it a step further by 'imagin[ing] yourself as one of those people in that situation'.[19] What are they thinking at that moment? What emotions are they feeling? What brought them to that place? Another way to develop empathy is to take an acting class, something that many fields outside theatre, including M.F.A. programs and medical schools, are encouraging students to do. While it may not be possible to require all workshop participants to take an acting class, we can talk about some acting techniques that we might·

---

[16] Pink, p. 113,
[17] Pink, p. 160.
[18] Ibid., p. 161.
[19] Ibid., p. 179.

mine when we write, ways in which actors understand their characters in order more effectively to portray them. I often ask my students early in a workshop whether any of them have any acting experience. Usually, some of them do (theatre majors often take writing classes at the university where I teach; they are complementary disciplines) and I make note of who they are so that I can mine that knowledge in class. For example, in discussing a passage where an author is trying to show a character's emotion rather than tell it, I might ask 'Candace', one of my actors, how she would interpret a line of dialogue if she were portraying that character.

What I'm trying to develop in a workshop is an awareness of how the 'senses' students are developing in my course and as writers can help them outside my classroom, and how they can enhance their cultivation of those 'senses'. In doing so, I want them to start seeing that stories are in play everywhere, not just in a book or a drama or in a fellow classmate's novel excerpt, and that empathy is a universally critical skill not just in creating strong characters but in relating to one's boss or client or seatmate on a plane.

Finally, I don't want my students' inquiry into the culture around them to end with my workshop; I want it to begin there. Nothing makes me happier than when a student sends me a message about a new book, article, blog or cartoon that is a 'must read', because it shows me that they have turned their 'curiosity' outward where it is likely to stay. I don't want to make mini versions of myself out of my students; I recognize that the world that they are embarking on from my workshops is radically different from the one I entered into from my own workshops in the 1990s and that their paths will ultimately be quite different. But I want the workshops I organize to be useful to them in *their* worlds, and so if I could choose one characteristic to pass to them, it would be a writerly interest in the world around *me* that serves to keep me current in literary culture in important ways that lead to success. I want nothing less for my students. Like Leahy, I want them to be curious! I want them to be nerds![20]

---

[20] Leahy, p. 52.

Writing Exercises

1. Think about articles and books (poetry, fiction, nonfiction, etc.) that you've read that relate to the culture you're living and working in, in the early twenty-first century. Choose one that you think a peer should read, and write a letter to them explaining why they should read it and how it will help them develop as a writer.

2. Create for yourself a one, three, five and ten-year plan. Write about where you want to be in your development as a writer in each of these stages and how you plan to achieve it. Hint: Try to be as specific as possible, i.e. instead of 'Write best-selling true crime novel and retire to the Caribbean', for year five, consider a list of items: have established a regular writing routine, live in a place that makes it possible for me to write, surround myself with people who understand my need to write regularly, and so forth.

3. Think of story you have written (by story I am not limiting you to a short story but referring to any kind of writing that features a complete unit of narrative). Write the title here and then list five other ways/formats through which you could tell the same story.

Books on Contemporary Culture and Creativity

Csikszentmihalyi, Mihaly, *Creativity: Flow and the Psychology of Discovery and Invention* (New York: Harper-Perennial, 2008)

Csikszentmihalyi, Mihaly, *Flow: The Psychology of Optimal Experience* (New York: Harper-Perennial, 2008)

Flaherty, Alice Weaver, *The Midnight Disease: The Drive to Write, Writer's Block, and the Creative Brain* (New York: Houghton-Mifflin, 2004)

Florida, Richard, *The Rise of the Creative Class and How It's Transforming Work, Leisure, Community and Everyday Life* (New York: Basic Books, 2003)

Friedman, Thomas L., *The World is Flat 3.0: A Brief History of the 21st Century* (New York: Picador, 2007)

Gladwell, Malcolm, *Blink: The Power of Thinking Without Thinking* (New York: Little, Brown and Company, 2005)

Jenkins, Henry, *Convergence Culture: Where Old and New Media Collide* (New York: New York University Press, 2008)

Lloyd, Carol, *Creating a Life Worth Living: A Personal Course in Career Design for Artists, Innovators and Others Aspiring to a Creative Life* (New York: Harper, 1997)

Maisel, Eric, *Fearless Creating: A Step-by-Step Guide to Starting and Completing Your Work of Art* (New York: Tarcher, 1995)

McGonigal, Jane, *Reality is Broken: Why Games Make us Better and How They Can Change the World* (New York: Penguin, 2011)

Pink, Daniel, *A Whole New Mind: Why Right Brainers Will Rule the Future* (New York: Riverhead, 2006)

Pink, Daniel, *Drive: The Surprising Truth About What Motivates Us* (New York: Riverhead, 2011)

Pink, Daniel, *The Adventures of Johnny Bunko: The Last Career Guide You'll Ever Need* (New York: Riverhead, 2008)

Robinson, Ken, *The Element: How Finding Your Passion Changes Everything* (New York: Penguin, 2009)

Tharp, Twyla, *The Creative Habit: Learn it and Use it for Life* (New York: Simon and Schuster, 2005)

Works Cited

Coles, Robert, *The Call of Stories: Teaching and the Moral Imagination* (New York: Mariner Books, 1990)

Fenza, D.W., 'Creative Writing and Its Discontents, *AWP Chronicle* (2001)

Golman, Daniel, *Emotional Intelligence: Why it Can Matter More than IQ* (New York, Bantam, 2006)

Kim, J., '10 Digital Competencies for Every Graduate', *Inside Higher Education* (2010). Available at:
http://www.insidehighered.com/blogs/technology_and_learning/10_competencies_for_every_graduate

Leahy, Anna, 'Who Wants to Be a Nerd: Or, How Cognitive Science Changed My Teaching', *New Writing: The International Journal for the Practice and Theory of Creative Writing* 7.1 (2010), pp. 45-52

Pink, Daniel, *A Whole New Mind: Why Right Brainers Will Rule the Future* (New York: Riverhead, 2006)

Twelve syllogisms in search of an editor

Fiona Sampson

1. Language is occasional word-use.

    1.1. Language lives primarily in the ear and in the eye.

    1.1.1. This 'eye' is here taken to include an equivalent spatial mnemonic, through touch, used by people with visual impairment.

    1.2. In the contemporary West, every occasion of language use either occupies, or implies the use of, both ear and eye.

    1.2.1. Although degrees of implication are involved. When someone without literacy solves the problem of getting a stranger to read them a timetable by pretending to have lost their glasses, a different degree of proximity between eye and ear is exploited than that which opens up when an interviewee speaks 'off the record'.

2. Text is an occasion on which particular words are used in a particular order.

3. The literary text has a sense of occasion about its particular words and the order in which they're used.

4. This sense of occasion has some analogies with rite.

    4.1. As with rite, the individual experience is vested in and produced by an intrinsically public occasion.

    4.2. And the occasion on which a specific literary text occurs may be temporally diffuse, that is non-simultaneous, but is self-limiting.

    4.3. In other words, a literary text, which stages its own beginning, middle and end, is essentially performative.

    4.3.1. The same may be said of some but not all non-literary texts. For example, a shopping list is clearly performative, not in the sense that it is a cue to actions but in the sense that one can 'come to the end of it'. On the other hand, an advertising slogan, which one may encounter repeatedly and which would ideally like to address one near-constantly, from a range of media, is designed *not* to be 'got to the end of', in the crude temporal sense.

4.3.2. Within the temporo-spatial occasion of its 'performance', the literary text is also, because of its multiplicity of possible readings and resonances, uniquely unsusceptible to paraphrase: *vide* the controversy that inevitably accompanies literary translation. Therefore, unlike a shopping list, it performs not only its own symbolic function – or 'meaning' – but its whole own self.

5. The literary text is a particular kind of occasion in which there is a dialectic between the individual experience, of both reader and writer, and the public form

5.1. This dialectic is necessary but varies according to the individual involved.

5.2. Their necessary but varied relationship with the textual occasion is an equivalence between readers and writer in their relation to that text.

6. The diffuseness of the literary text thus allows for a particular degree of variation in individual experience.

6.1. Other textual occasions may also be temporally diffuse, but their relative lack of sense of occasion means they have limited ability to stage a discrete experience for the individual.

7. It is therefore difficult to establish some individual experiences – versions or reactions – of a literary text as having more authority than others.

8. Poets and their readers unite in potential, and sometimes actual, mistrust of the intervention of editorial choice in the broad church of individual literary experience.

8.1. Literary editorship is a profession under threat – from the economic collapse in publishing; from the squeeze in public subsidy of the arts, and the redirection of that subsidy towards less controversial, non-literary, social criteria (such as access and representation); and from the rise of bar-room ready-reaction in the blogosphere, whose central tenet is that expertise in reading and writing cannot be developed because it does not exist.

8.1.1. After the death of God in the twentieth century, the twenty-first century embraces the death of value, in which every opinion is equivalent.

8.1.2. Surely, the argument goes, there is nothing beyond personal self-interest. The writer wants her text, and the reader his opinion, to be heard as loudly and widely as possible. An advertising slogan takes hold not through the intrinsic pleasure of the text, but by sheer repetition. This is the egalitarian, post-value model. Excellence has been replaced by success.

8.1.3. It is also a post-literary model. The literary is precisely that which *does* have a sense of its own occasion, celebrates its own spatio-temporal boundaries, and does not look to resources outside itself to create that sense of occasion.

8.2. It is foolhardy indeed to try to earn your living as an editor and critic in the twenty-first century.

9. To be foolhardy enough to do so, you must have a sense of the persistence of the literary beyond the death of value.

9.1. You must also believe it persists beyond the particular occasion.

9.2. The rule of three states that three is the minimum number of protagonists required for arbitration. Only with the arrival of a third protagonist is there a potential referee.

9.3. The persistence of the [principle of the] literary is the third force in any disagreement between individual experiences of a literary text.

9.3.1. Although under the doctrine of absolute equivalence of views, differences of experience should not logically be treated as disagreements.

9.4. It is not the role of these syllogisms to suggest the essential nature of the literary – is it ahistorical, or consensual? – nor its place in society. These important questions require a whole volume to themselves.

10. The editor may be defined as the reader who brings a wider, non occasion-specific, sense of the literary to the reading room.

    10.1. 'The literary' is the collective identity and qualities of every individual literary text, or occasion.

        10.1.1. This does not mean that it is done collectively, but that it is a collection of innumerable individual actions and experiences.

    10.2. The literary is the name of a set of *practices* – that is, of *what is done* – rather than of a discipline or of abstract knowledge.

    10.3. The literary is itself, therefore, performative.

11. When the literary text says, *I am what I do*, it means both that it should be judged and experienced in its own terms and that if it fails in those terms – if it leaves something unexpressed or confused, for example – it has failed.

    11.1. Literary texts can fail as well as succeed.

12. When an editor says, *I am what I do*, she means that she is only reading from and for the literary. She doesn't read for friendship or out of prejudice or ambition, for example.

    12.1. Literary editing can fail as well as succeed.

Writing Exercise

There are several ways to practice editing. The first two are a bit like playing air guitar.

First: since, of all publications, literary magazines bear the strongest marks of editorial intervention, take a look at several issues of a few different periodicals, and ask yourself which you enjoy and why. Now ask yourself what you think their weak points are. Finally, imagine you are the editor of the issue you have in your hand. Assume that the material already in the magazine is all you have available to work with: a typical editorial experience. Would you:

1. Change the order of work,
2. Edit any pieces more closely – pruning them or changing passages (and how) and,
3. Delete the single weakest piece?

Secondly, once you've done this to a magazine, try doing the same with a single author book – poetry or short story collection, or full-length prose volume. This is harder to do, because this material is less differentiated – but try not to think of the book as one artistic whole that cannot be modified. Instead, view it as a series of poems, passages, or even 'pages of text', and ask yourself (using the strategy above) what needs changing.

The third exercise asks you to imagine that your own manuscript, or portfolio, doesn't belong to you but is someone else's work. It's being submitted to you for publication in a high-profile edition – and you do want to publish it. But at the same time its weak points – every lapse from completely authoritative professionalism, from typos to weirdly over-written passages – will undermine your own professional credibility. They will also undermine the author's own success – and your role is to protect them from their own weaknesses in this way. Now, what would you change?

Permission, Potency and Protection in the Creative Writing Workshop

Adam Baron

Action research is a methodology that allows continuing professional development within teaching practice through a cycle of active teaching and reflection upon it. This reflection can be subsequent to teaching or part of the cycle of any one teaching moment (lecture, class, seminar etc.). This short paper will use Action Research to investigate the behaviour of students beginning a Creative Writing Degree through the application of Eric Berne's theories of Transactional Analysis.[1] Specifically it will look at good or bad seminar attendance and the subsequent participation or lack of it within seminars. How do the previous (pre-university) experiences of students within educational and familial contexts inform their ability to learn within tutor-guided small groups? Can established behavioural patterns within a 'Berne-ian' Parent/Adult/Child model be either reconfigured or enhanced to provide more productive learning transactions?

My desire to research in this area comes from my practice of Creative Writing teaching within the context of a student body comprising a widely varying quality of pre-existing skill sets. Kingston University is attended by a hugely diverse range of students coming from almost every educational, social and racial background imaginable. I have taught students of great talent and enthusiasm but also students with poor basic skills and little desire to engage with their studies. The limited success I have had in drawing the seemingly less able students towards higher achievement levels has instilled in me a desire to better understand the effect that the Higher Education template has upon them when they arrive here. My equally limited successes in upping seminar attendance and active participation of all attending students has led me to reflect critically on two things. Firstly, why have some of the methods I have used failed while others have succeeded? Secondly, how can I place these successes within a theoretical framework, to achieve more consistently positive results?

Berne's two seminal works (*Games People Play* and *Transactional Analysis In Psychotherapy*) externalise Freudian theories of the SuperEgo, Ego, and Id. They have demonstrated to me convincingly that personality states can radically inform the approach people take to the kind of interpersonal

---

[1] Eric Berne, *Transactional Analysis In Psychotherapy* (1961); (2001) and *Games People Play: The Psychology of Human Relationships* (1964).

relationships that are essential to effective learning in Creative Writing. By placing just two students within Berne's model I hope to show that optimum attendance and participation will be a boon to student learning. Only by drawing students slowly towards a state in which complementary transactions can occur will the desired attendance/participation be achieved.

As an experienced writer it was a temptation to believe that my role as teacher was the transference of knowledge. For example, introducing eight characters on the first page of a novel is confusing for the reader and it is much better to begin with one or two, and seed the rest of the characters in later. Is my role not, therefore, simply to convey this piece of scholarship, relevant to my field? Anne Brockbank and Ian McGill demonstrate that a greater personal commitment to teaching practice is required, a 'transformative' result being achieved that promotes 'reflective learning in student learners'.[2] While this and many other theories of learning begin to seem self evident (and seem to say little specifically about seminar attendance) I found in revisiting texts from my own field, an approach more relevant to Creative Writing teaching that complements my reading of Berne. Janet Burroway talks about writing workshops as 'a democratisation of the material for college study' and stresses the need for 'mutual goodwill' within them.[3] She quotes the writer Robert Morgan who does not believe that Creative Writing knowledge can be passed on from instructor to student in the way that ideas in physics can. He sees the writing teacher as someone who builds up students' confidence levels so that they effectively teach themselves. In another course book Burroway identifies a problem central to the teaching of Creative Writing. The students' academic output is writing and 'all writing is autobiographical as well as invented'.[4] From this I realise that knowledge of Creative Writing craft cannot be passed on without viewing the student holistically. Techniques must be employed to encourage attendance and participation if personal hurdles to learning are to be overcome. Without participation there is no learning. Participation however is more than an active engagement with the seminar and a wiliness to make comments or read out work. As Robert McKee points out, success in writing (and in writing-learning) can only come with increased self knowledge.[5] The work is an objective correlative of their inner

---

[2] Anne Brockbank and Ian McGill, *Facilitating Reflective Learning in Higher Education* (1998), p. 119.
[3] Janet Burroway, *Writing Fiction: A Guide to Narrative Craft* (2007), p. xii.
[4] Janet Burroway, *Imaginative Writing: The Elements of Craft* (2007)), p. xxii.
[5] Robert McKee, *Story: substance, structure, style, and the principles of screenwriting* (1998), p. 66.

states and can only be produced with an active engagement in seminar (i.e. complementary, adult-to-adult transactions).

I have already mentioned my desire to make correlations between where students come from educationally and their willingness to engage in Creative Writing seminars. It is by using Berne's theories that I will try to counteract these assumptions, demonstrating that such an action is not an Adult one but the act of a Child. Berne splits our ego states into three: Parent/Child/Adult. To begin with the Parent state, he asserts that it is characterised by received ideas that have been unchallenged since they were instilled in childhood. If I extend this to what I will call childhood learning states (pre-university) I can see immediately the relevance of Berne to my Level four Seminar.

Student Felix has not been equipped with sufficient grammar skills in childhood (crucial to Creative Writing). He has also been viewed as a poor student and sees himself as such (without putting that to the test). He attends seminar rarely and says little but he is perfectly capable of punctuality and participation as his active engagement in a rap band makes clear. When dealing with his peers, Felix acts in the way he wants to, but when he approaches seminar he reverts to previously internalised ideas about himself ('I am a poor student with poor skills. I now have freedom not to engage in learning that makes me feel useless, so will not.') It is not the study itself that he doesn't want to engage with because I make it perfectly clear that he can write rap in class. It is, in fact, me (as representative of authority) he wants to avoid because he cannot help but revert to a Child/Parent relationship that actually no longer applies to him.

It is up to me, therefore, to break Felix out of this and draw him towards the Adult: i.e., a logical assessment of whether seminar attendance would benefit him. The answer is 'yes' because he is a passionate rapper and we could study good examples in this form to find out how they work. But unless I can help him change his attitude towards learning as it is now (towards adult learning from child learning) he will not see this. I need to break his habit of transferring feelings he had during childhood towards authority figures, to me.

I would like to have the opportunity to apply Berne's theories directly to Felix in the context of Action Research. It would be instructive to work in tandem with a psychotherapist trained in Berne's theories to see if his seminar attendance and participation improve. As it is, by asking Felix to perform his rap at our Awards and Achievements show I was able to make him realise that he can bring his passion into an educational context. I did this by moving my relationship with him into an Adult/

Adult one. I did this through what Berne terms 'Stroking'[6]: Instead of telling him to study certain rappers I told him which ones I liked. They were of course outdated sources and he was able (while appreciating that I had some knowledge) to interact with me on the subject, advising me of better rappers than the ones I'd mentioned. The transaction was now what Berne termed Complementary. I was communicating from my Adult state and Felix was replying from his (no longer the badly equipped child). Felix realised that the structure of our seminar was one he could fit into without being reminded of childish states that were unrewarding. His membership of a band had shown that he was, as Berne put it, 'structure hungry'.[7] I was able to show him that the structure of seminar and learning was one he could engage with.

The Child ego state represents not the received learning we have within us but the actual way we respond to the world. The Natural Child responds as s/he sees fit, to events and people, genuinely expressing themselves. The Adaptive Child does not. Rather, s/he has gained a sense of what wins parental approval and acts accordingly. In my Level four seminar, Jane attends every week. She answers questions when asked, presents her work, and fulfills all assessment requirements. Her work is well punctuated and clear, Jane having learned all the necessary skills to please her former teachers. In an Adult Learning environment however she will not achieve her potential (or the First she badly wants). She has transferred her Adaptive Child status and I cannot interact with her in a way that is complementary. Rather, our transactions are crossed. I approach her from an Adult state and want an Adult response. I want her short story to be about her in a real way. I want her to be honest in it and reveal herself. What I get is a decent piece of prose with no insight into who she really is. Jane is curtailing herself and her creativity by her desire to achieve my approval. To my Adult she responds dutifully and enthusiastically, but as a Child.

How could I help Jane to better learning using Transactional Analysis, twinned with Action Research? Berne speaks about Permission. I can, firstly, free Jane from sharing her work in class (knowing she will definitely do it). I can talk not about her work but its context: not the rather anodyne scene in the nightclub that she wrote, but what Jane and her friends actually do when they go out. I can show her that unlike in her Childhood state, I am not there to make judgement on her or her behaviour. She can

---

[6] Berne defined a *stroke* as the 'fundamental unit of social action'. A stroke is a unit of recognition, when one person recognises another person either verbally or non verbally.

[7] Berne, *Games People Play*, p. 17.

share her real ideas with me in class and then in her work and we will then have complementary transactions.

Another tool in this example would be the notion of Potency and Protection. Vigour and self assurance will let Jane know that I really am not going to let her hide within her Adaptive Child status. Protection means that if Jane really does let go of her true thoughts and feelings, I will be (subsequently) supportive to her both academically and pastorally. She will be losing me as a surrogate parent by entering a complementary transaction with me. This may be too traumatic for her and she may be reluctant to take this path. Like many students who begin their studies as good, competent, solid, she may end just the same. How do I convince her to take the leap? One way to move her towards a more Adult/Adult learning zone would be to free myself of the need to mark her work. If I tell her, as I will, that someone else will be doing that, she might feel a sense of release. She might be able to engage with me, and other tutors, rather than trying to impress us.

A brief look at Transactional Analysis in the context of seminar attendance and participation shows me that even the most cursory psychological investigation of the student body can reap great rewards. By understanding the position of each of our students on a Berne-ian scale we can help move them towards more fruitful educational transactions. It would help draw our weaker and less motivated students into the learning environment in a way that is meaningful for them. It would also stretch the students who seem to be more able and who often slip under the radar, writing perfectly acceptable work week after week. And while Berne's model may seem formulaic and all encompassing, it really can help to create productive adult relationships within the seminar room.

Writing exercise

To find a character's voice write a harangue, or rant, in which he or she blurts out their opposition to something or someone they despise. Take ten minutes to do this and write without pausing.

Works Cited

Berne, Eric, *Transactional Analysis In Psychotherapy* (1961); (London: Souvenir Press, 2001)

---. *Games People Play: The Psychology of Human Relationships* (Harmondsworth: Penguin, 1964)

Brockbank, Anne and Ian McGill, *Facilitating Reflective Learning in Higher Education* (Milton Keynes, Open University Press, 1998)

Burroway, Janet, *Writing Fiction: A Guide to Narrative Craft* (Pearson Longman, 2007)

Burroway, Janet, *Imaginative Writing: The Elements of Craft* (Pearson Longman, 2007)

McKee, Robert, *Story: substance, structure, style, and the principles of screenwriting* (London: Methuen, 1998)

The Queerosphere: Musings on Queer Studies and Creative Writing Classrooms (On Poetry, Creativity, and the Fleetingness of Things)

(For Steve Butterman and his extraordinary students)

Maureen Seaton

1. Whenever I think of the Queerosphere I think of the first time I went to my friend Steve's Queer Studies class and I was a big queer about to talk about queer queer queer. I wasn't *too* self-conscious, with a Big Q carved into my forehead and Queen Latifah tattooed on my right ankle. No, really, my first time in Steve's classroom I was nervous because I was no longer with the woman I'd been with in the book of poems his students had just finished reading and were going to ask me questions about and that just seemed wrong. (Steve has his students make up questions, and unlike a lot of students in other classrooms in other places, they actually do make up questions.) Now I've been to Steve's *queerospheric* classroom (a term he made up) many times, and I think of his students with great warmth. In fact, these musings could be called 'Steve's Students', because it is about them, really, at the heart – all of their faces turned upward with what I can only call queer anticipation.

2. With my own student poets I am less comfortable being that queer. It's because I'm afraid of stepping on their toes and/or eliciting responses of not exactly homophobia but something more like a judgment that might sound like this: *That queer only wants to teach us about other queers.* I know, this isn't giving my students a lot of credit, but I have to admit I have trouble when anyone's curriculum, including my own, is heavily weighted in any direction. Right now I'm not talking about a Queer Studies classroom, but a Creative Writing classroom, so my mind is a bit confused, which I actually take to be the first step in either the queer impulse or the creative writing impulse – any impulse that ends in creating anything, in fact. So perhaps my confusion is seeking an answer and perhaps there is an answer, and

my queer impulse, which gets mixed up with my creative writing impulse, which is okay, really, is seeking this particular answer. But answers seem anti-queer unless they are simply lighted upon for a second, a proboscis extended into the flower's honey, and then the creature moves on. My classroom is not a queer studies classroom, yet I am a study in queer. Steve's classroom is a queer studies classroom and Steve is also a study in queer. We've known each other a while now. We both like to create things and we both like to eat. We both like to look at lakes (which we're doing right now) and we both like to fly, but not in planes. Steve's students love me for being their queer guest writer. My own students have more ambivalence about me because to them I am like a teacherly mother of some sort and they actually don't like to think of me having any sex at all, with anyone.

3.   *...in constant motion/mutilation.* This phrase interests me and it raises another memory from the Andy Goldsworthy documentary Steve and I just watched where the sculptor talks about destruction. I'm all for destruction as a part of creation. So constant motion must mean mutilation, although the word destruction appeals to me a little more than the word mutilation because mutilation seems to come from without, whereas destruction, to me, can come from within. Am I judging that? One of the basics I embrace is 'Don't judge.' Also: 'Don't limit.' This may make me more queer than who I sleep with, certainly, and perhaps extremely queer in the way I create and teach, because if all is in constant motion, which it is (and we are), then nothing can be judged because nothing stays itself long enough to be judged. Or analyzed. Well, anything may be judged or analyzed, but perhaps it is queer to remember that one is only analyzing a certain iteration of a certain thing (or a certain person) that exists in a single moment of time and space. Speaking of Fernando Pessoa (which Steve and I were doing a few minutes ago), I would love to be able to wrap my mind around the idea of a poet writing extensively in more than 72 personas. (Pessoa called them his heteronyms.) I'd settle for the ability to write as even one other person. I do often speak in parentheticals, which could be a sign of someone lurking. (A woman just walked by with beautiful hair. Maybe her.) What does this have to do with teaching?

4. I guess there are many ways to and around the pedagogy of poetry. A wise lesbian once suggested to me that poetry was not generally accessible simply because its ideas had not been thought of yet by the general population, that its nature was of 'one who has yet to come'. (Quotes mine.) In this way it spearheads creativity and perhaps culture itself, leading us forward through its images and metaphors. This consoled me then and it consoles me now but has little (?) to do with our topic of the day, which is about the queerospheric classroom. I would say that poetry is not inherently a queer literary genre but that because poetic license exists even in the mind of the general population as an accepted possibility, poetry lends itself to a queer literary genre a bit more than the others. I'm troubled by theory, but that would be like saying I'm troubled by the message of Christ or the teachings of Buddha or the way Isis mothers us or Moses leads us into the sea. And I am. There's a coot moving across the lake now. I am like him in that I am moving like a shadow across a larger body than mine, because I am dedicated to the other side of the lake and therefore preoccupied with my vision. This is where my life resembles the life of Mary Shelley, the way she sat down with a few friends one night and said, 'Let's see who can write the scariest story ever written'. I am like that about so many things, trying to scare myself and everyone else with my inability to paddle in a straight predictable line.

5. It's like watching a person move from the sun to the moonlight, no, vice versa – there is a shift, who cares in which direction? Neither is elite, neither from a place of sore loser. I can't ever remember when I was sure. I've been so queer for so long I can't remember any other name besides Slim Shaky. (This is not a heteronym, Steve, please don't expect a letter from Slim anytime soon.) Am I hopelessly unable to write analytically at this point? Do I want to do that in this piece of writing that borders on the prose poem? The prose poem, now there's a queer genre, if ever. Yet it seems to have been appropriated quite solidly by straight white men, which is okay, isn't it? Was Baudelaire gay? Rimbaud? Stein? I want to stay here now, sitting in the sun until my vitamin D level rises above sea level. Why are the gulls upset? How do I know they're upset? Am I frustrated because I haven't written a damn thing from my left brain all day and my right brain is mutating with each stroke of the keys. No. It is all the

same, all light and all the moon's umbra. Who else is so lucky they get to do this, sit and feel this thin soft moment? What is queer about the classroom is that it is always moving like those coots, those gulls, that it defies definition but not in a defensive way. It simply falls through the fingers like lake water. Organic. Authentic. Is this too much to want? Is *queering* a fractal situation or do fractals live deep in the bodies of queers as they live in anyone? That is the joke *and* the bible story – the truth, you might say, if there was such as thing as truth, if there was such as thing as you.

Writing Exercise

Exquisite Ekphrastic 'Sonnet' (for two)

Poetic collaboration, especially when your composed lines are initially hidden, offers fabulous opportunities to shake up the process – alter it, stretch it, gloss it, queer it. So once my students have traveled the raucous road of surrealist games together (Exquisite Corpse, etc.), I present the Exquisite Ekphrastic Sonnet:

1. *Pick your collaborator.* (Be choosey, but open.)
2. *Pick a work of art you can both talk to.* (This poem is in second person. The 'you' of the painting/sculpture/ photo may be animal/vegetable/mineral. Just make sure you're compelled to address it, whatever it is: 'If ever a building deserved a friend, it's you.')
3. *Write seven lines each quickly, trust first thoughts, do not show your partner yet.* (Sit by the painting – at a museum or gallery or on your computer screen – with your paper and pen. Write to the curly dog running wild through sheep: 'Your rear end is missing, but you are strong'.)
   a. Collaborator 1: Number your seven lines with odd numbers.
   b. Collaborator 2: Number your seven lines with even numbers.
4. *When finished, read lines back and forth in order.* (Laugh with merriment, embarrassment, wonder.)

P.S. You may choose to leave the 'sonnet' as is, fourteen lines of fantasticness, or you may be compelled to give the sonnet its 'turn' by moving lines around. Tinker in any way you like – or not, it's up to you. It's a collab: odd, imperfect, lovable. Try variations: 'about', not 'to'; or in a larger group with any number of lines; or set your own rules or non-rules. Type up. Perform queerly.

(Thanks to Neil de la Flor, who maniacally played this with me, summer 2010, in New Mexico and Florida: 'Inside you are a princess holding a lamb with a silver head.')

Carnival Girl (after Rodney Hatfield)

1. You wear chicken legs like a contortionist wears tights.
2. Surrounded by blood, you look like a spaceman.
3. How many times will you steal a human's head?
4. Your own head is a square that cuts you off at the neck.
5. Your arms are barely there.
6. Your pigtails are chopped and fading.
7. Where is your crown?
8. Where are your hands?
9. You lost your right breast to a collector.
10. You're divided into 3 parts.
11. You're shaped like a rectangle.
12. In the mirror you look like a girl in the mirror.
13. Your mouth is a perpetual hole, your eyes dumb.
14. Where is your mother?

The Archive of Imagination: Using Oral Tradition in the Teaching of Creative Writing

Éilís Ní Dhuibhne

The context of the curriculum

In September 2006 U.C.D. (University College Dublin) introduced a one year full time M.A. programme in Creative Writing. This M.A. is taught in the context of current educational principles and agreements, most notably the Bologna Process of 1999.[1] Ireland is one of 46 signatories to this agreement between European Education Ministers which, as Geraldine O'Neill comments, 'provided many European universities with a blueprint for supporting staff in developing transparent learning outcomes and as a consequence facilitates student mobility'.[2] The credit-based modular system of the European Credit Transfer and Accumulation System (ECTS) was introduced to U.C.D. as a result of the Bologna Process, as was the stipulation that universities supply and publish module descriptors and learning outcomes.[3]

Nationally, the dominant influence on the design of all curricula in U.C.D., including Creative Writing, is the National Framework of Qualifications, established in 2003 – the N.F.Q.[4] The N.F.Q., drawing on the Bologna guidelines, established a qualifications framework 'which is precise, transparent and internationally acceptable'.[5] According to the N.F.Q.'s Grid of Level Indicators, an M.A. programme is a Level Nine qualification. This Grid lists eight specific learning outcomes, encompassing competencies, skills and knowledge, which are expected of a graduate from a Level Nine programme.[6] The

---

[1] Bologna 1999: http://ec.europa.eu/education/higher-education/doc1290_en.html.

[2] Geraldine O'Neill, 'Initiating curriculum revision: exploring the practices of educational developers', *International Journal for Academic Development*, 15.1, (2010), p. 64.

[3] http://ec.europa.eu/education/lifelong-learning-policy/doc48_en.htm.

[4] University awards and the National Framework of Qualifications (NFQ): *Issues around the design of Programmes and the Use and Assessment of Learning Outcomes* (FIN, 2009), p.6. Also online

[5] Ibid., p.6.

[6] See http://ec.europa.eu/education/lifelong-learning-policy/doc/eqf/ireland3_en.pdf.

curriculum for the M.A. in Creative Writing in U.C.D. has inevitably been influenced by Bologna and the N.F.Q.: e.g. the programme is modular and awards ECTS credits. Since 2007, it has published on the U.C.D. website Module Descriptors and Learning Outcomes.

It is likely that the expansion of the curriculum from the traditional workshop model, to include more structured modules, results from the influence of Bologna and U.C.D.'s compliance with its requirements. Traditionally, academic creative writing programmes in the U.S. and the U.K. emphasised process and praxis, rather than product. They were loosely structured and heavily based on the workshop model,[7] and the first Irish programmes followed this template.[8] While the workshop method has stood the test of time, it has its limitations. Graduates can complain that in that type of programme 'nobody taught me anything; people talked about my work'.

The principles of educational agreements such as Bologna and the N.F.Q. tend to emphasise product (or content) rather than process (or practice). How suited these blueprints are to 'studio-subjects' like art, music or creative writing, is debatable. However, the requirement that fourth level university courses meet certain standards as far as product is concerned, i.e. that as well as providing opportunities for praxis, feedback, and apprenticeship, they also 'teach something', is essentially welcome. And even though Creative Writing is such a new subject, taught by writers (like me) who have not themselves taken a degree in Creative Writing – such programmes did not exist in Ireland until very recently – the requirements of the ECTS system provides guidelines which have been useful aids to designing an innovative and stimulating curriculum which goes 'beyond the workshop'.

The Curriculum in Creative Writing needs to tread a tightrope between over-systematisation and such vague construction that it is not really an academic curriculum at all, but a Listowel Writers' Week extended over two semesters on a campus.[9] It needs to support the freedom which is essential to creativity, but also to provide students with the knowledge and the gateways to knowledge which they are so eager to acquire – it should 'talk about' and encourage their work but also needs to *teach something*. The frameworks of Bologna and the N.F.Q. have

---

[7] See Mark McGurl, *The Program Era, Postwar Fiction and the Rise of Creative Writing* (2009).

[8] For example, the Oscar Wilde Centre Trinity College, Dublin http://www.tcd.ie/OWC/.

[9] Established in 1970, the Listowel Writers' Week in North Kerry has been recognized as the primary event in Ireland's literary calendar http://writersweek.ie/.

ensured that the curriculum of the M.A. in Creative Writing in U.C.D. has avoided – or been rescued from – the danger of excessive informality: of having no academic curriculum at all. The central requirements of transparency, structure, and goal-directed teaching, which underpin these processes, are precisely what the discipline of Creative Writing needed to design a thoughtful curriculum and to justify its place in the university.

The U.C.D. curriculum in Creative Writing, designed after the Bologna agreement, mixes apprenticeship with structured modules, process with product, and thus offers a package which may be more satisfactory to a talented writing student eager to develop her own creativity, but also eager to learn new skills and acquire knowledge.

Beyond the workshop

One of the competencies specified in the Irish N.F.Q. is '"Learning to Learn", to self-evaluate and take responsibility for continuing academic/professional development'.[10] This is a clear goal of the curriculum of the U.C.D M.A. in Creative Writing. Students are taught to educate themselves, as writers and readers. For instance, modules on 'Reading and Writing the Novel', 'Reading and Writing Poetry', and 'Reading and Writing the Short Story' combine textual analysis with creative writing practice, and highlight the close connection between reading and writing.

The module entitled 'The Archive of Imagination' is another course that fulfills the 'Learning to Learn' requirement, and which blends process and product. The course was introduced in 2008, and is a good example of how innovative product-oriented teaching can blend readily with the traditional workshop pedagogy, with outcomes as exciting and rewarding as they are unpredictable.

Originally the idea behind 'The Archive of Imagination' module was that students of creative writing would be introduced to the U.C.D. archive of literary manuscripts, which contains the papers of important Irish writers (many of them graduates of U.C.D.) such as Mary Lavin, Edna O'Brien, Frank McGuinness, Colm Toibin, Maeve Binchy, among others.[11] However, another extremely important archive in U.C.D. is that of the National Folklore Collection, formerly the Department of

---

[10] http://ec.europa.eu/education/lifelong-learning-policy/doc/eqf/ireland2_en.pdf, p.86.
[11] http://www.ucd.ie/archives/html/collections.htm.

Irish Folklore and prior to that, the Irish Folklore Commission.[12] This archive contains more than a million manuscript pages of stories, songs, ethnography, and other kinds of oral tradition, a huge sound recordings archive, and a substantial collection of photographs, film, and other visual records. The Irish Folklore Commission was established in 1935 and its collections moved to U.C.D. in 1972.

I decided to try using the Folklore Archive in my teaching of creative writing, partly because I am very familiar with it, having studied Folklore there myself and having frequently drawn on its resources in my own fiction and drama. Since beginner writers have a huge appetite for 'triggers' and, to paraphrase W.B. Yeats, are often in search of a theme, an acquaintance with the superabundance of themes available in the folklore collection was likely to be useful to them, purely at the level of idea or content. In addition, from an educational point of view, it is important for students of creative writing in U.C.D. to be aware of the existence of the National Folklore Collection, one of the great literary treasures of the university, and of the world.

How, specifically, can oral narratives be useful to writers?

Folklorists have always observed and investigated the fertilization of literature by oral tradition, which is especially evident in medieval literature, since early writers often drew their stories directly from oral sources and wrote their own versions of them, essentially participating in a process of dissemination similar to that in which oral narrators engage (i.e. hearing a tale, retelling it, passing it on). However, folklorists generally stress the stylistic and technical difference between oral narrative and written literature. Oral narrative observes conventions, many of which result from the exigencies of the process of storytelling and listening: for instance, narrators need tricks or techniques to aid the memory; listeners need a clear uncomplicated narrative strand if they are to understand what they are hearing. Devices such as repetition, and the insertion of stock descriptive passages ('rhetorical runs', in Irish tradition), are examples of devices that make the task of remembering and telling long stories easier for the oral narrator. Such tricks are of no particular benefit to the writer, who is not under pressure to remember and perform as s/he creates. Readers, also, have an easier time of it than listeners. If concentration lapses or the text

---

[12] http://www.ucd.ie/folklore/en/.

becomes complicated, a reader can always turn back the pages and re-read. People listening to a story haven't got this luxury; they need to follow the thread of the story and it has to be linear. 'Meanwhile, back at the ranch' does not work in oral narrative.

While early writers used the content of oral stories – the plots, characters and ideas – they discovered early on that they had much more stylistic and compositional freedom than storytellers. The distinction between oral and literary narratives is famously described by the Danish folklorist, Axel Olrik, in his essay 'The Epic Laws of Folk Narrative', written in 1908, but still one of the most useful descriptions of oral narrative technique and structure.[13] Olrik was one of the first folklorists to describe the narrative patterns of oral stories. Although his implication that narrative obeyed some sort of universal super-organic imperative that is independent of the individual narrator has long been disproved, in general his analysis of patterns in oral stories holds good, especially if one replaces the constraining word 'Law' with a less rigid term, such as 'trend' or 'tendency'. Olrik noted common patterns, to which he gave memorable names such as 'The Law of the Single Strand', 'The Law of Repetition', 'The Law of Opening and Closing', and 'The Law of Three', to name but a few. 'The Law of Opening and Closing', for example, describes the tendency of oral narrators to move gradually into the story, with a formulaic statement such as 'Long long ago', followed by an introduction of character and place, and equally to withdraw slowly from the tale, giving listeners an opportunity to move gradually from the heightened atmosphere of fiction to their own ordinary real world.

As well as naming the 'Laws' of oral narrative, Olrik demonstrates that these formulaic features of oral stories were gradually eliminated from written narrative as written literature developed from classical antiquity onwards. For instance, one of the most striking and immediately obvious patterns in oral narration is the 'ruthlessly rigid' Rule of Three: the widow has three sons, the dragon has three heads, Rumpelstiltskin visits the princess three times. Olrik points out that:

> Nothing distinguishes the great bulk of folk narrative from modern literature and from reality as much as does the number three. Such a ruthlessly rigid structuring of life stands apart from anything else

---

[13] Axel Olrik, 'The Epic Laws of Folk Narrative', in *The Study of Folklore*, ed. Alan Dundes (Englewood Cliffs: Prentice Hall, 1965), pp. 129-41.

[....] Everywhere in classical antiquity, and in the European Middle Ages, one sees how narrative slowly detaches itself from the number three.[14]

Written narrative gradually detached itself from many of the other features of oral narrative structure. 'Get in fast and get out fast' is common contemporary advice for writers of short stories. This is precisely what an oral storyteller would never do; they 'get in slowly and get out slowly', according to Olrik's 'Law of Opening and Closing' (which, by the way, suggests that the 'plunge in' advice is not appropriate for radio stories; but possibly listeners' expectations of how stories work is informed by their experience of reading).

If the history of literature is progressive, it has progressed inexorably away from oral narrative, with its formulaic compositional methods allied to wildly fantastical subject matter. The alliance of predictable form and surrealistic content, which is the hallmark of, say, the wonder-tale (also known as the Märchen or fairytale) has given way to an alliance of realistic content and unpredictable form in the novel. How, then, can contemporary students of creative writing benefit from revisiting ways of storytelling which a writer such as Chaucer decided was old hat more than 600 years ago?

Fairytales: Finding the imagination

When the module 'The Archive of Imagination' began, I was apprehensive about how students who had registered for a Master's in Creative Writing might respond. I had no clear idea of what the results, in the form of students' own creative writing, would be. It is true that I have been inspired by folklore myself, but that was after deep immersion in the subject over several years of post-graduate research and study. The M.A. students were going to get a rapid introduction to this new subject over the course of a 20-hour module. It felt risky. Apart from the challenge of introducing writing students to a new field, there was, as in other modules in the U.C.D. M.A. programme, the challenge of combining product and process, of offering new knowledge to students, while simultaneously providing them with plenty of opportunities to apply that knowledge to their writing. In other words the module had to be both a class or lecture, and a workshop – with the consequent obvious danger of falling between two stools.

---

[14] Olrik, pp. 133-4.

At the outset, I had high hopes of introducing students to several genres of oral art: songs and ballads, legends, jokes, modern legends, the fairytale, children's lore. I wanted to show them everything in the folklore shop. I offered short introductory lectures on a smorgasbord of folkloric genres. Students responded fairly well – some being interested in children's lore, others in the wonder-tale, and one or two in the actual methodology of folklore collecting, which was not a result I had ever foreseen: one student interviewed and recorded the personal memoir of an old relative, following the example of folklore collectors – and this in particular is a good example of how even a quick introduction to a new discipline can revolutionise the way a young writer works, and broaden their horizons and sense of what literature is. (The resulting work was excellent, and challenged my conception of what creative writing is.)

However, I soon found out that a 'stuffed' curriculum for this module had more disadvantages than otherwise. The knowledge students gained of the various genres was superficial, at best. I learned that the content of the course had to be reduced to manageable proportions, if students were to experience some depth rather than just catch a quick, sometimes confusing, glimpse of a ragbag of genres.

The challenge, then, was to select one or two forms of oral tradition from the rich range available, and abandon the rest with regret. It was not difficult to decide on which genres to concentrate on. In the context of fiction writing, the most relevant forms of oral narrative are undoubtedly the wonder-tale, which can be regarded as an antecedent of the novel, and the migratory legend, which has plenty in common with the short story. Therefore I decided to focus on these two genres – although children's lore, songs and ballads, local history lore and memorates,[15] can obviously provide instructive and inspiring material for creative writers.

What do we actually do in the module?

First of all we visit the archive, the National Folklore Collection. Simply moving physically out of the seminar room is an exercise that is always beneficial. Going on a journey, even a very short journey along the corridors of Belfield, activates the imagination. The mere discovery of where the archive is, the exposure to its

---

[15] An anecdote describing a remembered experience, usually autobiographical.

visual art, its sound recordings and handwritten manuscripts, its stacks of index cards, has been of itself an inspiration to some students. And once the location is familiar, they are aware that they can always return and read or carry out research – which a few have done.

The remaining classes are held in the more ordinary context of the classroom, where we read and discuss wonder-tales and legends, and review new stories, poems, and other work, inspired directly or loosely by the oral texts. We begin with an introduction to the international wonder-tale, or fairytale. This is the most exciting genre of oral, and perhaps of any, story. In the wonder-tale the human imagination enjoys its fullest fling. Fantastic, highly stylised, symbolic, poetic, its richness of imagery and symbol contrasts with its simplicity of structure and the flatness of its characterisation. As Max Lüthi comments in *The European Folktale: Form and Nature*, 'The European folktale has a very special power. Not only the children of each new generation feel its attraction, but adults experience its magic again and again as well'.[16]

We look at the index of international folktales compiled by Hans-Jörg Uther, *The Types of International Folktales*, possibly the most inspiring work in the history of indexing.[17] We read examples of Irish and international versions of a small selection of wonder-tales, e.g. 'The Girl as Helper in the Hero's Flight', 'The Dragon Slayer', 'Cinderella'. The concept of variation – that the same story exists in thousands of versions, told by different tellers, in some cases all over the world – is a revelation to many students.

Students are introduced to some work on the style of the wonder-tale, and some interpretations – Bengt Holbek's *Interpretation of Fairytales* and Lüthi's *The European Folktale: Form and Nature* are the best introductions to exploration of meaning and form, respectively, in this kind of narrative.[18] And it is on this significant combination that we focus – the rigid structures, and the accompanying wild cornucopia of fantastical imagery. Some students are particularly interested in structural aspects of tales – responding to what Lüthi claims to be the source of the wonder-tale's power: 'The secret power of the folktale lies not in the motifis it employs, but in the manner in which it uses them –

[16] Max Lüthi, *The European Folktale: Form and Nature* trans. John D. Niles (1986), p. 1.
[17] Hans-Jörg Uther, *The Types of International Folktales: A classification and Bibliography, Based on the System of Antti Aarne and Stith Thompson* (2004).
[18] Bengt Holbek, *Interpretation of Fairytales* (Helsinki: Academia Scientarum Fennica, 1987).

that is, its form'.[19]

The stylised patterning of the narratives – their one dimensionality, their flatness, their use of a limited palette of colours, the use of repetition for emphasis, and particularly 'The Law of Three', fascinate students. Although literary writers abandoned these patterns in the Middle Ages, it is illuminating to revisit the old rules, and to play around with devices such as repetition, triplication, exaggeration, in writing about contemporary subjects. One student's story entitled 'Three Monsters' simply applied the rule of three to a story about mental illness encountering the Irish health service, with brilliant results. Here the juxtaposition of the traditional archetypal structures with contemporary realistic material was outstandingly effective. When I, as a teacher, read that particular student story, I began to reach some understanding of what Creative Writing meant, and what a programme can do to release a student's potential for original invention: cross fertilisation seems to lie at the heart of creativity. In bringing writers to a cultural crossroads, encouraging them to combine old and new ways of composition, one is guiding them towards the liminal space where the imagination is activated and where real innovation and creativity can begin.

While the structural aspects of the fairytale can be inspiring and provide opportunities to experiment with the form and shape of fiction, the symbols and images, the 'motifs' of the traditional tales have a more immediate and obvious appeal – most people find them more powerful than Lüthi would have it. Interpretation of archetypal symbols leads to an expansion of the imagination, a liberation from the shackles of realism.

The (anthropomorphised) North Wind. A loaf of bread wet with human milk. The Impossible Tasks. The ring at the bottom of the well. Stables thatched with feathers and no two feathers from the same bird. Eagles who talk and give lifts on their wing to girls in distress. Transformations – the little white goat who is a goat by day and a handsome prince by night. The magic tablecloth, which when spread on the ground is automatically decked with the best food and wine. The magic comb which when applied to hair turns it blond. The dog who digs a hole in the ground and reveals a flight of stone stairs leading down to another world. These motifs occur in just one version of one fairytale, a version of 'The Girl as Helper in the Hero's Flight' told by a Donegal storyteller, Sorcha Mhic Ghrianna, in 1936.[20] Students often select just a single image or a motif from a story

---

[19] Lüthi, p. 3.

[20] Sorcha Mhic Ghrianna, 'Ri na Fásaighe Duibhne', in *Field Day Anthology of Irish Writing*, Vol. IV, ed. Éilís Ní Dhuibhne (2002), p. 1237 ff.

and create their own fiction around it: Mhic Ghrianna's story, packed with powerful and unusual images, stimulated several good, highly original and unusual stories in U.C.D. in 2009 (some of which later found publishers).

The second form of oral narrative to which students are introduced is the migratory legend. Legends provide an interesting contrast with the wonder-tale – these two oral genres are often defined by juxtaposition with one another, originally in the Grimms' dictum: 'Das Märchen ist poetischer, die Sage ist historischer'.[21] They relate in a way that is not entirely dissimilar to the relationship of the novel to the short story. Wonder-tales are long, multi-episodic and concerned with the overcoming of obstacles by the hero or heroine on the quest for happiness (in the form of wealth and love). Their locations are more or less surreal, and their connection with reality is symbolical rather than representational. Legends, by contrast, are short, realistic, and usually involve the direct encounter of a human protagonist with a supernatural being: a typical legend, popular in Ireland, is the story called by folklorists 'The Man Who Married the Mermaid'. This tells of a man who finds a mermaid's cloak on the beach, takes the mermaid as his wife, and hides her cloak (without which she cannot get back to the sea.) Several years later she finds the cloak hidden in the roof-thatch, and goes back to her natural element, sometimes taking the children of the marriage with her.

This legend has been used by Irish writers including Seamus Heaney and Nuala Ni Dhomnhaill as the basis for poems,[22] and exerts a powerful fascination on my writing students. Other legends, describing the meeting of people with fairies, ghosts, or other such beings, have the same power. New versions work well. Indeed, the structure of the legend, its focus on a single key episode in the life of its protagonist, its realism, relate it to the modern short story. In the modern Chekhovian or Joycean short story, 'the veil over reality lifted to reveal a deeper truth' as Heather Ingram remarks in her study, A History of the Irish Short Story.[23] This moment of illumination, of contact with a deeper truth, a world other than the familiar, is central to the oral legend. This makes it a useful model for students trying to

---

[21] The fairytale is more poetic (i.e. fictional), the legend more historical (i.e. realistic); http://www.br-online.de/wissen-bildung/collegeradio/medien/deutsch/maerchen/arbeitsblaetter/maerchen_inter_6.pdf.

[22] Seamus Heaney, 'Maighdean Mara', in Selected Poems (London: Faber and Faber, 1980), p. 146-47, and Nuala Ni Dhomhnaill, 'An Mhaighdean Mara', in An Dealg Droighin (1981), p. 34.

[23] Heather Ingram, A History of the Irish Short Story (Cambridge: Cambridge University Press, 2009), p. 85.

understand the shape of the short story, while the mixture of realism and fantasy in the legends liberates their own imaginations, and encourages them to move beyond realism.

Changing your mind

In the M.A. classes, the emphasis is on exposing students to new material, new knowledge, but encouraging them to explore aspects of this material which resonate with them on a personal level. Oral narratives survived because they express deep emotions and ideas about the human condition, often by way of imagery and symbolism which is universal, archetypal, and as timeless as it is ancient. Exposure to the forms, patterns and imagery of oral narrative opens the imagination to new ways of thinking and creating, which happen to be very ancient ways of thinking and creating. And it is precisely this liberation of the imagination that I have found to be the greatest benefit of introducing creative writing students to oral narrative.

A great deal of teaching is inevitably focused on what is essentially editing, or editorial advice, and when market values come into play the focus can be on what not to write, rather than anything more nurturing. Noah Lukeman's *The First Five Pages: A writer's Guide to Staying out of the Rejection Pile*,[24] the long shadow, not of flamboyant Joyce, but of minimalist Carver, rigorous Hemingway, the cutting editorial whip of 1940s Iowa Paul Engle,[25] exert a powerful influence on the creative writing class, particularly in the workshop context. The rich imagery of oral narrative provides a counterpoint to textual economy. Use of oral material cannot be an encouragement to meaningless fancifulness in writing. There *is* no meaningless fancy in oral narrative – stories that are specious do not survive for a day in oral tradition. But the richness and playfulness of meaningful fantasy, which is the driving force of the wonder-tale and the supernatural legend, provides a healthy antidote to realism and minimalism.

In the context of a fourth level university degree in an Irish university that participates in the ECTS, the module on folklore and writing plays a significant role. It provides one key taught or product element in the Creative Writing M.A. programme.

---

[24] Noah Lukeman, *The First Five Pages* (New York and London: Simon and Schuster, 2000).
[25] Paul Engle (1908-91) the long-time director of the Iowa Writers' Workshop and founder of the International Writing Program (IWP), both at the University of Iowa.

Students acquire new information, and techniques of literary analysis. This new information however, operates as a direct and extremely effective inspiration to new creative work. The classroom and the workshop, learning and writing, analysis and imagining, synthesise or fuse in this particular module.

As one student put it: 'It changed the way my mind works.'

This, perhaps, is what creative writing programmes should aim to do.

Writing Exercise

A. Find a version of 'The Animal Bride' (ATU 402) in the library or archive, or on the internet, (e.g. Grimms' 'The Frog Prince')

B. Write a story or poem based on the tale or some part of it.

Or

C. Write a story using a few of the formal devices of oral narrative technique, e.g. 'The Law of Three', 'The Law of Contrast', 'The Law of Opening and Closing.'

Works Cited

Holbek, Bengt, *Interpretation of Fairytales* (Helsinki: Academia Scientarum Fennica, 1987)

Ingram, Heather, *A History of the Irish Short Story* (Cambridge: University Press, 2009)

Lukeman, Noah, *The First Five Pages* (New York and London: Simon and Schuster, 2000)

Lüthi, Max, *The European Folktale: Form and Nature*, trans. John D. Niles (Bloomington: Indiana University Press, 1986)

McGurl, Mark, *The Program Era, Postwar Fiction and the Rise of Creative Writing* (Cambridge, Massachusetts: Harvard University Press, 2009)

NFQ (2009): University awards and the National Framework of Qualifications (NFQ): *Issues around the design of Programmes and the Use and Assessment of Learning Outcomes.*

Ní Dhuibhne, Éilís, 'International Folktales', in *Field Day Anthology of Irish Writing* Vol. IV, ed. Éilís Ní Dhuibhne (Cork: Cork University Press in association with Field Day, 2002), p.1237 ff

Olrik, Axel, 'The Epic Laws of Folk Narrative' (1909), in *The Study of Folklore*, ed. Alan Dundes (Englewood Cliffs: Prentice Hall, 1965), pp. 129-141

O'Neill, Geraldine, University awards and the National Framework of Qualifications (N.F.Q.): *Issues around the design of Programmes and the Use and Assessment of Learning Outcomes* (F.I.N., 2009)

O'Neill, Geraldine, 'Initiating curriculum revision: exploring the practices of educational developers', *International Journal for Academic Development*, 15.1 (2010), p. 64

Uther, Hans-Jörg, *The Types of International Folktales. A classification and Bibliography. Based on the System of Antti Aarne and Stith Thompson* (Helsinki: Academia Scientarum Fennica, 2004)

Writing Without a Safety Net: Guidance for Writing after the Creative Writing Classroom

Siobhan Campbell and Patricia Clark

The term begins and students find their way into a classroom. Some know each other, calling out a 'hello', throwing down books and laptop onto a table next to another student. Others enter the room shyly, bundled into coats and hoods, not making eye contact. It is an ordinary room with four walls, tables and chairs at a university. The students finding their way into the room begin as strangers and individuals but will gradually begin to form a group. In sharing poems, in reading poems together and discussions of language, of writers, of where words spark and dazzle and where they fail, the group will create a place of safety, constructive criticism, and support. We will share our work all semester long – about intense moments in life – of joy, dread and sorrow; work which is socially or politically engaged and work which comments on or emerges from the cultural debates of our time. Words will be written on paper and shared with relative strangers, at least at first. Everyone in the room works toward good writing, improving one's own writing, and toward pertinent, yet tactful, commentary. By the end, the writers here have made progress. Now, can we show them for the future, for their lives beyond classrooms, how to venture out boldly, to tell their particular stories vividly and precisely and to continue their writing in the wider world?

In many senses, then, the writing workshop experience is like life. Though it is development-oriented, there is no way of predicting how the writing of individuals will turn out over a semester or even over a year-long or degree-long course. All writing teachers have had the experience of watching previously confident and original writers go through a phase of producing derivative and imitative work because they are in the process of changing their writing styles, and conversely, of seeing previously tentative writers develop exponentially within the 'safe place' created by the workshop.

This paper is concerned with enabling student writers to move beyond the workshop by taking the skills they have learned in that environment into their writing lives beyond that safety. It may be useful to capture some of the broad differences, which are demonstrated in the Table 1 below:

Table 1. The writing workshop vs. the non-writing workshop

The Writing Workshop	Writing without workshop
Imposed	Voluntary
Formal/planned	Informal/appointment with the self
Mechanistic – but allowing for the organic	Organic – may require some mechanism
Collaborative	Individual
High predictivity – a result in mind	Low predictivity – what is the result?

At a glance, it's clear that the move to writing without the backup of the workshop experience might prove to be too much of a challenge for many graduating students. And so it will always be. As writing teachers, we know that many of those we teach will go on, not to make writing creatively part of how they earn their living, but to do a variety of other things, some of which will entail transferring those communication and expressive skills. Here however, we are concerned with the student who does hope to make writing part of their post-workshop lives.

While the latter may seem self-evident, it can serve as a stark reminder to us as creative writing teachers. How often might we think of the semester's writing workshop as going well when all the participants are producing work that has some merits of technique and content? Might it behove us to then address whether we are also aware of the role of the workshop in learning to go beyond it, 'learning for change' as it were? Might we not then relook at our own role in teaching the developmental skills required to enable and enhance that self-reflective learning for change?

Creative writing tutors from both sides of the Atlantic may use differing language, but our aims for 'learning outcomes' are similar. Often, those associated with the 'writing workshop' will emphasise most those skills related to knowledge and understanding (knowledge of the codes and conventions of a variety of forms and genres, the ability to reflect constructively on your creative activity and to identify the weaknesses and developing strengths of your own writing etc.). However, it is where we begin to define the hoped-for practical and professional skills that we encounter those most pertinent to the present discussion. An amalgamation of sample phrasing of such learning outcomes could include:

- An understanding of methods of stimulating creativity and the use of research

- The ability to construct and present sustained, coherent and persuasive written and oral arguments

- An understanding of the potential uses of information technology, social networking and the blogosphere for research processes and for generation of ideas

- The ability to sustain self-assessment methods, including the skills of revision and redrafting, to improve ongoing performance

While we might quibble about terms ('performance' is possibly questionable), we can see an attempt here to articulate the 'beyond the workshop' concept. Given that many of the learning outcomes of writing workshops may imply, rather than articulate, such outcomes however, we want to outline some ways below in which current practices could be tweaked or adapted to allow for more emphasis on developing skills for the ongoing writer.

Students devise their own assignments

Students may be writing poems and stories in response to prompts in some creative writing classes at undergraduate level and it is an excellent exercise – perhaps in the final year – to ask them to devise some of their own assignments. They can work in pairs to raid both their own degree-experience as well as creative writing pedagogy texts. A fully written-up assignment (based on a template provided by the tutor) could be brought back to workshop, presented and discussed. Those that most attracted the interest of the group could then be attempted. Time given to a discussion of the results of such assignments will enable students to continue to 'set their own assignments' when they move beyond the workshop.

A particularly helpful text in this regard is Robin Behn and Chase Twichell's *The Practice of Poetry: Writing Exercises from Poets Who Teach*.[1] A class session or sessions might focus on a handful of the exercises from the text with the goal of understanding the reasoning behind the assignments. The tutor might encourage

---

[1] Robin Behn and Chase Twichell, *The Practice of Poetry: Writing Exercises from Poets Who Teach* (2005).

discussion questions in advance: What are the aims of the assignment as it stands? How would you adapt this to your own poetic practice? Knowing the work of others, are there suggestions you can make as to other adaptations that would suit a different kind of writer. The follow-through here is to have students devise some of their own assignments and subject them to the same scrutiny before they are attempted.

Students employ self-reflective practice beyond the workshop

We can see that the requirement to develop new practice by the early-career writer will involve ongoing self-evaluation. Such self-reflective practice will have been taught in most workshop situations which allow for an element of self-reflective writing, either as an informal addition to assessed work or as part of an assessment. Self-reflective work by writers would tend to allow them to recognise that technical, structural or other problems are shared by others and are not exclusive to oneself. Typically, the writing tutor will have given examples of how other writers have solved the dilemma in question, often by providing specific reading samples. In discussion, or in their self-reflective writing, the student is encouraged to foreground the nature of the writing challenges discovered in the process of producing the work. Discursive work like this would also allow for the build-up of options, a recognition that there are possibly several ways of approaching the challenges of writing a given text, and it also allows for augmentation of self-confidence and competence in identifying and addressing issues that arise.

Core criteria for self reflection used in U.S classrooms focus on specificity and also global thoughts about one's own writing future. When students write about 'progress' in their work, they are asked to identify specific works of theirs where growth has occurred, as well as identifying the area of growth (sentence length, imagery, etc.). Though it may be especially difficult for upper level undergraduates to write about their future work, it is still vital to ask if they are able to identify areas where they know their work still needs attention. From seeing other students' work in a workshop, for example, a student may feel that 'texture' is a feature missing in his or her work. How will they address this? What writers do they feel they could read who might 'influence' their work by an infusion of this trait?

To push this forward to the non-workshop setting, students could be encouraged to develop their own checklist of elements to think about when moving to self-assess their own writing.

This could fall into two broad-brush categories and the challenge to students is to add to and hone the list of topics under each:

Technical and Stylistic Challenges

Might include: form chosen, language register, pacing, point of view or line and stanza breaks where applicable.

Thematic or Content-based issues

Could list tonal play and authorial intent, ethical or political considerations, reader-awareness and its effects, as well as a sense of discovery or insight and its implications.

Students will find it stimulating to foreground the areas that most concern them in their own work, and typically this exercise results in each writer adding a number of touchstone topics to their own working checklist. The aim, of course, is not to over-mechanise but further to enable a systematic way of thinking.

What we are suggesting here then is that a close look at how already-established learning outcomes might be predicated on a set of understandings that in themselves suggest ways in which they might be adapted, post-workshop, to guide a new set of self-generated practices.

This is usefully characterised by Patrick Easen, in an article entitled 'The visible supporter with no visible means of support',[2] where an approach is outlined which helps to:

- Explore, clarify and make sense of existing practices and value systems
- Replace the set of understandings or meanings, which underpin existing practices with a new set of understandings that can guide the development of new practices.

In essence, the move from the workshop situation to writing without one is a move from the collaborative environment to that of individual practice. But while we know that we all face the blank page or the blank screen alone, what writer is writing without reference to the tradition and to the presence of the writers in that tradition who have gone before them or who are contemporaneous? The creation of exercises which can be begun within the workshop but which have real purchase afterwards

---

[2] Patrick Easen, 'The visible supporter with no visible means of support', in Colin Biott, ed., *Semi-Detached Teachers* (1990), pp. 85-96.

may be one of the most enabling actions that writing tutors can take for their students.

Two such exercises are: **Write your own Manifesto** and **Create your own anthology,** both outlined below in the Writing Exercises section at the end of this chapter.

The outcomes of teaching the workshop with an awareness of the 'beyond the workshop' situation may enable us as tutors to value even further the skills developed in collaborative work which can be redeployed into work by an individual. At its simplest level, we want the student to have learned that the stimulus of having to produce work to share at workshop is partly rendered by the very appointed nature of a workshop time and place. Many of us already encourage our students to make a writing appointment with themselves as part of their ongoing practice. To push this further, we would encourage identification for students of the element of self-reflection on group process that occurs in workshop. While many of us do this in informal ways, it may be useful, perhaps towards the end of each session, to identify the overall thrust of the processes of giving and receiving criticism, engagement with the technical aspects and the content of the work, and to contextualise what has occurred that day in workshop with a view to how it has been a learning experience for all concerned.

Sometimes this may take the form of characterising what has taken place in terms of the collaborative context of the workshop with a view to reminding students that they are in a process of going beyond the collaborative. It may be that asking the students to reflect on some questions is enough:

- What might you take from today's workshop to apply in your own writing?

- How would you have addressed the texts we read today if you were reading them on your own?

- Might you identify ways of thinking that have arisen today as particularly useful to bring forward into your own ongoing practice?

It's clear that the apparently 'non-creative' elements of the workshop may have as much to teach the ongoing writer as the creative elements. To that end, it is interesting to note the wide variety of non-creative assessments devised by writing tutors in both the U.S. and the U.K. It appears to be normal practice that writing students will often be asked to produce an accompanying critical, reflective or contextualising piece.[3] In our own teaching these elements of non-creative engagement have taken several forms and are termed in a variety of ways including self-reflective essay, response to process, self-assessment, auto-critique, commentary, writing journal, poetics, critical commentary and introduction to the work or critical preface.

Such an emphasis is corroborated in the A.W.P. hallmarks of the required features in successful creative writing programs.[4] A sampling from here shows an equal emphasis on skills that can be taken out of and beyond the workshop:

- **An Emphasis on Revision:** Creative writing courses are by definition writing-intensive, and they should emphasise revision of successive drafts in response to feedback from peers and extensive written comments by instructors.

- **Grading, Testing, and Evaluation:** Criteria for grading in undergraduate courses should be based on the levels of each student's mastery of rhetoric, literary terminology, literary forms, critical approaches, and the writer's craft. Grades for the course should also weigh students' verbal and written feedback on each other's work.

What links all of the above is clearly an attempt to engender key reflective and self-reflective skills, and by implication, that these are attributes which the student can take onwards into a productive writing life. Behind this is the recognition that it's now imperative, for almost all writers, to be able to articulate their own project. In practical terms, this is not only useful in any media situation (profile, interview, radio appearance, etc.) but also in the writing of grant applications which have become more and more concerned with elements of originality and impact on the wider community as government agencies for the arts are pressed to provide 'value for money'. The exercises outlined below, then, can be seen to not only enable a writer in productive self-reflection towards further writing, but also to equip them for the outward-looking facets of a writing life.

The action of creative writing tutors in the creation and monitoring of all the above does, of course, require self-reflective teaching. It may be worth asking what in-service backup there is

---

[3] See for example, the National Association of Writers in Education, *Creative Writing Subject Benchmark Statement/ Creative Writing Research Benchmark Statement* (2009), p. 9.
[4] The Association of Writers and Writing Programs. Online.

for teachers of creative writing to continue to reflect on their own practice. Most of us have module evaluation questionnaires or the equivalent, but how many of these allow for an element of concerted self-reflection on the methods used and their actual efficacy in the classroom? Perhaps, at a basic level, it could be a matter of allowing an open-ended question into the existing mechanisms for reporting on Creative Writing modules. What techniques has the tutor employed to enable the members of the workshop to view themselves as writers in the longer term? How has the tutor raised the issue of redeploying workshop skills in the non workshop-based writing life? If we begin to understand the writing workshop as not just an end in itself but an environment with specific powers to enable for the future, it's possible that a small set of adjustments to our teaching will have a large impact on our students' thinking. In this way, we begin to implement the punchy *one-two* approach outlined by Easen, and mentioned above.

Writing Exercises:

1. Create your own Manifesto Exercise

(Or: What I Believe about Creative Writing and Poetry/ Fiction/Drama Non-fiction writing.)

1. Make a list of your passionately held beliefs about the creative process. These should reference or react to seminal statements on writing from recognised practitioners. 'No ideas but in things.' (William Carlos Williams); 'The truth should conform to the music.' (Richard Hugo); or Marianne Moore's statement, Poets create 'imaginary gardens with real toads in them'.
Be sure to consider ways of generating material. Discuss the variety of ways you, as writer, find subjects and/or generate 'material' for poems (personal experiences, research, reading, artwork, history, etc.)

2. Consider the ethical implications of your creative writing. (Are you committed to socially aware writing, or do you believe in art-for-art's sake? Do you use aspects of the lives of others in your work and have you addressed issues of privacy? What is your opinion on the social or public obligations of an artist?)

3. Technical aspects of your genre, including Form, Tone, Language, Imagery, Sensory details, Symbolism, etc.

4. Ways a piece of work could proceed towards its ending.

5. Ways a piece of writing can go wrong and how to identify these.

6. Ways you know that you have read a striking poem or a successful piece of fiction or drama.

7. What you expect from a piece that aspires to the status of literature.

This should be a decisive statement of your beliefs, referencing other writers and/or texts as you feel necessary. The statement should show where you are today with your own work and it should outline your 'first principles' as a writer. Again, think 'Where do I stand?' in relation to those seminal statements about poetry or the creation of literature.
[Note for tutors: this **Create your own Manifesto** exercise can be adapted for undergraduates at the early stages of their degree and lends itself to being revisited toward the later stages as the new manifesto generated by students at that stage will clarify their own development to themselves in potentially satisfying ways.]

2. Build your own Anthology Exercise

You are invited to edit your own poetry anthology. The choices you make will reflect your current creative and critical engagement with the canon and with contemporary work. The writers you invite in, and the list of those you keep out, will also reveal how you would like your own work to be valued.

This is your chance to draw a creative line through the centuries of written artistic expression, in an attempt to place yourself and your own work into a space that you define for yourself along that line.

Decide on a title and, if necessary, a subtitle for your anthology (you may find it easier to do this towards the end of the process).

You can employ any of the three approaches below, or you can adapt these to make your own distinctive strategy, which you will fully articulate in your introduction:

a) **The context-driven anthology**

   This might include representation of what you consider to be the defining poetic movements (anything from the Metaphysicals and Romantics to Beats and Black Arts, through Conceptual and Confessional, Flarf, Language Poetry, Negritude, New York School, Objectivist, Surrealist, Symbolist, etc.).

b) **The thematically driven anthology**

   This allows you to group poems from whichever century you choose together, possibly placing classic works beside more experimental texts to draw out what they may have in common. Typical themes of interest might include poems about war and conflict, poems that emerge from a feminist poetic, or poems that are ethically driven by an eco-awareness or other ethical or political stance. Some themes will intertwine and you may discuss how one theme leads to another in your introduction.

c) **The chronological anthology**

   This challenges you to fully draw a line through the tradition of centuries of literary endeavour until you reach your own work. You might begin with the ancients (Is Homer or Sappho your earliest poetic parent or does that honour belong to Liu Xiang or another?). The best chronological anthology will try to select at least two works from each century but the majority of texts may be from the nineteenth to twenty-first centuries.

For reference consult poetry anthologies of form as well as the survey texts that you find most useful (suggested texts appear below). Read widely and take notes on why certain writers who were originally 'in' are put 'out' in the end. You will find that a discussion of those you have discarded will form an interesting paragraph or two in your introduction as it requires that you articulate your own developing aesthetic. Remember to keep all references correctly (using M.L.A or M.H.R.A. guidelines) from the beginning.

1. Include at least one of each of the following in your anthology: elegy, ode, sestina, villanelle, ballad, pantoum, sonnet.

2. Include at least three pieces which encompass the following: a narrative poem, a dramatic monologue, a poem in free verse, a stanzaic poem, a prose poem.

3. Include up to ten poems (but at least five) from contemporary sources such as *Poetry*, *American Poetry Review*, *The Boston Review*, *Jacket*, *Agenda*, *PNReview*, *Versal*, *Magma*.

4. Include up to five of your own poems (but at least two). Choose carefully where you place these. If chronological, placement will be obvious but if you have selected a thematically driven approach, you will want to select the positioning of your poems alongside those to which they appear to relate.

5. Write an introduction to the anthology which reflects upon your decision-making process. You may use the first person and address the reader. Your aim is to write a clear introductory text which contextualises the work and describes the approach you chose to take.

6. Write a 'works cited' appendix that gives full reference detail for each work used. Add a bibliography with the details of the books, journals and websites you consulted.

7. Bind your anthology in an easy-to-use format. Number the pages. Produce a contents page and a title page which highlights your book title and your name as editor.

Congratulations, you have edited your first poetry anthology! The critical reading skills you display, along with your attention to text and your understanding of your chosen approach will be graded, as will your overall attention to citation and reference.

[Note for Tutors: The **Build your own Anthology** exercise can be adapted for the level you are teaching by small adjustments in the requirements and the consequent time-frame that you give for completion. It can be adapted to apply to other genres of writing with ease. In survey courses at level four (U.K.) or freshman year, it may be that a challenge to students to choose two texts from each century in their core survey text is amply stimulating and paves the way to apply the full exercise at a later stage. This exercise can be adapted easily to apply to short fiction, non-fiction writing or the novel. It can be shortened by asking for a list of references on writers who would be included by a particular student if editing their own book. The discussion about who has been 'left out' is, like all debriefing after the publication of an anthology, often the most interesting part! Tutors may elect to have students work on this exercise in pairs or even in groups, particularly those at an early stage where the gaps in the reading of one student can hopefully be filled in by the knowledge of another. In classroom use, this exercise has generated perhaps the most lively and engaging debates of a semester's teaching. It forces students who feel that they have a complete grasp of the tradition back to look at movements that they may have glossed over in the past. They find that this process of retrieval is both creatively and critically challenging. The skills of the ongoing anthologist of course are those that many students will need both actually to edit works in the future but more importantly perhaps, to maintain their own 'reading-for-writing' in a concerted way.]

The four approaches outlined here: Devising Assignments, Amplified Self-reflective Practice, Manifesto Writing and Anthology Editing, are designed as ways to enable tutors to articulate an ongoing 'beyond the workshop' agenda while still within the workshop. In sharing our practice, we have clarified both our commitment to the workshop experience and its capacity to have long-term positive effects on our students. The debate around 'beyond the workshop' approaches is worth joining and will become even more pertinent as the constraints on our discipline tighten. Two key places to join this debate are the A.W.P. pedagogy forum and *New Writing: The International Journal for the Practice and Theory of Creative Writing* (Routledge). The authors look forward to encountering new thinking on these issues in the open space of shared pedagogic practice in the future.

Suggested Texts

Behn, Robin and Chase Twichell, *The Practice of Poetry: Writing Exercises from Poets Who Teach* (New York: HarperCollins, 2005)

Enright, D.J., ed. *The Oxford Book of Contemporary Verse, 1945-1980* (Oxford: Oxford University Press, 1980)

Hall, Donald. *Breakfast Served Any Time All Day: Essays on poetry new and selected* (Ann Arbor: University of Michigan Press, 2004)

Hoover, Paul, ed. *Postmodern American Poetry: A Norton Anthology* (New York: Norton, 1994)

Hulse, Michael, ed., *The New Poetry* (London: Bloodaxe, 1993)

Kaminsky, Ilya, and Susan Harris, eds. *The Ecco Anthology of International Poetry* (New York: Ecco, 2010)

Morrison, Blake, ed., *The Penguin Book of Contemporary British Poetry* (London: Penguin, 1998)

Nelson, Cary, ed. *Anthology of Modern American Poetry* (London: Oxford University Press, 2000)

Plimpton, George, ed., *Writers at Work: The Paris Review Interviews*, eighth series (New York: Penguin, 1988)

Ramazani, Jahan, Richard Ellmann and Robert O'Clair, eds., *The Norton Anthology of Modern and Contemporary Poetry*, 2 Vols. (New York: W.W. Norton, 2003)

Redmond, John, *How To Write a Poem* (London: Blackwell, 2005)

Riley, Denise, ed. *Poets on Writing: Britain 1970-1991* (London: Palgrave Macmillan, 1992)

Salzman and Wack, eds., *Women's Work, Modern Women poets writing in English* (Bridgend: Seren Books, 2009)

Scully, James, *Line Break: Poetry as social practice* (Evanston: North Western University Press, 2005

Contributors' Notes

Adam Baron is Principal Lecturer in Creative Writing at Kingston University, London. He is an internationally renowned crime novelist whose work has been translated into French and German. He has published four novels with Macmillan: *Shut Eye, Hold Back the Night, Superjack* and *It Was You*. *Shut Eye* and *Hold Back the Night* have been broadcast on BBC Radio 4.

Siobhan Campbell is the author of five books of poetry, most recently, *Cross-Talk* (Seren, 2009). She has been shortlisted for the Michael Marks Award and has won prizes in the National, the Troubadour and Wigtown competitions. Represented in the major contemporary anthologies, she publishes regularly in the U.S. and the U.K. Founder of the Military Writing Network at Kingston University, London, she also acts as Managing Editor for Kingston University Press.

Patricia Clark is Poet-in-Residence and Professor in the Department of Writing at Grand Valley State University. Author of three volumes of poetry, Patricia's latest book is *She Walks into the Sea* (Michigan State University Press, 2009). Her work has been featured on Poetry Daily and Verse Daily, also appearing in *The Atlantic, Gettysburg Review*, and elsewhere. She is also the author of a chapbook, *Given the Trees*, in the Voices from the American Land series (2009). New work is forthcoming in *The Cimarron Review, Superstition Review*, and elsewhere.

Jenny Dunning's short stories and essays have appeared recently in *Literary Mama, North Dakota Quarterly*, the *South Dakota Review, Tusculum Review, CutBank, Beloit Fiction Journal*, among others. Her story 'Reva' received a Special Mention in the 2008 Pushcart Prize anthology. She is Assistant Professor at St. Olaf College in Northfield, Minnesota.

Deidre Fagan is an Associate Professor of English at Quincy University. She is author of the *Critical Companion to Robert Frost* and has published articles in *The Emily Dickinson Journal, Americana Review, South Asian Review, Creative Writing: Teaching Theory & Practice*, and *The Explicator*. She has also published creative work in *Grey Sparrow Journal*, *Bartleby Snopes*, and *Boston Literary Magazine*, among others. Her interests include, but are not limited to, American poetry, memoir, and creative writing.

Ursula Hurley is Senior Lecturer in English and Creative Writing at the University of Salford. She has a particular interest in creative non-fiction; her work in this area won first prize in the Unbound Press First Chapter competition and was short-listed for the Tony Lothian Prize 2010. She publishes poetry with Shearsman and Erbacce Press. Her research on writing pedagogy has resulted in contributions to *How to Write Fiction (and think about it)* (Palgrave, 2007) and *Everything You Need to Know About Creative Writing (but knowing isn't everything)* (Continuum, 2007).

Margaret Lazarus Dean is Assistant Professor of Creative Writing at the University of Tennessee and lives in Knoxville. Her novel, *The Time It Takes to Fall*, was published by Simon & Schuster in 2007.

Nigel McLoughlin is Professor of Creativity and Poetics at the University of Gloucestershire. He is the author of five collections of poetry, most recently *Chora: New & Selected Poems* (Templar Poetry, 2009) and is Editor of *Iota Poetry Journal*. He also writes on the pedagogy of writing and creativity.

Éilís Ní Dhuibhne is Writer Fellow at University College, Dublin. She is the author of many novels, collections of short stories, plays and works of non-fiction in both English and Irish. Her works include *Blood and Water, The Bray House, Eating Women is Not Recommended, The Inland Ice* and *The Pale Gold of Alaska*. She has won the Bisto Book of the Year Award, the Readers' Association of Ireland Award, the Stewart Parker Award and an Oireachtas. *The Dancers Dancing* was shortlisted for the Orange Prize for Fiction in 2000.

Paul Perry is Lecturer in Creative Writing at Kingston University, London, and the author of a number of critically acclaimed books of poetry including *The Drowning of the Saints*, *The Orchid Keeper*, and most recently *The Last Falcon and Small Ordinance* (The Dedalus Press, 2010). His work has appeared in the *TLS*, *The Irish Times*, *The Best American Poetry 2000* and *The Best Irish Poetry 2007*. His translations include *108 Moons: The Selected Poems of Jurga Ivanauskaite*. He is the current curator for the dlr Poetry Now Festival in Dun Laoghaire.

Joseph Rein is co-editor, with Chris Drew and David Yost, of *Dispatches from the Classroom: Graduate Students on Creative Writing* (Continuum, 2011). His fiction, poetry, and essays have appeared in numerous journals and anthologies, most recently *Laurel Review*, *Wisconsin Review*, and *New Writing: The International Journal for the Theory and Practice of Creative Writing*. He is Assistant Co-ordinator of the Creative Writing Program at the University of Wisconsin–Milwaukee, where he is pursuing his doctorate in fiction writing.

Ben Ristow is a Ph.D. candidate in Rhetoric, Composition, and the Teaching of English at the University of Arizona (Tucson, Arizona). His scholarly essay 'Because of Wendy: A Bibliography of Wendy Bishop's Creative Writing Scholarship' appears in *Composing Ourselves as Writer-Teacher Writers* (Hampton Press, 2011) and his most recent short story 'St Jerome and the Dumpster Girls' was a finalist for the *Mississippi Review* Prize and the Black Warrior Review fiction contest before it was published in *BOMB Magazine* (Issue 114) and featured in their podcast series 'Fiction for Driving Across America'.

Fiona Sampson's books include *Rough Music, Shelley: Poet to Poet* and the 2010 Newcastle/Bloodaxe Poetry Lectures. Shortlisted for the Forward and T.S. Eliot Prizes, she has been awarded a Cholmondeley Award and the Newdigate Prize. Forthcoming from Chatto are *Beyond the Lyric*, (Autumn, 2012) a critical survey of contemporary British poetry, and her next collection, *Coleshill* (January, 2013). She is Senior Researcher in Creative Writing at Kingston Writing School, Kingston University, London.

Maureen Seaton is Associate Professor in Creative Writing at the University of Miami. Her work has appeared in *The Best American Poetry, The Atlantic Monthly, Paris Review, New Republic*, and many other publications both on and off line. A recipient of many awards including a Piedmont College, she is the author of several collections of poetry including *Cave of the Yellow Volkswagen* (Carnegie Mellon University Press, 2009).

Heidi Lynn Staples teaches English at Piedmont College, Georgia. Her work has appeared in *Best American Poetry, Chicago Review, Ploughshares, Women's Studies Quarterly*, and elsewhere. She is the author of four collections, including *Noise Event* forthcoming from Ahsahta Press.

Todd Swift has published seven full collections of poetry, including *Seaway: New and Selected Poems* (Salmon, 2008) and *Mainstream Love Hotel* (Tall-lighthouse, 2009). He has edited or co-edited many anthologies, including *Poetry Nation, 100 Poets Against The War*, and (with Evan Jones) *Modern Canadian Poets* (Carcanet, 2010). His poems have appeared in leading publications, including *Poetry* (Chicago), *Poetry London, Poetry Review, Jacket, The Guardian*, and *The Globe and Mail*. Forthcoming publications include *Lung Jazz: The Oxfam Book of Young British Poets* (Cinnamon Press, 2011), co-edited with Kim Lockwood, and *When All My Disappointments Came At Once* (Tightrope Books, 2012). He is a lecturer in Creative Writing for Kingston Writing School, Kingston University, London.

Michael Theune is the editor of *Structure and Surprise: Engaging Poetic Turns* (Teachers & Writers, 2007) and the host of the blog structureandsurprise.wordpress.com. His poems, essays, and reviews have appeared in numerous publications, including journals such as *College English, Jacket*, and *Pleiades*, and books such as *Mentor and Muse: From Poets to Poets* (Southern Illinois University, 2010) and *The Monkey & the Wrench: Essays into Contemporary Poetics* (University of Akron, 2011). He is Associate Professor of English at Illinois Wesleyan University.

Stephanie Vanderslice is Associate Professor of Writing at the University of Central Arkansas and Director of the Great Bear Writing Project. She is co-editor, with Kelly Ritter, of *Can It Really Be Taught? Resisting Lore in Creative Writing Pedagogy* (Boynton Cook, 2007) as well as co-author, with Kelly Ritter, of *Teaching Creative Writing to Undergraduates: A Resource Guide and Sourcebook* (Fountainhead 2011) and sole author of the forthcoming, *Rethinking Creative Writing in Higher Education: Programs and Practices that Work* (Professional and Higher, 2011).

UK Ltd.

001B/4/P